PAPA JACK

The golden smile, ca. 1930. *(Library of Congress)*

PAPA JACK

Jack Johnson and the Era of White Hopes

Randy Roberts

THE FREE PRESS
A Division of Macmillan, Inc.
NEW YORK

Collier Macmillan Publishers
LONDON

The Free Press
A Division of Macmillan, Inc.
866 Third Avenue, New York, N.Y. 10022

Collier Macmillan Canada, Inc.

Printed in the United States of America

printing number

1 2 3 4 5 6 7 8 9 10

Library of Congress Cataloging in Publication Data

Roberts, Randy
    Papa Jack: Jack Johnson and the era of white hopes.

    Includes index.
    1. Johnson, Jack, 1878–1946. 2. Boxers (Sports)—
United States—Biography. I. Title.
GV1132.J7R62 1983   796.8′3′0924   [B]   82-49017
ISBN 0-02-926640-8

92
Johnson, J.

To Ilsa and Cardigan,
who were always there.

Contents

Acknowledgments

THE RESEARCHING AND WRITING of this book were at once both a very personal and a shared experience. In the hours I spent alone sifting through long-unread documents and trying to make sense out of a very complicated life, I came to certain conclusions about Jack Johnson. These views are my own, and if they are found lacking I alone am responsible. However, between the hours of isolation I have had numerous occasions to discuss Johnson with friends and colleagues, and they have helped me clarify my own thoughts. In the summer of 1981 a National Endowment for the Humanities seminar permitted me to discuss my research with a group of intelligent and encouraging scholars. Philip Rieff, the director of the seminar, constantly tried to sharpen my theoretical vision, and James Sterrett, with whom I stayed during the summer, was supportive in a number of ways, particularly as an example of a totally humane person. Also during that summer I enjoyed the hospitality and insightful opinions of Melvin Adelman when I was doing research in New York.

Similarly, my colleagues at Sam Houston State University have been very helpful. John Payne read the entire manuscript and improved it with his gentle criticisms. Terry Bilhartz helped with proofreading chores. Jim Olson improved every idea I discussed with him. Gary Bell and Don Coers allowed me to talk too much about Johnson on our long rides to Austin for research. And Lee Olm was as encouraging a chairman as I could hope for.

A special thanks goes to Gary Phillips, who generously shared his research on West Coast boxing with me. Always friendly and helpful, he aided me throughout the writing of this biography. And at The Free Press, Joyce Seltzer supported and improved my work in its later stages. I was also well treated by the staffs of the National Archives, the Library of Congress, the New York Public Library, the Rosenberg Library, and the university libraries at Sam Houston State University, the University of Pennsylvania, the University of Texas, and Columbia University.

Finally, to Ilsa I offer more my apologies than my thanks. My friends had to tolerate my research interests; she had to tolerate me.

Prologue: Scars

JACK JOHNSON'S BODY was lined with scars. Some, including the ridged tissue above both eyes that no longer sprouted hair, were the result of his profession. Most, however, were those of a laborer raised in poverty where accidents were common and doctors scarce, scars caused by the substitution of coffee grounds for the needle and thread of a surgeon. The most disconcerting scar was on his left leg, an ugly, thick line that ran from his upper thigh to the middle of his knee. It was a legacy of the months he spent working in racing stables. A nervous horse had kicked him, ripping open the skin and breaking the femur. Surprisingly, the bone had healed without leaving him with a limp, and skin had re-formed over the nasty gash. When he was nervous he would occasionally run his fingers over the scar, much as one might touch a mustache or a lock of hair in a moment of quiet contemplation.

As Jack Johnson spoke in his own defense, his hand wandered aimlessly toward his left thigh. He was in trouble—serious trouble—but his face didn't register it. Instead of a worried frown he wore an inscrutable smile. Although on trial for violating the White Slave Traffic Act, he refused to look contrite. His voice registered nothing but scorn for Harry A. Parkin, the United States Assistant District Attorney who was questioning him. Yes, Johnson said, he had known many white prostitutes, and he had traveled across America with a

few of them. And yes, he knew the government's star witness, Belle
Schreiber, particularly well. But, Johnson told Parkin, he had never
broken any laws with Belle. Jack said he had seldom even seen Belle
since the passage of the act that forbade the transportation of women
across state lines for immoral or illicit purposes. Yes, there were a few
times when the two spent some nights together, like the time in August 1910 when Belle came to Jack in Atlantic City. She came to him,
he emphasized, and why shouldn't she? After all, he had just beaten
the great Jim Jeffries for the undisputed heavyweight championship.
Parkin asked: "Did you buy her meals or pay her hotel bills or give
her any money?" Johnson answered defiantly: "I never gave her
nothing that trip at all." Question: "Did you buy her meals?" Answer: "Never—nothing." Question: "Pay her hotel bill?" Answer:
"Nothing, never even bought a drink." Question: "So she spent her
own money at that time?" Answer: "She must have—she did not
spend mine."

The exchange was typical of Jack Johnson in his prime. He was
an uncompromising man, even when confronted by the overwhelm-
ing power of white authority. He touched his leg and spoke his mind
and was content to allow the twelve white jurors to think what they
wanted. In his mind he was Papa Jack, a name he signed on the pictures of himself that he gave to close "lady friends." Papa Jack, the
best lover and talker and boxer in the world. But even being Papa
Jack was not enough in a white world. He already stood convicted
simply because he was black, and it was better to go to prison with
dignity than to shuffle there with his hat in his hands. You could control only so much of your destiny. In the ring he was totally confident, because he had nearly absolute control. Outside the ring, however, he tended to lose the reins of his life, moving at a speed that
even his reflexes could not handle. And sometimes he crashed—he
wrecked cars, beat women, and suffered from nervous exhaustion.
But, in control or out of control, he didn't toady to anyone.

Perhaps because of his public bravado his private life suffered.
His challenge to the standards of white America was such that he isolated himself from even his closest friends. Certainly there was no
other famous black American of his day who so utterly resisted racial
barriers, no other who so openly assaulted white middle-class attitudes. Undoubtedly his reckless and disorderly private life was the
price he paid for the flawless control he demonstrated publicly.

It is only in his private world that one glimpses Johnson's otherwise invisible scars, the marks caused by humiliation and degradation

and painful abuse. It was always nigger this and nigger that and the world champion's a nigger in the newspapers and at every fight. But the insults never erased his smile or caused him to lose his composure. It was only in private—usually with a white woman—that the hurt surfaced and manifested itself in violence.

The invisible scars were as old as Johnson. One doesn't need a psychologist to see the origins of his complex personality. There were a crippled father and a childhood that had ended far too quickly. There were the lessons that blacks raised in the Jim Crow South learned early, the rules that if not closely followed could cost a black man his life. There were the Battle Royals where black youths fought each other for the pennies and nickels thrown into the ring by laughing white men. There was plenty of pain.

Johnson learned. He fought for the white man's pennies, and when he grew bigger and much stronger he battled for the very symbol of athletic and physical dominance—the heavyweight championship of the world. And he was victorious. He was the true Battler Royal. And, instead of picking up pennies off of the floor, he was handed checks for thousands of dollars, which white bank tellers were pleased to cash for him. Further and further he drifted into the white man's world. He hired a white man to drive his car, another to manage his boxing career, and another to help him dress in the morning. He spent money on white prostitutes, and he married a white woman. Perhaps in a limited way he even believed that he was accepted in his new world. But he wasn't. He was still simply picking up the pennies. It was just that there were more of them.

It was then that the invisible scars became inflamed, and hate like pus seeped out of them. He was no longer a champion, but just another black boy in Galveston.

Ego! It is the great word of the twentieth century. If there is a single word our century has added to the potentiality of language, it is ego. Everything we have done in this century, from monumental feats to nightmares of human destruction, has been a function of that extraordinary state of the psyche which gives us authority to declare we are sure of ourselves when we are not.

Norman Mailer
Existential Errands

1

Flourishing in the Dark

NO ONE THOUGHT MUCH about holding church services that Sunday, so the few churches left standing were empty. Even the priests and ministers had better places to be. The winds that had swept along the Texas Gulf Coast on Friday, September 7, 1900, hit Galveston Island in the early hours of Saturday. They blew with greater force as the day progressed. By eight thirty in the evening, the hurricane winds exceeded 110 miles an hour. Houses collapsed, shattering slate roofs. The fragments of slate, sharp enough to decapitate a person, and mixed with bricks and pieces of wood, acted like shrapnel in the high winds. The next day it was discovered that scores of people had been killed or mutilated by the flying debris. In the worst disaster ever to visit North America, more than six thousand people were killed.

The loss of life was compounded by the destruction of property. The stately Victorian mansions of the town's commercial elite and the disease- and rat-ridden huts of its poor were treated alike by the storm. Over two-thirds of the buildings in Galveston were destroyed. Pictures of the city taken after the flood had subsided have an eerie, desolate quality; they resemble photographs of war-ravaged Dresden. In every manner the inhabitants of Galveston and the Island suffered greatly. The winds of that Saturday carried a grisly fame. They made Galveston synonymous with disaster.

1

In the wake of the tragedy, loss and suffering became relative terms. Some people lost their lives. Others lost close relatives. Still others lost their homes. The ones who survived were considered fortunate, and those who lost only their homes even more so. Their situation was not usually noted by the reporters. However, a few observers described their plight. Joel Chandler Harris, journalist and author of the Uncle Remus stories, had traveled to Galveston to report on the storm: "The condition of thousands of those who have been spared is far more pitiable than that of the dead. Their resources have been swept away by the wind and tide, and they are desolate in the midst of desolation."[1]

One of the desolate was Henry Johnson. Compared with others, he lost little in physical and financial terms. As far as can be ascertained, he did not lose any of his immediate family, and in a storm that swept away more than $10,000,000 in property, his financial losses hardly stand notice. Nevertheless, this crippled black man lost every possession he owned. He had worked for years to buy a plot of land and build a house. According to the assessor's records, before the storm in 1900 he owned a lot worth $600 and a house valued at $500. Then the storm came and took away his house. Afterward Henry Johnson dropped out of all historical records. Although he did not die in the storm, his life's work was still lost in the winds and water of September 1900.[2]

When Henry Johnson came to Galveston is unknown. Born a slave in Maryland, he is reputed to have entertained wealthy planters as a bare-knuckle fighter. It is also said that Johnson served under Robert E. Lee in the Civil War. Such stories, however, are unverified by any written sources. Henry Johnson did not enter the historical records until the 1870s, when he was first listed in the Galveston city directories. The 1878 directory identified him as a woodcutter, but that was the last year he practiced that trade.[3]

In 1880 Henry Johnson stepped into sharper historical focus. The federal census report of that year described him as a forty-two-year-old black man who could neither read nor write. He was listed as a laborer, but his physical condition evidently was not good. Under the general questions about health, the census worker had scribbled "paralyze." Neither the nature nor the extent of Johnson's infirmity was noted.

In the 1880s Henry found a more permanent home and a new job. Early in the decade, he acquired a small plot of land in Galveston at 808 Broadway and started to build a house. The assessor's office in 1881 estimated the land to be worth $350 and valued the improvements at $50. Over the next two decades the land value leveled at $600, and the house Henry built—a small, one-story frame dwelling with a basement and an enclosed porch—was priced at $500. By the standards of the neighborhood, neither figure was impressive; Henry's holdings were meager even in a poorer quarter of Galveston. But he did own the land and house outright, and for an ex-slave this in itself was a considerable accomplishment. Later in the decade Henry found a job that did not unduly tax his strength. For a few years he worked as a porter at a saloon, and in 1888 he became a janitor at a public school for black children. In the early 1890s he became the janitor for the entire East School District. He remained at this job for the next decade. Again, by middle-class white standards Henry was still a poor man; yet he had made the difficult transition from slavery to freedom and had both a steady job and a secure home.[4]

Quietly Johnson had established roots. He had married Tiny, a woman nineteen years his junior, when she was in her early teens. Soon afterward they started a family: Lucy was born in 1872, Jennie in 1875, Arthur in 1878, Henry in 1880, Fannie in 1885, and Charles in 1887; three other children died at birth.[5] Both parents were pious, and both valued education. The Johnson children were raised in the shadows of church and school; all six learned to read and write. The picture of the Johnson family that emerges from official records is one of solid respectability. Like most ex-slaves—in fact, if not in fiction—Henry Johnson got on well as a freedman. He settled down with one woman and provided for his children. He neither roamed from city to city nor moved from job to job. If Henry Johnson could not enjoy all the rights of a free man, he could and did accept a free man's responsibilities.[6]

It was only because of his first son that Henry is remembered at all. Arthur John Johnson was born on March 31, 1878.[7] At that time Galveston was the largest city in Texas, and its port was one of the finest in the United States. With a population of some 25,000, Galveston mixed small-town life with big-city optimism. While the rest of the South struggled through a depression, the *Galveston Weekly News* boldly prophesied that there was money to be made in cotton and therefore in land.[8] But Henry Johnson lived in the shadows of this optimism, and Arthur John ''Jack'' Johnson was born into a race of laborers, men who picked cotton they did not sell, plowed fields they did not own, and unloaded ships they could not ride. They did not write letters, keep diaries, or otherwise document their existence. They worked, they died, and they were not widely remembered. When, rarely, one of them became famous, his life became a fitting subject for all sorts of myths. What has been recorded of Jack Johnson's background is more what people chose to believe than what actually happened.

Johnson's mother, Tiny, a squat, broad-featured, hard-working woman, overshadows Johnson's father as an influence in his life. It is she who is credited with having taught Jack to fight back. Tiny insisted that her son was once the rankest of cowards—a boy who had to be defended in schoolyard scraps by his sister. Many a time, she remembered, Jack would return home bruised and crying. Finally, Tiny told her son that if he were beaten again a worse whipping would be waiting for him at home. The lesson was learned instantly; never again did Jack lose a schoolboy fight. The same sort of story is told about most men who become champion fighters. Such accounts make them more human, soften character lines made hard by poverty and casual violence. This act of transformation must be accomplished by the mother, who traditionally represents humanity, gentleness, and sympathy.[9]

Too little is known about Henry Johnson to judge the psychological impact he had upon his son. However, in his son's autobiography Henry Johnson appears to represent the very values Jack Johnson challenged. His father, Johnson wrote, was "a man of a pious turn of mind," who had "served faithfully" as a school janitor. He was a cripple who was attached to home and job. He was a man whose reach never exceeded his grasp. By contrast, Jack was physically quick where Henry was slow, a wanderer rather than rooted, and challenging instead of accepting. He was the reverse image of his father. If Henry resembled Uncle Tom, Jack was a combination of Brer Rabbit and Stagolee.[10]

Jack Johnson's first idol was Steve Brodie. In his largely fictional autobiography, Johnson claimed that his single ambition as a youth was to meet Brodie, who had won fame as the first person to jump off the Brooklyn Bridge and survive. According to Brodie and several of his friends who claimed to have witnessed the leap, in mid-July 1886 he had jumped and had been picked out of the river by a passing barge. Brodie's claim was supported mostly by his Irish charm, and more than a few skeptics claimed that a dummy had been thrown off the bridge and that Brodie had merely swum to the barge. In any case, Brodie parlayed the fame he acquired into riches, first as a saloon keeper and then as an actor in the play *On the Bowery*, in which he reenacted his historic leap.[11]

On another undocumented—and universally unbelieved—occasion, Jack Johnson said he had run away from home to New York City to meet Brodie. Only twelve at the time, Johnson rode the rails and traveled as a stowaway on ships until he arrived in New York. He then walked to the Bowery and became friends with Brodie. At least, this is what Johnson wanted his readers to believe. The truth of the assertion lies not in the physical actuality but in the unconscious wish. Like many writers of autobiographies, Johnson reveals more about himself when he invents than when he tells the truth. Johnson, like Brodie, refused to recognize boundaries, either on his actions or on his imagination. Brodie tempted fate—he cheated death—and lived. Johnson also successfully challenged the currents of his time. While Booker T. Washington was advising fellow blacks to swim with the currents of racial prejudice and injustice, Johnson was struggling mightily against the flow.

Jack Johnson belonged to the first generation of American blacks to be born free. Because of the nature of historical inquiry, more is known about how whites responded to the end of slavery than about the blacks' response. Most Southern whites expected emancipation to have disastrous results. Beliefs that blacks would be unable to cope with freedom were often voiced. The Negro race, Southerners reasoned, was notoriously carefree and prone to laziness, drunkenness, and disease. Indeed, without white supervision, the race would surely decline. Census reports in 1870 and 1890 were interpreted as scientific proof of these predictions. Other whites feared that the black population would grow more rapidly than the white. Noting "the remarkable fecundity of the African," Dr. Edward W. Gilliam projected that in 1980 the black population would exceed 192 million. Eventually, Gilliam predicted, "mere numbers must prevail over wealth, intelligence, and prestige," and the "dark, swelling, muttering mass along the social horizon, gathering strength with education, and ambitious to rise, will grow increasingly restless and sullen under repression, until at length, conscious through number of superior power, it will assert that power destructively, and, bursting forth like an angry, furious crowd, avenge in tumult and disorder, the social law broken against them."[12]

Demographic theories aside, few white Southerners viewed black advancement as anything less than a threat. Freedom had erased the lines of caste; black codes, which had been designed for race control, were outlawed. Avenues of social and economic advancement, at least in theory, were opened to blacks. The most farsighted of Southern leaders knew that once cracks in their social system appeared, they could never be totally mended, and that theoretical freedoms would in time become actual ones. When that occurred, there would be racial war. Writing in the *North American Review*, Senator John T. Morgan of Alabama warned that the further blacks progressed away from slavery, the closer they moved toward a racial showdown: "The greater their personal success may be, the more they will feel the pressure of caste, so that race prejudice will forever remain as an incubus on all their individual efforts." More to the point, as Dr. Gilliam observed, "The advancement of the blacks . . . becomes a menace to the whites." Thus, any social, educational, or economic gains made by the blacks were interpreted as steps toward a final collision between the races.[13]

More than any other black of his generation, Johnson gave flesh to the whites' jeremiads. He was the black man who, freed from the restraints of slavery, would go forward toward the ultimate confrontation. Other black leaders, such as Booker T. Washington and even W. E. B. Du Bois, spoke cautiously. Johnson, however, moved boldly, refusing to maneuver around obstacles or to check his speed. He would live by his own rules or not all all. In so doing, Johnson threatened order. He embodied the white man's nightmare of racial chaos.

What influences and events shaped Johnson's character are unknown. He attended five or six years of elementary school, where he learned to read and write. After classes he helped his invalid father sweep the floors and clean the grounds of the school. When his years of formal education ended, he took what work he could find. By his own accounts he trained horses, painted wagons, baked bread, and unloaded ships.[14]

Johnson's real education came about during endless hours of drifting about Galveston and south Texas. He learned that he was physically superior to other youths, that he was quicker and could punch harder. Before choosing the ring as a career, Johnson fought because he enjoyed fighting and because it helped to define him as a man. His first taste of organized fighting came in Battle Royals. This form of boxing contest was more ritual than sport; it served to debase black youths before the white enforcers of the Southern racial system.

Battle Royals had only one theme but a number of variations. The single theme involved black youth fighting black youth in front of white spectators, who threw pennies and nickels to the victor. The lesson was obvious: rewards came from defeating your brother, not from joining him. Only rarely did a Battle Royal entail a single man-on-man confrontation. Usually eight or more black youths were told to get into the ring and fight a free-for-all. No rules were observed, and only the last person left standing won any money. Occasionally, to add to the amusement of the spectators, the youths were blindfolded. Then the fighting became directionless, with spindly black kids striking out wildly at unseen opponents and being hit by unanticipated punches.

When the dignity of a one-on-one battle was permitted, it usually involved some other twist to subtract from the fighters' self-respect. For example, as a preliminary to the Johnson–Joe Choynski fight of 1901 in Galveston, two one-legged "colored boys" fought each other. To the cheers of the all-white audience, they hopped around the ring as if fighting on pogo sticks. Other one-on-one contests saw fighters tied together by the arms or the ankles, or forced to take turns hitting each other, or even to fight nude.[15]

Most accounts of Battle Royals were written by white reporters, who seemed to share the amusement of the other white spectators. The description that most closely reveals the truth of the events is the fictional one written by Ralph Ellison: "Blindfolded, I could no longer control my emotions. I had no dignity. I stumbled about like a baby or a drunken man. . . . My saliva became like hot bitter glue. A glove connected with my head, filling my mouth with warm blood." And through the sightless horror the voices: "Let me at those black sonsabitches! . . . Get going, black boy! Mix it up! . . . Uppercut him! Kill him! Kill that big boy! . . . That's right, Sambo."[16]

Ultimately these were events without winners, only losers. The pennies did not pay for the lost dignity. Their sole function was to reinforce racial stereotypes. Like the blacks in minstrel shows, blacks in Battle Royals conformed to white expectations. Blindfolded or tied together, blacks were made to look more comical and less dangerous. It was difficult to take seriously one whose masculinity and dignity were so totally compromised. Emasculated before each other and the white audience, the black youths were given painful lessons about the nature of caste.

By all accounts Johnson was proficient in the Battle Royals. Even when his opponents joined forces against him, Johnson usually won. He taunted his foes and, backing into a corner, fought them one at a time. As much as possible he tried to maintain his dignity under circumstances that tended toward humiliation. Yet total dignity was unattainable, and there were times when he was forced to wear a Sambo mask. One time he was matched against a relative in a fight staged in Galveston. The fight was dull, and the promoter, an old-time heavyweight named Jim Hall, told Johnson to fight harder or get ready for a real beating. Johnson replied in the patois all blacks were assumed to use: "You see, Marse Hall, dis nigger am mah brother-in-law and ah can't hit him hard, cause if ah tries it de whole tribe will jes beat me to death when ah gets home." Hall replied he did not care what happened to Johnson when he returned home, but he'd better fight.[17]

The story, though told and reported in 1909, could have been taken from a nineteenth-century description of the typical slave. Johnson assumed the role of the slave who believed he could trick the master, but of course he could not, for the master understood his naturally lazy and shiftless nature. In the eyes of white society, no slave was as intelligent as a master. Johnson was caught in his deception and forced to work. He was made by a symbol of absolute authority—in this case a white fight promoter—to perform as he was supposed to.

But Jack Johnson rarely behaved as he was supposed to. As he grew older, signs of rebellion began to surface. He left home at more frequent intervals, roaming around the country, taking jobs as a sparring partner or a laborer. Seldom did he last long at any single job. When he was at home, his tendency toward changing jobs was just as evident. From 1896 through 1898 Johnson held at least three different jobs. He worked as a porter, a barber's helper, and a dock worker. However, as he reported, he was more fond of fighting and shooting craps.[18]

When Johnson was in Galveston he lived with his family. By 1900 the small Johnson dwelling and an even smaller house in the rear of the lot were occupied by eleven or twelve people. Besides Henry and Tiny Johnson, five of their children still lived at home, including one who was married and had three children of her own. Henry no longer worked, but Henry, Jr., and Augustus Rhodes, the son-in-law, were laborers. And by then Jack was fighting professionally at private clubs in the Galveston area. None of the males made much money, but the house was paid for and expenses were few. Then came the storm, and family bonds of the Johnson household dissolved.[19]

The great flood ended Jack Johnson's family life. Johnson's biogra-
phers insist that he was married by that time to a light-skinned black
girl from Galveston named Mary Austin. Their source for this information is Johnson's autobiography. Jack said they married in 1898,
traveled together in Colorado, split up, reconciled for a trip to the
West Coast, and permanently separated in Denver in 1901. "Mary
was a splendid woman," he recalled, "and I recall my life with her as
one of the happy periods of my existence." Certainly a woman
named Mary Austin did travel with Johnson for a few years, and he
did introduce her as his wife. But they were never legally married. In
the 1900 census reports Johnson is listed as a single male living at
home with his parents, and no female named Mary lived there. Further, when Johnson applied for a marriage license in 1913 he asserted
that he had never been married.[20] The confusion probably originated
in Johnson's habit of introducing female traveling companions as his
wife. Whoever was living with him at a given time became "Mrs.
Jack Johnson," and in his championship years this caused considerable confusion. At various times, two or three "Mrs. Jack Johnsons"
might be found in the city where Johnson was staying. Mary Austin
may very well have been the first official unofficial "Mrs. Jack Johnson."

Just as Johnson distorted his exact relationship with Mary Austin, he invented stories of his travels in the late 1890s. The tales read
well, drama always being more important to Johnson than mere fact.
Until the end of his life he had a tendency to view his career as an un-
finished novel, a thing to be tinkered with, a fact changed here or an
event added there. He had an eye for consistency in the whole of his
life—he longed for a moral to his story—and so was not above using
a Procrustean hand in molding individual episodes. A case in point
was his wanderings in the West. In the late 1890s, Johnson wrote, he
left Galveston with "no particular destination in mind." Thereupon
began a series of conflicts with symbols of white authority. He
clashed with "hard-boiled train crews" and "police officers and con-
stables," with "road detectives and watchman" and small-town
judges. He spent nights in jail and days in hobo jungles. He rode the
rails throughout the Midwest and the Rocky Mountain states. When
he needed money, he got a job as a sparring partner or fought in a
professional match.[21]

In truth, most of Johnson's trips and adventures were imaginary.
City directories, census reports, and boxing record books place him
in Galveston for most of the months during those years.[22] The importance of Johnson's testimony rests not in its factual accuracy but in

its psychological truthfulness. He interpreted even his early career in terms of a conspiratorial racial conflict. His every physical movement, he believed, was curtailed by white authorities. They booted him off trains, chased him from boxcars, beat him with clubs, arrested him, jailed him, sentenced him. They attempted, in short, to restrict his mobility and lock him away. These early conflicts illuminate the fears that governed Johnson's life. Authority represented repression, and mobility symbolized freedom. This is why the police and automobiles were so omnipresent in Johnson's mind: He rebelled against any symbol of authority and often said he enjoyed nothing more than a fast car. Confinement was slavery for him, just as movement was emancipation.

By the time Johnson reached his late teens, he was locked into an occupation. He was a fighter. He started as a sparring partner for better fighters and sometimes fought circus boxers who roamed the country taking on all challengers. On a less formal but often more serious level he battled other black men in alleys and on the docks. Though slender, he was well muscled and quick, and he usually won the street fights that came his way. Recognizing his aptitude in the profession, and looking for a way to make more than a laborers' wage, Johnson turned to professional boxing in the closing years of the nineteenth century.

Prizefighting in Texas—as in almost every other state—existed in a curious limbo. It was widely followed, generally encouraged, normally tolerated—and forbidden by law. It was a subculture that was scorned by reformers but admired immensely by millions of men who never saw a professional fight but who had the vague notion that prizefighters were a special breed. In 1893 *The Nation*, an organ of respectable America, remarked that the clientele of prizefighting "consists almost always of the scourings of human society—gamblers, thieves, drunkards, and bullies. . . . The pugilists themselves . . . are generally persons whose manners and morals are a disgrace to our civilization." Concurrent with this opinion was another that whispered the name the Great John L. as if it were a religious invocation. Indeed, Professor William Lyon Phelps of Yale remembered reading the newspaper to his saintly Baptist minister father the day after the Sullivan-Corbett fight: "When I came to the headline CORBETT DEFEATS SULLIVAN, I read that aloud and turned the page. My father leaned forward and said earnestly, 'Read it by rounds!' "[23]

Texas law first took note of prizefighting in 1889, when a statute was enacted that lumped boxing together with dog-fighting, bullfighting, bull-baiting, and bear-baiting. All such contests were permitted, but a tax of $500 was levied for each performance. In 1891 the law was changed to prohibit boxing. Now anyone involved "in a pugilistic encounter between man and man, or fight between man and bull or between man and other animal" was guilty of a felony punishable by a fine between $500 and $1,000 and by a jail term between sixty days and one year. Because the 1889 law was never specifically repealed, there was a period of general confusion about the status of boxing. The question was settled in 1895, when Dallas sportsmen arranged to have the Corbett-Fitzsimmons heavyweight championship fight staged in their city. The way for this bout was seemingly cleared when Judge J. M. Hurt ruled that the 1889 law was still in effect. However, Governor Charles Culbertson held another opinion, and as governor of "the Great State of Texas" his opinion counted. Spurred on by a personal controversy with several members of the Dallas sporting fraternity, he saw his gubernatorial duty as defending of the 1891 law. In the end the governor prevailed, and in September 1895 a new law was passed that was essentially the same as the 1891 statute except that it provided for a penitentiary sentence of between two and five years for those who engaged in prizefighting.[24]

Of course, the law did not actually stop prizefighting. No matter how tightly it was worded, the statute left room for a certain amount of local interpretation. For example, prizefighting was legally defined as any encounter "for money or other thing of value, or upon the result of which any money or anything of value is bet or wagered, or to see which any admission fee is charged." For many turn-of-the-century sports fans, this definition did not rule out exhibitions for which no money was paid, on which no money was bet, and to which no admission fee was charged. Under this set of assumptions, the Galveston Athletic Club in 1899 invited Joe Choynski, a nationally prominent boxer, to come to Galveston to act as the club's physical training instructor. The members of the club agreed to pay Choynski $500 a month for his services, and the famous boxer agreed as one of his duties to give a "scientific demonstration" of his trade against a local heavyweight named Jim Hall. Of course, neither Choynski nor Hall would be paid for the exhibition, nor would any of the club members either bet on the outcome of the exhibition or be charged for watching the demonstration. That, after all, would make the exhibition a prizefight, and in Texas prizefighting was strictly forbidden.[25]

Into this Alice in Wonderland world of professional, but technically nonprofessional, boxing Johnson entered in 1897. Johnson's

record for the first several years of his career is sketchy. Because boxing was illegal, club fights were not normally reported in the local
newspapers, and even on the rare occasions when they were covered,
only the main attractions were mentioned. Johnson was not a main
attraction. He fought in obscurity. The *Ring Record Books* listed five
fights for Johnson for 1897 and 1898, but he probably fought more.
For the most part these were years of learning his trade, and at that
stage education was more important than results.

By 1899 Johnson had begun to move up. He now was fighting
and defeating the best of the local fighters. Although his relaxed
fighting style struck some spectators as lazy, it was effective. Johnson
appeared to win without extending himself. After defeating a local
favorite named Jim McCormick in March, Johnson decided his talents had outgrown Galveston. He went to Chicago, the stamping
ground of such prominent boxers as Jack Root, Peter Maher, Billy
Stift, Frank Childs, Marvin Hart, and Tom Sharkey. From men of
this quality, Johnson began his graduate education in pugilism. As a
sparring partner he learned to slip punches, hook to the kidney, and
perform other tricks of the trade.[26]

He learned, but he did not prosper. The money he made as Jack
Root's sparring partner was negligible, and without a reputation he
was not in demand for real fights. He ate poorly and slept irregularly.
Then his chance came, and he failed. On May 7, 1899, he was
matched against a good black boxer whose *nom de guerre* was Klondike Haynes. Johnson, who was underfed, was described as "nearly
starved" when he entered the ring, but for the first few rounds he
outboxed Klondike. Then he started to weaken under Klondike's
body attack. In the fifth round Johnson decided that he had fought
enough and abruptly quit. Chicago was unimpressed with the debut.
Johnson went back to Galveston for another season in the minor
leagues.[27]

Nineteen hundred was a bad year for Johnson and a worse one
for Galveston. Along with houses and stores, the flood washed away
local boxing events. Johnson is credited with only one fight for that
year, a twelve-round win against Josh Mills in Memphis. If Johnson's
autobiography is to be believed, he also traveled throughout the
Rocky Mountain states with a boxing troupe that included Tom
Sharkey and Mexican Pete Everett. But in 1900 Sharkey fought on
the East Coast and Everett on the West Coast. In truth, Jack Johnson was as much obscured by the storm as was his father. Like so
many other Galvestonians, he was lost in the flood.[28]

He resurfaced early in 1901. On February 25 of that year he was matched against Joe Choynski, one of the greatest fighters of the late nineteenth and early twentieth centuries. Choynski was a Jew and a legend. His father published *Public Opinion*, a muckraking San Francisco newspaper that exposed anti-Semitism in American society. Like his father, Joe also fought against Jew-baiters. In 1889 he fought future heavyweight champion Jim Corbett on a grain barge anchored in San Francisco Bay close to Benecia. Corbett won in twenty-seven savage and bloody rounds. Thereafter Choynski fought and defeated many of the best fighters of his era. He battled John L. Sullivan and Bob Fitzsimmons, Kid McCoy and Tom Sharkey, Jim Jeffries and Joe Walcott. He fought the greats and the near greats, from lightweights to heavyweights. By 1901, when he fought Johnson, his skills and his ambition were declining.[29]

In 1900 Choynski was knocked out by Kid McCoy, Joe Walcott, and Tom Sharkey. He was old but still had a reputation; Johnson had no reputation but possessed what A. J. Liebling has called "the outrageous fortunes of chronology."[30] A victory over Choynski would vault Johnson into the national heavyweight scene and allow him to return to Chicago in style. Johnson was anxious for the match and had full confidence that he would win.

The fight was something of a social occasion for Galveston. Although the wet night air seeped through the cracks in the walls of Harmony Hall, no "political meeting or ordinary entertainment" had ever attracted such a large crowd. Before the main event black minstrels and a quartet from Houston sang a few songs; then the two one-legged "colored boys" boxed in a Battle Royal. Finally, referee Herman Bernau gave a short talk on the necessity of maintaining order during the interracial bout. This done, the two fighters entered the ring and the fight started.

If Choynski could no longer defeat champions, he could still handle newcomers. For two rounds Johnson looked good; he moved well and landed as often as he was hit. Early in the third round, Choynski feinted with a left, which pulled down Johnson's guard, and crossed with a right. Johnson fell forward into Choynski's arms and then gradually sank to the floor, face downward. Everyone expected Johnson to rise; reporters did not believe that the punch had carried knockout power. But at the count of ten Johnson was still stretched out on the canvas.[31]

But the action was just beginning. As soon as the referee finished his count, Captain Brooks and four other Texas Rangers climbed into the ring and arrested Choynski and Johnson. The arrest was orderly, but Johnson, still groggy from Choynski's right cross, was confused and had to be helped out of the ring. Afterward Brooks told reporters that he had acted on orders of the governor; he was told to allow Galveston authorities to prevent the fight, but if they failed to do so, he was to stop it. And, faithful to his duty, stop it he did. When the first "real punch" was landed—the knockout blow— and the count completed, Brooks arrested the offenders.[32]

The issues behind the arrest were more political than pugilistic. Governor Joseph Sayers was a genteel, high-minded man who, although not a progressive on the issue of prizefighting, believed in the enforcement of state laws. He had seen Galveston overcome the effects of the flood and regarded boxing as a small barrier to the general progress of the community. Publicly, he stated that the people of Galveston could decide whether or not to enforce the statute against prizefighting, but the governor's actions spoke otherwise. He employed a forceful attorney, John Lovejoy, to prosecute the case and made sure that the bench was sympathetic to the state's position.[33]

Prominent Galvestonians, however, were determined to protect their manly enjoyments. Alderman Robert Webber said the $5,000 bond under which Johnson and Choynski were held was worse than in a murder case. Is it "a greater crime against the great state of Texas to engage in a friendly boxing contest than to shoot your neighbor down without notice?" Webber demanded. He knew boxing was criticized as brutal, degrading, and demoralizing; he knew the argument that it attracted the rowdier sorts of people. But in Galveston the sport was good clean fun that had a following among the "best citizens" of the community. Charles L. Davis, president of the Galveston Athletic Club, agreed. Neither the fighters nor the promoters were guilty of anything more than staging a wholesome "scientific exhibition" of self-defense, one whose purpose was moral uplift and physical improvement.[34]

In jail Johnson and Choynski were told that their bond would be reduced and that they would be released as soon as the court heard the charges. Eleven days after the fight Judge Allen was presented with the writ. His reaction was not what the fighters expected. In presenting the case to the grand jury, he emphasized that Texas had abolished prizefighting for salutary reasons. The sport, he said, was a "species of brutality before which most Americans blanched." Prizefighting "accustoms people to cruelty and begets a taste for brutal pastimes;" it "dulls man's ordinarily sympathetic natures." Addressing the grand jury, he added, "but with the reason of the law you have nothing to do; it is sufficient that the law is on the statute book and your sworn duty is to act under it. And it seems the law of Texas has been deliberately and openly violated and defied." As Allen spoke, Johnson's and Choynski's faces registered their concern. They had expected to leave the courtroom free men, or at least free on bond. Instead they were returned to jail.[35]

Not that jail was bad, at least not this one. Both prisoners were well treated. They were celebrities of sorts, and their case was special. Sometimes they were allowed to spar for the amusement of jail authorities and the inmates. In these sessions, Johnson learned the subtle moves of the profession that only a master could teach. Professionally, for Johnson the time spent in jail was like a training camp. The two even posed for pictures, looking out from behind bars as their captors held rifles and handguns as if they had just bagged a pair of prize elk. In truth, their time in jail resembled a charade that had gone sour but could not be ended. Jail life was not bad, but after a few weeks it began to pall.[36]

Judge Allen showed no desire to end the charade. While the grand jury reviewed the evidence, Allen went to Austin and conferred with the governor. He returned more convinced than ever that lawbreakers must not go unpunished. However, the grand jury was not so outraged. After a leisurely review of the evidence it failed to find grounds for an indictment. Allen was shocked and angry. After some discussion, Allen said that the grand jury had not understood his instructions; he therefore denied the motion to dismiss the case.[37]

Choynski was irritated. He told the court that his only reason for coming to Galveston was to take a job as athletic instructor for the Galveston Athletic Club. Calling himself a "has-been," he said his exhibition with Johnson was purely for the purpose of instruction. When asked if he had knocked out Johnson, he replied: "No, sir, he just found a soft spot and laid down. I have given exhibitions with other people and had them do the same thing. . . . Johnson just got tired and quit." Judge Allen was unimpressed. He ordered the grand jury to reconsider its findings and sent Johnson and Choynski back to jail.[38]

Determined as Judge Allen was to keep Choynski and Johnson locked away, the grand jury was just as determined that they should go free. Finally a truce was reached. On March 20 the fighters' bond was reduced to $1,000. Two days later the bonds were paid and the boxers freed. They had spent twenty-four days in jail, and both were bitter over the experience. Choynski told reporters that he was through with boxing; he would return to his wife in La Grange, Illinois, and devote himself to other pursuits. Johnson, too, was through—but only with Galveston. He left for St. Louis, where he expected to engage in other "scientific exhibitions." Both said they would return to Texas when their case came to trial. It never did.[39]

The emotions of the day soon calmed. Choynski returned to boxing and fought for three more years. Johnson was back in Galveston within a month, as were "scientific exhibitions" of pugilism. Boxing was returned to the *de facto* local option status it had enjoyed before the Johnson-Choynski affair. Before the year was over, Johnson fought at least eight more times in Galveston, all in matches that were as much ignored by the newspapers as they were enjoyed by the spectators. By the summer of 1901 it was clear that Johnson was far better than any of the other local fighters. Once Jim McCormick, a top Galveston boxer, had fought draws with Johnson; now Jack toyed with him.[40]

In Galveston Johnson had flourished in the dark. His successes went unobserved and unnoticed. He was a good fighter and knew it, but as long as he stayed in Galveston no one else would know it. He had made tentative forays into the boxing world beyond Galveston, but always he returned. Galveston meant home—his family, a house at 808 Broadway, and Mary Austin. It meant familiar surroundings and security. After the flood proved security an illusion, it was easier for Johnson to break his ties with Galveston. Late in 1901, when he was twenty-three years old, he left the city. Galveston would never again be his home.

2

Black Boss Man

WHITE BOXING FANS GENERALLY felt uncomfortable about interracial matches. Too many things could go wrong; the white fighter, who was expected to win, might for any number of reasons lose, and then blacks were sure to misinterpret the result. This was especially true in the South. In 1897 the Mississippi Pleasure Company arranged a fight between Joe Green, a black, and a white boxer called simply "the Swede." Shortly after the fight began, Henry Long, described as "a loyal Southerner" by the *New Orleans Daily Picayune*, stopped the contest, explaining: "The idea of niggers fighting white men. Why, if that darned scoundrel would beat that white boy the niggers would never stop gloating over it, and, as it is, we have enough trouble with them." Watching boxing was no fun for whites when racial tranquility was riding on the outcome.[1]

Some felt more than tranquility was at stake. Americans, proud that they produced the best fighters and apt to place a cosmic interpretation on any event, constructed satisfying theories around their ring dominance. They nurtured the best fighters because in the Social Darwinistic sense Americans were the most fit people in the world. When John L. Sullivan was champion, the *New York Sun* commented that he was "the most phenomenal production of the prize ring that has been evolved during the nineteenth century." This led to a thrilling syllogism: Sullivan is the greatest fighter in the world;

Sullivan is an American; *ergo* America is the world's greatest country. In the ring the "march onward and upward" and the "progress of the species" were visible. As Dale A. Somers said, "When the prize ring produced men capable of beating all rivals in such rigorous, primeval struggles, it seemed to justify America's competitive system and to prove the value of the system's scientific underpinnings."[2]

Such heady theories became blurred when blacks fought whites. White theorists could not use a victory by a black fighter over a white boxer as an indication of America's special fitness; indeed, such an outcome tended to diminish the "scientific" racial stature of white Americans. Therefore, in the last decade of the nineteenth century matches between blacks and whites were generally avoided in championship fights, even though black fighters dominated several of the lighter divisions. When the practice was overlooked—as it sometimes was in the lighter divisions—the results were often dismaying for white spectators. In 1892 George "Little Chocolate" Dixon was pitted against Jack Skelly, a white boxer. Dixon administered a frightful beating to Skelly. The fight was staged in New Orleans, and the *Chicago Tribune* noted that the white fans "winced every time Dixon landed on Skelly. The sight was repugnant to some of the men from the South . . . the idea of sitting quietly by and seeing a colored boy pommel a white lad grates on Southerners." Southern newspapermen readily agreed. The editor of the *New Orleans Times-Democrat* said that it was "a mistake to match a negro and a white man, a mistake to bring the races together on any terms of equality, even in the prize ring."[3]

Such problems did not occur in the heavier divisions, where men weighed more and therefore, whites reasoned, more was at stake. John L. Sullivan understood the symbolic importance of being world heavyweight champion, and he made it clear that no black should ever be given a chance to win such an exalted title. In 1892 he issued his famous challenge to fight all contenders: "In this challenge I include all fighters—first come, first served—who are white. I will not fight a Negro. I never have and I never shall." True to his word, the Boston Strong Boy never did. Black fighters might fight for and win titles in the featherweight and lightweight divisions but not in the middleweight, light heavyweight, and heavyweight divisions, for these were the championships that mattered. Most Americans equated pounds with importance, and especially when the scale tipped at one hundred seventy-five and a championship was being contested, the nation took note. In these contests race was a crucial matter; opportunity was strictly for whites only.[4]

Even when the title was not on the line, important interracial heavyweight fights aroused heated emotions. The most admired black heavyweight of his day was Peter Jackson, a boxer from St. Croix. He was universally acknowledged to be noble in the ring and gentlemanly outside it. Yet he was never allowed to fight for the championship, and when he fought white fighters at all he was often subjected to the vilest racial insults. The white attitude toward Jackson was shown in a drawing by future prime minister Winston Churchill. In 1892 Churchill saw Jackson defeat Frank Slavin at the National Sporting Club in London. Churchill was seventeen at the time, and the match provoked his deepest racial prejudices. The picture he drew of the fight shows an apelike—long-armed and hunch-shouldered—Jackson standing over a frail-looking Slavin. Churchill called this curious piece of juvenilia "Knockout," but the emotions that produced it were far from innocent. When big men—one black and the other white—fought, white jaws tightened.[5]

When Jack Johnson left Galveston, then, he was not in pursuit of the world heavyweight championship. He was a black heavyweight and therefore expected to fight other black heavyweights. And for the next three years that was exactly what he did. There were occasional fights against lesser white heavyweights—white fighters so unimportant that they had no reputations to lose to black boxers—but generally Johnson was matched against the very best of a very good crop of black boxers. In those days the best blacks had to fight each other or find another profession.

From Galveston Johnson drifted to the West Coast. He loved the sea and, all things considered, preferred to live in warm climates. California, not unlike Galveston in these respects, was a logical place for Johnson to go. Beyond weather, by 1900 it was the national center for boxing. Of course, prizefighting was illegal in California; the first session of the legislature held in the state in 1850 enacted a law making it a felony for two persons to fight each other for any sort of prize. This law was amended from time to time but never so as to make prizefighting lawful. Yet like certain customs in Hamlet's Denmark, it was a law honored more in the breach than in the observance. In every major section of the state, prizefighting was a booming, profitable, and legally undisturbed enterprise.[6]

In the fall of 1901 Johnson wandered into Bakersfield. He was known only by word of mouth—generally his own—and attracted little attention. Bakersfield had a reputation as a rough desert town, and the addition of another man who boasted that he could fight was scarcely noticed. After several months of self-advertising, however, a few men began to listen to Johnson. Frank Carrillo was one who thought this boastful twenty-three-year-old was worth a second look. Carrillo was a heavy-set man of Mexican-American ancestry who most definitely did have a reputation. He owned a saloon and carried a gun, and few men crossed him. As a saloon owner, he was also a sporting man whose interests embraced horse racing, gambling, and boxing. Eventually he agreed to manage Johnson, matching the Texan against a leading West Coast heavyweight named Hank Griffin. Johnson looked good, even though he lost the decision. The next month—December—the two were rematched in a fight staged in Oakland. This time they fought to a draw. For Johnson it was a considerable pugilistic step.[7]

After working as a sparring partner for Kid Carter in the Oakland area, Johnson was again struck with the need to move on. He went back to Chicago, the scene of his earlier failure. But without an established reputation or following, he was unable to get a fight. Moving to the East Coast, he also failed to find any matches. Then he was called back to Chicago by a local promoter to fight Frank Childs. At that time Childs was considered one of the best black heavyweights in America; indeed, he was so good that Fred Russell, a white boxer, backed out of a scheduled match with him. Johnson was pressed into action as Russell's replacement, and on only two days notice he acquitted himself well. Johnson started off fast and almost knocked out Childs in the second round. But the travel and lack of meals took their toll, and Childs won the six-round decision.[8]

From Chicago he went back to the East Coast, where he defeated Dan Murphy, a relatively unknown boxer, and then headed for warmer climates, first to Galveston and then back to California. In California, Carrillo had arranged several more fights. With each success, Johnson's stock rose. His fights in Chicago and in the East had been reported in California. He was no longer unknown; in four short months he had acquired a reputation. Carrillo used this quickly won fame to match Johnson with Joe Kennedy, who the previous year had fought world heavyweight champion Jim Jeffries. The fight attracted a large crowd to Oakland's Reliance Club, and Johnson was impressive. He was well trained and against the flabby Kennedy appeared even better than he was. After taking a series of uppercuts in the fourth round, Kennedy fell to the canvas and was unable to rise. Commenting on the fight, the *Oakland Tribune* called Johnson a "hard and willing worker" who should be given the chance to fight in the premier California Clubs.[9]

After a few more wins Johnson was matched against Jeffries. Not *the* Jeffries though; this was Jack Jeffries, Jim's brother. Jack Jeffries, like other brothers of famous champions, was a mediocre fighter who because of his genes was considered to have outstanding potential. Johnson fought him in Los Angeles. Never before had so large a crowd turned out to see a fight in that angelic city. Though many came to see Jim Jeffries, who attended the match, still more were intrigued by the black-white confrontation. The most money was bet on Jack Jeffries, whose physique reminded one reporter of a Greek god. By contrast, Johnson was described as "a long, lean, bullet-headed, flat-chested, 'coon.' "[10]

The excitement of the night did not seem to touch Johnson, who sat in his corner "half asleep and yawning like a big cat." And for the first few rounds Johnson boxed as if he were only half-awake. As Jim Jeffries, dressed in a gray, sleeveless undershirt, looked on, his brother moved well and landed a few good punches. Johnson glided, fighting a defensive battle and throwing few punches. In the fourth round Jeffries landed a hard blow to Johnson's nose. The punch seemed to wake Johnson, who thereafter "glared like a wild beast." In the next round, after a hard right uppercut, Jeffries fell to the canvas. The champion watched sadly as his brother was counted out.[11]

Before Johnson defeated Jeffries, he was a fighter whose personality was unknown to the sporting pages of California papers. After the fight sportswriters began to take notice. In their view he was a typical black boxer—talented, but indolent and frivolous. To white reporters Johnson looked sleepy and moved with the slow grace of an uncaring and unemployed dancer. His body expressed controlled, even hidden, power. He was "a good-natured black animal," wrote one journalist. He was no different from the stereotypical slave— lazy, powerful, happy, carefree. Yet reporters sensed something deeper, a carnivorous potential for violence. He was "good natured" but still a "black animal"; he moved defensively, but when hurt his eyes "glared like a wild beast's." Even his laziness was compared to that of a "big cat." The black cat image would become a stock metaphor in any description of Johnson. Its implications are significant, carrying overtones of destructiveness and infidelity, lawlessness and lust. Johnson was to play the same role in white America's mind as the black cat plays on the canvas of Manet's "Olympia"—tail raised, defiant at the feet of the naked white harlot.[12]

Johnson's dress accentuated his rebellious tendencies. Traditionally boxers fought in the colors of turn-of-the century respectability—black and white. Occasionally an Irishman might add a dash of green to his raiment, but brighter colors were seldom seen in the ring. Johnson scorned such customs. For the Jeffries fight he wore pink pajamas as boxing tights. And not an "inoffensive" pink, but what a *Los Angeles Times* reporter described as "one of those screaming, cater-wauling, belligerent pinks." The spectators laughed when they saw Johnson's colorful flouting of ring tradition; they were yet to realize that Johnson's clothes reflected the defiance of the man. Johnson, always a fastidious dresser, *was* his clothes. "Cater-waul": the cry of a cat in heat. The *Times* reporter was closer to the truth than he knew.[13]

In everyday dress Johnson aligned himself with other black and white sporting men. One reporter claimed Johnson had no fewer than twenty-one suits, changed clothes three times a day, and always dressed for dinner. What was even more unusual for a black, the journalist continued, Johnson's clothes were "tasty, too." Another reporter said that it was always "high levee" on Spring Street in Los Angeles when Johnson trained at the Fourth Street Gym. After training he would answer questions and entertain other blacks. On one such occasion it was reported, "The boss dingy, resplendent in a new suit, with a cane, dress suit and the very latest thing in golf caps [held] forth on the sidewalk." Even in these early years Johnson was a hero for many blacks. They listened to and laughed at the comments of a black man who by any material standard was a success— and, more important, a success on his own terms.[14]

Part of Johnson's pose was imitation. A sporting man was expected to dress and act in a carefully prescribed manner. Style—the gaudier the better—was most important. Johnson viewed himself as an extraordinary individual and therefore acted in extraordinary ways. He sipped beer and vintage wines through a straw; he laughed loudly, rolling his head backward to a ninety-degree angle with his back; he employed a maid just to look after his clothes; he prided himself on his gold teeth. In this manner, he was similar to Jelly Roll Morton, the Ragtime musician. Morton liked diamonds; he wore them as shirt studs and cufflinks, and he had one implanted in a front tooth. For a Sport that was style, and Johnson greatly admired it.[15]

A Sport even moved in a special way—slow and graceful, never rushed. Morton, a legend among black Sports, once said Ragtime could not be hurried or accelerated; its rhythms had to be slow and stylized. On the streets Jack Johnson walked that way, and in the ring he fought that way. Boxing, like music, is a rhythm activity. Even its exercises—jumping rope, punching the speed bag, shadow boxing, sit-ups—are in essence rhythm. Every great fighter has his own rhythm and style. Some move in jitterbug bebops; some shuffle to an internal slow-drag blues. Johnson shuffled; he boxed the way Morton played the piano, with an emphasis on style and grace, not speed and power. It was a style well loved by the Sport.[16]

As Johnson boxed, he lived—like a Sport. A Sport gambled, enjoyed the night life, and frequented "sporting houses." Marriage—or if married, fidelity—lacked style. By the time Johnson went to California he was through with Mary Austin; yet he always longed for the comfort of a semiconstant companion and, if money permitted, two or three. While Johnson was in Philadelphia in January of 1902, he met Clara Kerr, a beautiful black woman who was probably a prostitute. When Johnson left Philadelphia for Chicago, she followed. Eventually they lived together in Bakersfield, where she assumed the customary *de facto* title "Mrs. Johnson." According to Johnson's autobiography he loved her deeply, but she was unfaithful and eventually left him for a horse trainer and well-dressed Sport named William Bryan. In his version Johnson played the cuckold. Not only did Clara run off with Bryan; the man had been sharing quarters with Johnson and Clara. Moreover, the ungrateful pair took Johnson's clothes and money when they left. From that point Johnson's story gets melodramatic. He tracks the two across the continent, finds them, and is reconciled with Clara; a few months later she leaves him, again taking wardrobe and ready cash along; he turns to a life of dissipation—gambling, drinking, not eating—and almost dies; reaching a low point, through the force of will he returns to boxing and goes on to win the championship. Years later he discovers Clara in prison at Tom's River, New Jersey, on a murder rap. "I employed lawyers for her," Johnson wrote, "and provided her with other funds and aid. She was acquitted of the murder charge and shortly afterward I helped her to acquire a small hotel which she has conducted successfully since."[17]

It is an extraordinary story, but then Johnson was fond of such tales. The truth of the relationship was probably less melodramatic and a bit more sordid. Years later, when Johnson was charged with a violation of the Mann Act, a Bureau of Investigation agent in Philadelphia located Charles Horner, a friend of Johnson, who knew him during 1902. Horner, who had once been Johnson's sparring partner, told agent Carbarino that Clara could "tell a great deal about Johnson compelling her to lead the life of a prostitute and give him her earnings." According to Horner, Johnson stayed with Clara until he began to have sexual relations with white women, at which point he left Clara. Carbarino, an exceptionally thorough agent, recommended that the government subpoena Horner as a witness. Horner, he reported, "is an intelligent negro, above the average, and would make a very good witness." Unfortunately, Horner died a month after being interviewed by Carbarino, and Johnson's relationship with Clara was never thoroughly explored.[18]

Certainly, Clara was not the last prostitute whom Johnson lived with; indeed, he was seldom attracted to any other kind of woman. Yet in later years there were never any suggestions that he was a pimp or that he profited in any other way from prostitution. That his women companions practiced prostitution while he was involved with them did not bother Johnson. But they were always allowed to keep the money they earned. Probably Johnson followed the same procedure with Clara: they lived together when it was convenient, and when it was not Johnson went his way and Clara went hers. Pimps were usually Sports, but beyond Horner's story there is no indication that Johnson was such a breed.

In California Johnson developed both his street style and his ring style. The first depended upon the second. Without pugilistic success Johnson lost his street appeal. He realized this and was careful about his craft. After defeating Jack Jeffries, he went back on the road. In Memphis he knocked out Klondike Haynes, who had knocked him out three years before. In Chicago he fought a draw with Billy Stift, a very good black heavyweight. Back in Los Angeles he was matched against Hank Griffin, whom he had fought several times before. The fight, sponsored by the Century Athletic Club and staged in Hazard's Pavilion, was scheduled for twenty rounds, and it went the distance. Griffin was a smart defensive fighter who for most of the bout was content to allow Johnson to lead. After Johnson tired in the thirteenth round, Griffin controlled the action. When the fight was judged a draw, few people complained.[19]

By mid-1902 Johnson was recognized as a skillful heavyweight. Though light by heavyweight standards—he weighed only 180 pounds—he was exceptionally quick and had a good right uppercut. But his main talents were defensive. He generally fought with his weight on and his shoulders directly above his back foot. His hands were held only chest high, and he always had a clear view of his opponent. He looked like an artist leaning back from a canvas to evaluate the picture from a distance. And he fought the same way—almost as if he were detached or wanted to stand above the action. It was a style that was more admired than enjoyed. Most spectators preferred action; they liked aggressive, free-swinging punchers. For some, Johnson's balanced defensive style seemed lazy, and they normally attributed this flaw to his color.[20]

In fact, race undoubtedly contributed to his style. All of the great black heavyweights of the first quarter of the twentieth century were noted more for their defensive than their offensive abilities. Hank Griffin was a superb defensive boxer, but so too were Denver Ed Martin, Sam McVey, Harry Wills, Sam Langford, Peter Jackson, and Joe Jeannette. In part, this was ascribable to economics: a good aggressive black could not get lucrative fights with white boxers. It actually paid a black boxer never to look too strong or too good against a white opponent. Such great fighters as Johnson and Langford often confessed that they carried white boxers and withheld the full measure of their abilities. For them, greatness lay in the ability to just barely defeat a vastly inferior white boxer.

Yet more than economics contributed to the development of the black defensive style. It was also cultural. Much of black humor and black culture is based on the ability to retort and defend. The black ritual of insult—variously called the Dozens, Sounding, Woofing, Joining, Screaming, Cutting, or Chopping—emphasizes the facility of verbal reactions. Because blacks only insulted other blacks when playing the Dozens, the ritual provided "a vehicle for deflecting aggression away from the white world where it was dangerous, into a permissive channel within the black world where it would have few serious consequences." In addition, it promoted self-discipline; resorting to physical reprisals was tantamount to an admission of defeat. As Lawrence W. Levine wrote, "the inculcation of this kind of discipline was one of the central objects of the ritual of insult. Developed at a time when black Americans were especially subject to insults and assaults upon their dignity to which they could not safely respond, the Dozens served as a mechanism for teaching and sharpening the ability to control emotions and anger; an ability which was often necessary for survival."[21]

The development of a defensive style in the ring served the same purpose for black boxers as playing the Dozens did outside it. Passivity was assumed to be a black characteristic, just as aggression was considered a white trait. In fact, aggression was seen as an indication of the amount of white blood in an individual. As late as 1930 Robert E. Park, a former teacher at Tuskegee Institute, characterized pure-blooded blacks as docile, tractable, and unambitious. In contrast, the mulatto was described as aggressive, restless, enterprising, and ambitious. Before the 1950s and 1960s this doctrine was generally accepted. Marcus Garvey even once criticized the NAACP for implicitly accepting the theory by staffing its offices with light-skinned blacks. Given these assumptions and expectations, black boxers conformed. White fighters like John L. Sullivan, Tom Sharkey, Robert Fitzsimmons, and Jim Jeffries developed styles centered on power and aggression; they attacked relentlessly and prided themselves on never taking a backward step. For them, the ring was territory, and the object was to hold it. Black fighters viewed both the ring and the object differently. The ring, like the world, was assumed to be the white man's territory, and the black fighter's object was to yield it without suffering physical punishment, allowing his opponent to defeat himself. This was accomplished through feints and deceptive defensive maneuvers. The black boxer waited for the white fighter to tire before moving on the offensive, but usually he did not turn aggressive even then.[22]

A look at knockout percentages, a yardstick for aggression, illustrates this point. Three of the great white heavyweights of the late nineteenth and early twentieth centuries were Sullivan, Sharkey, and Jeffries. Sullivan's knockout percentage was 71 percent, Sharkey's 68, and Jeffries's 71. For the same period the best black heavyweights were Jack Johnson, Sam Langford, Peter Jackson, Joe Jeannette, and Sam McVey. Johnson's knockout percentage was 40 percent, Langford's 39, Jackson's 44, Jeannette's 36, and McVey's 41. The difference was a matter of style. Spectators expected white fighters to be aggressive. Indeed, James J. Corbett, the white boxer who defeated Sullivan, was roundly criticized for his scientific and defensive style. Black boxers, however, were seldom criticized for their defensive methods. Culture had conditioned boxing spectators every bit as much as black and white fighters.[23]

After the Griffin fight Johnson was recognized as a premier black heavyweight, and promoters in the different centers of Western boxing were anxious to put his name on their cards. He traveled to Victor, Colorado, and fought Mexican Pete Everett. Like most boxers whom Johnson fought during this stage in his career, Everett has long been forgotten by all but dedicated followers of the sport, for this reputation was largely regional. But in 1902 Everett was one of the best heavyweights in America. In 1901 he had defeated Tom Sharkey on a foul, and he had fought Jeffries in 1898. By 1902 many ring authorities believed Everett was in line for a title fight. But he was no match for Johnson, who fought his usual skillful, cautious fight. After twenty rounds, Johnson was given the decision.[24]

Returning to Los Angeles, Johnson was once again matched against Frank Childs, whom George Siler of the *Chicago Tribune* had earlier called one of the two best black heavyweights in the country. For Johnson, it was more than just another match; it was a grudge fight. Earlier in the year he had had a dispute with Childs, probably over Clara. In later years Johnson told Nat Fleischer, the former editor of *Ring*, that his single object was to hurt and humiliate Childs. However, this was not how it appeared to the large crowd of spectators, who saw it as a slow, boring twelve-round win for Johnson.[25]

The victory over Childs enabled Carrillo, who was still Johnson's manager, to get his fighter a bout with a leading white boxer. He agreed to fight George Gardner in San Francisco. Gardner was an Irishman from County Clare and though small and light—slightly under 6 feet and 165 pounds—was highly regarded by fans in the Bay Area. He had fought the great Joe Walcott, and for a few months in 1903 he was light heavyweight champion of the world. Johnson, who had been ill, was weak throughout the match, but not too weak to win. The sportswriter for *San Francisco Chronicle* said the aggressive Gardner simply could not hit the "shifty" Johnson. Typically, Johnson failed on a number of occasions to force an advantage. Rather than try for the knockout he allowed Gardner to recover. But this was part of Johnson's style. Unless hurt himself, he never tried for the knockout.[26]

Johnson's last fight in 1902 was against Fred Russell, who was known as one of the dirtiest fighters of his day. Russell had fought—and fouled—the likes of Choynski, Griffin, and Walcott. He was known to hit a fighter when he was down, to butt, and to hit below the belt. Johnson, however, seemed unawed by Russell's reputation, and in the early rounds he toyed with his opponent. By the eighth round Russell was cut over both eyes and blood was smeared over his face and running from his mouth. The large crowd at Hazard's Pavilion did not like seeing a white fighter beaten so severely, and Johnson's ever present smile added to their discomfort. But in the eighth round Johnson won their sympathy. Russell, in desperation, hit Johnson low, and when Johnson doubled over in pain, Russell hit him below the belt three more times. Johnson fell to the canvas and was awarded the fight on a foul. Russell had to be saved by the police from what one writer euphemistically described as a "frenzied" crowd.[27] For Johnson, whose record for 1902 was eleven wins, three draws, and no losses, it had been a good year with a painful finale.

In California boxing circles the word spread that success had gone to Johnson's head. In Bakersfield, where he still lived, a warrant was issued for his arrest, the ostensible reason being failure to pay debts at several local stores, but his troubles went beyond that. It was believed by whites that Johnson and Clara had become "uppity." A writer for the *Bakersfield Daily Californian* came nearer the truth: "It is said that Jack has made himself somewhat obnoxious to various persons who . . . made the charge, claiming that he is living in the forbidden district and beating bills." The desert community of Bakersfield had few blacks, and those who lived there stayed in their own part of town. A black man living in a white area was more than many people in Bakersfield could accept. Carrillo told reporters that his fighter would pay his bills, but he avoided the touchy subject of where he would pay his rent.[28]

Actually, Johnson's wish to live in a white area was only one sign of his growing independence. In early January he split with Carrillo. The manager said "Mrs. Johnson" was behind the break. California sportswriters attributed it to Johnson's "swelled head." Perhaps it was a little of each. Carrillo was the first of many white managers Johnson would have. Women would come between him and other managers, but the central problem was that Johnson did not trust white men. He believed—often on good evidence—that because he was black, whites tried to take advantage of him. Ultimately he viewed managers in the same light as taxi drivers and lawyers: occasionally they were needed, but it was best never to keep one for too long.[29]

In early 1903 more than 4,000 wildly cheering spectators watched Johnson fight for the title. The champion was Denver Ed Martin, considered the best black boxer in America, and the fight was for the Negro heavyweight championship. Since blacks were not allowed to fight for the real crown, California sportswriters had created the need for a Negro heavyweight division. But only the West Coast reporters paid any attention to the championship. In New York and Chicago the division was ignored or viewed as another crazy Californian invention. The fight, however, was staged in Los Angeles, a little world unto itself, and so it did not matter how the rest of the country felt about the match.[30]

Denver Ed Martin was smooth. He was also big, fast, and a very clever boxer. Martin tipped the scales at 203, outweighing Johnson by 23 pounds. One reporter said Johnson looked "slender and boyish" next to Martin. Almost a "pigmy," said another. And everyone agreed that Martin's footwork was the best in the business. Yet Johnson had defeated some good fighters in 1902, and although Martin was the betting favorite, there was plenty of Johnson money to be found on Spring Street—the Los Angeles bookmaking center—in the days before the fight.[31]

For the first ten rounds both men showed a great amount of respect for each other. Martin's feints were foiled by Johnson's counter-feints, Martin's footwork neutralized by Johnson's footwork. Punches were tentative and harmless; clinches were many and long. The spectators were restless and bored, and there were a few cries of "fake" from the outer reaches of the audience. All this changed in the eleventh round. Johnson landed a right hook to Martin's neck. Martin went down, and the spectators jumped to their feet; one reporter, more excited than accurate, wrote, "Four thousand throats bellowed out a volume of whistles, cheers, yells and screeches so overpowering that it was impossible to hear yourself speak." But few wanted to hear anyway; most were content to scream and watch. They watched as Johnson knocked down Martin four more times in the eleventh round. Martin survived the round and even won a few of the later rounds. But Johnson easily won the twenty-round decision and the title.[32]

After Martin's defeat, only one black was left on the West Coast who was considered as good as Johnson. That man was a youngster named Sam McVey, who even by 1903 was inspiring legends in sportswriting circles. His fame rested less on his fighting ability—which was considerable—than on his visage. By the day's Anglo-Saxon standards, McVey was considered a very ugly man, with an exceptionally broad nose, thick lips, and projecting lower jaw. He was described as "African black"—which meant very black indeed. Even though his fight with Johnson was his first recorded match, the scar tissue around his eyes indicated he was not new to the sport. Any man who could look at McVey for twenty rounds, said a reporter for the *Los Angeles Times*, deserved "a good reputation for bravery," for the fighter's countenance "would scare back the rising moon."[33]

The racism implicit in such a statement tended to dehumanize black boxers; as long as brutality was treated with humor, whites need not take it too seriously. It had long been an article of faith among the followers of boxing that blacks were insensitive to pain. More than one hundred years before, Dr. Charles White in *An Account of the Regular Gradation of Man* recorded that blacks had harder and thicker skulls than whites. And in Johnson's time the ring authority Bohum Lynch wrote that "it was recognized from the first that the African negro and his descendants in the West Indies and America were harder-headed than white men, less sensitive about the face and jaw; most black boxers can take without pain or trouble a smashing which would cause the collapse of a white man." Following this arrant nonsense, one reporter, commenting on the Johnson-McVey fight, remarked: "They don't arrange these coon fights right. The afternoon before the fight they ought to run the fighters through a steam carpet-cleaning machine, and set a pair of men pounding them a while with meat cleavers. A little thing like twenty rounds of punching can't worry a coon like McVey much. He could stand up for twenty rounds lashed to a post and let the other man take an ax."[34] In short, McVey in particular—and blacks in general—formed an incipient species regarding tolerance to pain.

McVey and his backers arrived in Los Angeles with money to bet. It was estimated that McVey supporters lost $15,000 on the fight. McVey was no match for the skillful Johnson. The champion hit McVey with frightening ease, though he did not try for a knockout. For Johnson, showing his style was enough. He put on an exhibition showing every sort of punch, combination, and defensive maneuver. He sent the seventeen-year-old McVey back to Oxnard bruised but not seriously hurt. And though the crowd would have preferred additional gore, they were satisfied with the match.[35]

There were people in California who were not pleased with Johnson's performance outside the ring. Now even Frank Carrillo was one of the discontented. Ever since Johnson had dropped him as his manager, Carrillo had been waiting to even the score. After the Martin fight he had had Johnson arrested on a charge of "embezzling" a watch. The charge was soon dropped, but Carrillo was still mad. There were rumors that Johnson feared Carrillo's temper. For these and perhaps other reasons Johnson decided to leave California until tempers cooled. Traveling with his friend Joe Walcott, the great welterweight champion for whom he often had worked as a sparring partner, Johnson headed East. Along the way Walcott helped refine Johnson's boxing technique, and though arrested for such petty offenses as stealing a chicken several times along the way, the pair finally arrived in Boston, Walcott's adopted home, in April.[36]

Johnson had traveled in the East before, and he had friends in New York, Boston, Philadelphia, and Pittsburgh. When he needed money, he accepted a fight, although competition there was vastly inferior to that on the West Coast. In Boston he defeated Sandy Ferguson, a New England fighter who was white and overweight. A few months later he knocked out Joe Butler in Philadelphia. Boxing fans in Philadelphia were eager to see Johnson; they had heard that he was the best black heavyweight in America. But after watching him defeat Butler, they left the Washington Sporting Club impressed more by Johnson's plum boxing tights than by anything he did to his opponent. They were upset by Johnson's unwillingness to exert himself. Although he knocked out Butler in the third round, Johnson let everyone know that he considered the fight a joke. He treated Butler more like an upstart boy than a serious opponent.[37]

Nevertheless, two months later he again fought in Philadelphia. Rematched against Ferguson, once more Johnson refused to fight seriously. Though in excellent condition, he toyed with the out-of-shape Ferguson and chose not to end the fight with a knockout. Throughout the bout he smiled and laughed at Ferguson's futile efforts. In the sixth round—by Pennsylvanian law the last—Johnson, mocking Ferguson, asked, "Where do you want this?" He then slammed a short right to Ferguson's body and laughed. As the sportswriter for the *Philadelphia Inquirer* speculated, Johnson preferred to "suggest" what he could do rather than actually do it.[38]

After almost six months in the East Johnson decided to return to California. Much to the delight of West Coast sportswriters, he was even more flamboyant than when he left. Wearing his hair parted in the middle and speaking with an affected English accent (which he acquired from Walcott, a West Indian black), Johnson told reporters that from now on he wanted to be called J. Arthur Johnson. Furthermore, he wanted to fight Jim Jeffries for the title. If Jeffries had fought other black fighters like Hank Griffin, Peter Jackson, and Bob Armstrong, why not the current Negro champion? Jeffries, however, firmly refused to consider the match. When told of Johnson's challenge, he answered, "When there are no white men left to fight, I will quit the business. . . . I am determined not take a chance of losing the championship to a negro."[39]

Not only was Johnson more confident now, he had changed in other ways. For one, he was heavier. At 195 pounds he was just right for a heavyweight, and, as reporters noted, he was in perfect condi-

tion. There were a few displays of bad temper. Sparring in a Los
Angeles gym with Rufe Thompson, a good fighter at the end of his
career, Johnson was hit while clowning. Suddenly enraged, Johnson
angrily opened up on Thompson and beat him severely. Then, too,
his humor was more racially motivated. His challenges to fight Jeffries were more biting. Told that Jeffries would not defend his title
against a black, Johnson answered, "Ah waives de coloh line mah
self." Deference, a quality Johnson once could at least pretend, now
was totally missing from his bag of masks.[40]

In the ring he was also more ready to punish an opponent. Rematched with McVey for the Negro title, Johnson fought in a controlled rage. While he did not knock out McVey, he hit the Oxnard
fighter continually and hard. One reporter observed that McVey went
through the "worst hell" ever seen in a Los Angeles prizefight. Johnson, he said, might as well have "pounded a street car fender" as hit
McVey, whose face "looked as though a goat had chewed it." McVey
was badly cut and lost several teeth, and he was unable to hurt Johnson in return. Defensively and offensively, the champion was in perfect form. He was, reporters agreed, the best fighter ever seen in the
Los Angeles area. Billy Roche, McVey's manager, admitted his
fighter was outclassed and conceded that Johnson had a "magnificent style."[41]

The fight also impressed the promoters. It drew the largest gate
and crowd in Los Angeles history and stimulated at least $30,000 in
betting. That Johnson was the reason nobody doubted; he had par-
ticipated in the four most profitable fights in the area. His share of
the McVey fight was $2,796. Promoters reasoned that if Johnson and
McVey could draw a gate of more than $7,600, Johnson and Jeffries
would produce the largest gate in all boxing history. With visions of
the money, they said, "The color line gauge does not go now." The
public, promoters added, demanded the match, and if Johnson won
he would "wear the honor with decent grace." One article ended with
a sentence that would later become famous: "It is up to Jeffries to
say when." Jeffries quickly answered: "Never."[42]

Creditors similarly were pleased by Johnson's victory. Never a
very prompt bill payer, he still had a few unpaid debts, and lawyers
had served a writ of garnishment to the promoters of the Johnson-
McVey fight. Johnson, however, was not that easily separated from
his money. Before the fight he had signed a contract with Zeke Abrahams calling for the manager to get 100 percent of all of Johnson's
purses. Therefore, garnishment efforts failed. Called into court,

Abrahams modestly admitted that it was a fine contract. Asked how much money Johnson would receive, he replied, "He ain't gettin' nothin'." Johnson, Abrahams said, is a "witty fellow" who "lives off his wits and his white friends." Besides, he concluded, any money Johnson made he threw away on gambling and gifts for his "wife."⁴³

Johnson's creditors were frustrated several months later when the champion fought again. Matched against Sandy Ferguson in Colma, California, Johnson fought an uninspired fight. A leading San Francisco sportswriter, W. W. Naughton, called the match "barbeque boxing." Johnson and Ferguson, who genuinely liked each other, laughed and clowned for the entire twenty rounds. For his part Johnson had something to laugh about. Before the fight the law firm of Russell & Robinson had served a writ of garnishment to the sheriff of San Francisco county. Colma, however, is across the bay in San Mateo county. As a result of this error, Johnson was paid his entire purse.⁴⁴

The Ferguson match was Johnson's last fight in 1903. He had won all seven fights he had fought that year, and after Jeffries he was considered the best heavyweight in the country. But his personal life remained chaotic. His relationship with Clara was close to an end. She seldom traveled with him and sometimes even traveled with other men. Carrillo was still after Johnson's money, and he had been joined by other creditors. Even when he stayed in the "darkest Africa of West Oakland," bill collectors were able to ferret out the champion. On one such occasion Johnson threatened to return to Los Angeles and "clean out" the law firm of Russell & Robinson. For Johnson success had only complicated life.⁴⁵

A pattern of action was developing. When Johnson was confronted with personal problems, he caught a train. Trains provided an escape from contracts, creditors, lawyers, and women. They provided the mobility that governed the rhythm of his existence. In later years there would be periods when he would literally live on trains for weeks at a time. For now—1903—it was enough just to find one that was leaving San Francisco. When he found it, he was gone.

Early in 1904 Johnson went to Philadelphia. He had friends there and, better still, no creditors. After he spent the money he earned in the Ferguson fight, he started to look for matches along the East Coast. This proved difficult, for most of the good heavyweights were in California. After the repeal in New York of the Horton Law, which permitted fighting to a decision, Eastern boxing declined, and most of the top fighters went West. In Pennsylvania fights were not

allowed to be scheduled for more than six rounds, a rule that ruined
any opportunity for big-money fights in the state. Therefore, after
defeating a capable fighter named Black Bill in Philadelphia, Johnson decided to return to the West Coast money bouts.

The problem in the West was finding a good heavyweight opponent. The best white fighters—Jeffries, Bob Fitzsimmons, Jack
Root, Marvin Hart, and Gus Ruhlin—refused to fight him. For
them, drawing the color line was a convenient way to avoid unwanted
competition. The best black boxers would still fight Johnson, but he
had already beaten them all. Finally, for a quick payday, he agreed to
fight Sam McVey one more time. Nobody expected much of a fight,
so nobody was disappointed. For most of the twenty-round fight
Johnson carefully outboxed McVey. He sidestepped punches,
feinted, and fought, as one reporter noted, a "pretty" fight. This
clean style was unappreciated, and hisses, hoots, and catcalls punctuated each round. Then, with twenty seconds remaining in the final
round, Johnson knocked out McVey with a left-right combination to
the head. When McVey was revived he asked Spider Kelly, his popular
manager, "Was it a draw?" "Yes," answered Kelly, "and they
robbed us."[46]

But it was Johnson who was, in another sense, being robbed. Because of his race, he was locked out of the real money matches. And
his graceful defensive style went unapplauded. He returned to Chicago and fought Frank Childs, and was again criticized for his lack of
aggression. The leading boxing writer for the *Chicago Tribune*,
George Siler, wrote that the Johnson-Childs contest was a "brotherly
love" affair, a slow, dull, "unsatisfactory performance." Remember-
ing Johnson's earlier fights in Chicago, Siler remarked that the champion had "bungled the job" every time. He ridiculed Johnson's inability to knock out a "has-been" like Childs.[47]

Johnson returned to California determined to show that he
could, if he chose, fight aggressively. In a rematch against Denver Ed
Martin, Johnson went for the knockout from the first bell. In round
one he dropped Martin with a hard uppercut to the stomach and,
when Martin got up, worked over his opponent's kidneys in the
clinches. In the next round he knocked Martin down four times, the
final one for the count of ten. After the fight Johnson once again
challenged Jeffries, who once again refused. A few weeks before the
two had met in a bar in San Francisco. Jeffries told Johnson he would
fight him only in a cellar—alone. Supposedly, Jeffries put $2,500 on

the bar and said if Johnson came up the steps from the cellar first the money was his. "I ain't no cellar fighter," Johnson told Jeffries.[48]

And he was not. But by the end of 1904 a cellar seemed the only place Johnson would be able to fight Jeffries or any other leading white fighter. He had not lost a fight since his first match in California, but he was no closer to the title than he had been three years before. He was frustrated and broke, and Jeffries was the visible symbol of both problems. But by the end of 1904 Jeffries was tired of fighting altogether. He would soon retire, and the situation in the heavyweight division would change.

3

Changes in Attitudes, Changes in Latitudes

MARVIN HART SAID he did not dislike Jack Johnson in particular, it was just that, being a good Southerner, he did not like blacks in general. It was a few days before the match, and he was talking to reporters. He told them that his father had three wives and twenty-one children, and that he was the twenty-first. He wondered if being "the seventh son multiplied by three" would bring him luck. Turning the conversation to Johnson, Hart admitted that the black was a "clever fellow." "But," he asked rhetorically, "what has the coon ever done that should make him a favorite over me?" "Nothing," he answered. "No," he continued, "this coon will have to go some to beat me." He was sure that being white would work to his advantage. After all, it was commonly accepted that black fighters lacked heart, that they quit in a close fight. Hart would not quit; he had trained hard at San Francisco's Sheehan's Gym, and in a close bout he believed the hours of work before the fight would pay off. He even had a prediction: "Before the twentieth round is reached—probably several rounds before—there'll be a nigger prostrate on the canvas."[1]

The fight was Johnson's opportunity to show the boxing world that he was more than simply a gifted black fighter. Hart was a big, raw-boned heavyweight from Kentucky with an established reputation. He had fought and defeated most of the best white heavyweights of the day. There had been wins over Billy Stift and Philadelphia Jack O'Brien, and close fights with George Gardner, Joe Choynski, Gus Ruhlin, and Jack Root. While Johnson had been fighting blacks, Hart had been battling whites. Johnson's reputation was made on the West Coast, Hart's in the Midwest and East. They were about the same age, and both wanted a title fight against Jeffries. The match was a natural, and boxing fans in San Francisco knew it. William Pierce, sportswriter for the *San Francisco Post*, believed the fight would draw a $20,000 gate, for heavyweight fights pitting a good black against an equally talented white were rare. Pierce realized Johnson was faster and a better boxer, but he also knew that "Hart will try like only a white man can try."[2] The fight, then, matched the skill of a black boxer against the determination of a white fighter.

Alex Greggains, who promoted the fight, had only one worry— Johnson. He was afraid that Johnson would not be aggressive enough. He knew Johnson was capable of fighting a full twenty rounds, but he had reservations about the black fighter's desire. "I have notified Johnson," Greggains informed the press, "that he must fight all the time or the fight will be called 'no contest.' " Zink Abrahams, Johnson's manager, assured Greggains that Johnson was in superb condition for the bout and had every intention of being aggressive. To be on the safe side, however, Greggains agreed to referee the fight. A former boxer himself, he pledged that the fight would be honest. In fact, he said, he would permit the fighters only to wrap their hands in soft surgical bandages, and the wrapping would be done in the ring. There would be no doctored bandages or dogging boxers in a fight refereed by Alex Greggains.[3]

In the view of the white reporters the white spectators received exactly what they feared but expected. Hart was awkward but aggressive. Johnson was graceful but passive. Said W. W. Naughton, one of the leading sportswriters of the period, Hart was "persistently aggressive and steadfastly game." Though he took a frightful beating about the face, he was "indifferent to punishment" and displayed the "great pluck [of a] white man." Johnson, Naughton wrote, lacked "grit." He was by far the better boxer but not at all "stout-hearted." Naughton even commented that Johnson's white handlers "railed at the weak-hearted colored champion."[4] In short, the bout was fought along racial rather than pugilistic lines. It was a fight between a white whose name was Hart, and who had great heart, and a shifty, crafty, talented black.

Johnson came out of his corner laughing. His head was freshly shaved and he wore short, dark boxing trunks. Hart, in even shorter trunks, crouched low and jumped when he threw punches. Johnson landed consistently with his left jab. Welts rose on Hart's face. Hart threw a jumping left hook, which Johnson not only blocked but laughed at as well. There were numerous clinches and a lot of holding. On one occasion Hart tried to hold Johnson and hit him at the same time. He failed. Johnson found the maneuver laughable. The round ended.[5]

And so it continued. Johnson fought a smart defensive fight. He allowed Hart to force the action, then countered with straight lefts and rights. Tactically, it was the the sophistications of a Baron Jomini against the doggedness of a Sir Douglas Haig. Occasionally Hart landed good punches, but they had no effect on Johnson. For the first fourteen rounds Johnson coolly dominated the fight; if he lacked aggressiveness, he nevertheless controlled the contest. In the last six rounds he seemed to tire, and Hart, spurred on by cheers of "Hart! Hart! Hart!," started to land more often. Toward the end of the last round a sudden boom from a flash apparatus was interpreted by the fighters as the bell. Both began to walk to their corners, but Hart, realizing the mistake, rushed back at Johnson and landed his best punch of the fight. Before Johnson could resume a fighting position the bell ended the fight.

Greggains, the referee and sole judge, did not hesitate. He slapped Hart on the shoulder, proclaiming him the winner. Hart looked surprised, as if he expected no more than a draw. Afterward, explaining his decision, Greggains said he gave the fight to Hart because the white fighter was more aggressive. "Johnson," he added, "dogged it. He held at all times in the clinches. . . . I always give the gamest and most aggressive man the decision." Hart, on reconsideration, also believed he won. He agreed that Johnson was "a big, clever nigger" but felt if he had not hurt his right hand he would have knocked out the black boxer. Johnson said simply that he had been "robbed."[6]

Upset by the decision, Johnson once again left California. He believed Greggain's verdict was part of a plot to prevent him from fighting Jeffries. As long as he stayed on the West Coast and had to deal with California promoters, he would be barred from a heavyweight championship match. As long as he remained in the West, he would have to fight black boxers like McVey and Martin over and over again. He might not get a title bout in the East, but at least he could box a different set of fighters.[7]

He traveled light. He left behind Clara, Zink Abrahams, and a stack of unpaid bills. Rolling across America on a train bound for Philadelphia, future and past merged. The untested boxer who had left Galveston more than three years before had grown into a talented fighter, but with pockets still empty and a future still uncertain. And so it would remain for the next three years, as Johnson fought the best boxers in the country, black and white, but not the champions. He was ignored by various white titleholders. During these years frustrations turned into a quiet rage, and Johnson became even more conscious of the handicap of race.

Philadelphia sportswriters, like their counterparts in the West, were puzzled by Johnson. They knew he was talented, but they were suspicious of his casual attitude and unorthodox ring attire. In 1903, when Johnson fought Joe Butler there, reporters had commented on the black champion's plum-colored pajamas and the way he "fondled" his opponent in clinches. In sports page cartoons Johnson had been pictured as a coal-black, thick-lipped minstrel. This attitude did not alter in 1905 on Johnson's return to the East. Matched against Jim Jeffords, a good Eastern boxer, Johnson fought nonchalantly. In the second round, after dropping Jeffords with a right uppercut, Johnson leaned through the ropes and talked with the spectators. Johnson seemed content to allow the fight to go the distance until Jeffords landed a hard punch. Annoyed, Johnson knocked out the upstart boxer.[8]

Eastern sportswriters, although uneasy, were impressed. Their favorable opinion was confirmed on Johnson's next outing. He took on Black Bill at the old Knickerbocker Athletic Club and left no doubt concerning his fighting ability. In the third round he knocked Bill down five times, once for twelve seconds, a detail which the referee overlooked to keep the fight going and to give the spectators their money's worth. Bill, obviously displeased at being forced to continue the fight, absolutely refused to rise when he was knocked down in the next round. In less than ten days Johnson had knocked out two of the better heavyweights in the Philadelphia area.[9]

The problem with fighting in Philadelphia was that bouts could not be scheduled for more than six rounds, and consequently purses were small. Johnson was forced to fight more often. For example, a week after he knocked out Black Bill, he again was fighting at the Knickerbocker Club, only this time he fought two boxers on the same night. First he fought three uneventful rounds with Joe Jeannette, then he knocked out Walter Johnson in three rounds. Before the month was over, he fought the rugged Jeannette once more. Although the fights were well attended, the small purses and smaller newspaper coverage bespoke their insignificance.[10]

But, then, by mid-1905, boxing appeared everywhere to be fading in popularity and esteem. All of the sport's glory days seemed to be in the past. Less than a decade before boxing had been on the verge of national acceptance. During the 1890s prizefighting statutes were interpreted to the benefit of the sport. Even New York had accepted this trend. In 1896 the state legislatures altered their laws to allow "sparring exhibitions" held in buildings owned or leased by athletic associations. This change meant that for the first time championship fights could be openly staged in America's largest city. For the next few halcyon years, boxing fans reveled in the glory. In 1899 Jim Jeffries twice defended his crown at Coney Island. The second of those defenses, against Sailor Tom Sharkey, had been an authentic classic. Both were broad, powerful heavyweights, and Sharkey's chest, upon which was tatooed a sinking ship, gave the bout an epic quality. Adding to the ambiance were the bright, and consequently hot, lights that were hung ridiculously low so that the event could be filmed. The heat was overpowering. Many ringside reporters and spectators fainted, and as far back as the twelfth row men felt the oppressive electric heat. Jeffries said, "It was like standing at the mouth of a blast furnace, and hotter than the blast from a locomotive when the fire door is opened." For twenty-five rounds they traded punches, and the fight saw several dramatic shifts, as one fighter and then the next took command. The climax came in the twenty-third round, when Jeffries tore loose his left glove in breaking a clinch. Referee George Siler waved Sharkey back and grabbed Jeffries' hand, preparatory to restoring the glove. But Sharkey, too tired to understand, dodged Siler and threw a punch at Jeffries. Defending himself, Jeffries yanked his hand free and hit Sharkey with his bare fist. Finally the fight ended, and Jeffries was given the decision. It was a great fight, and the gate receipts—$68,000—made Coney Island the national center of boxing. So popular was the site that Jeffries defended his title there again the following year, this time in a minor classic against the former champion James J. Corbett. Boxing had never been so rewarding or popular.[11]

The period, however, proved to be more of a sunset than a dawn—golden and beautiful and soon over. In 1900 the political tide turned, and prizefighting was banned by law. Reform-minded politicians claimed that the manly art was "neither manly nor an art." There was nothing particularly "manly" about hitting and being hit hard. "Manhood in these days, even simple physical manhood, is gauged by higher standards, and the person who jumps into the water to rescue a drowning fellow-creature performs an act more manly than all the prize fights ever fought." Furthermore, one editorialist added, the "art of self-defense" is the "most useless of all arts" because in today's world there was not need to defend oneself with fists. Therefore, the Horton Law, which permitted boxing, was repealed, and the Lewis law, which prohibited boxing, was passed. Boxing had felt the first tremors of Progressivism.[12]

In the years that followed, Eastern boxing became a leading form of nonviolent entertainment. Spectator interest declined. The only serious fighting took place in the West, where, Easterners reasoned, moral standards were lax. According to a *New York Times* editorialist, San Franscisco was a city without a "moral sense." To end a fight there "by prearrangement, before one or the other of those taking part in it is disabled, is an offense against the unwritten moral code of the city." For Eastern reformers, boxing became more unsavory than ever. They delighted in exposing the seedier aspects of the sport. No fixed fight or ring death went unobserved in the Eastern press, although championship fights often went unreported.[13]

By 1905 these reformers believed that they were close to destroying the evil of prizefighting altogether. Like so many other aspects of Progressive reform, the crusade against prizefighting had strong class overtones. For example, the reformers did not oppose boxing—or sparring—as a form of healthy exercise. Indeed, many upper-class gentlemen noted that boxing inculcated worthy virtues in those who practiced the sport. Writing for the English publication *The Nineteenth Century*, E. B. Osborn claimed that "the lad who learns to box invariably becomes a law-abiding person and, if he *must* fight, will always fight like a gentleman." In America Dr. W. R. C. Latson wholeheartedly agreed. "Boxing is a form of exercise," he wrote, "which is not only of the most marked benefit in a purely physical way, but it is of the utmost value as a means of training the mental and moral faculties." This view was also endorsed by President Theodore Roosevelt, who believed that boxing was a "first class" sport and "not half as brutalizing or demoralizing as many forms of big business."[14]

These men, all from the upper classes and all sharing the prejudices of their Anglo-Saxon culture, opposed not boxing, then, but rather prizefighting. Roosevelt wrote, "When money comes in at the gate, sport flies out at the window." It bothered Roosevelt and men of similar interests that men from the lower classes might become rich by doing something that men from the upper classes did for exercise. That fighters were beaten senseless, often retired without a penny, or sometimes blinded or killed as a result of boxing does not seem to have weighed heavily on their minds. Rather, they saw corruption in the purses a champion could earn and the money bet on the outcome of a fight. "The money prizes fought for are enormous," wrote Roosevelt, "and are a potential source of demoralization in themselves, while they are often so arranged as either to put a premium on crookedness or else to reward nearly as amply the man who fails as the man who succeeds." In short, the rewarding of losers offended Roosevelt's sense of justice.[15]

Progressive attacks on boxing had begun by 1905 to deplete the interest in the sport. And as interest, especially of the wealthy, declined, so too did the size of purses. The profession was going broke. For this reason, on May 2 Jeffries announced that he planned to retire. Befitting his status as an American hero, he was then touring the country as the lead in a play about Davy Crockett. In Cincinnati he told reporters that his wife wanted him to quit boxing, but the real reason for his decision was that there was simply no money in the sport. Unlike Roosevelt, his sport was prizefighting, not boxing, and if he could not attract hefty purses, he would just as soon forgo the exercise.[16]

It had never been done before. No modern heavyweight champion had ever retired before losing the title. Symbolically, kings were supposed to be killed; they were not meant to retire. It was perplexing. How would a new king be chosen? There were no official ranking or boxing commissions to handle the transition. Jeffries, however, had an idea. Like retiring presidents and retiring business executives, he was concerned about who his successor would be. Encouraged by Lou Houseman, a writer for the *Chicago Inter-Ocean* and a manager of Jack Root, Jeffries agreed to referee a fight between Root and Marvin Hart and then name the winner the heavyweight champion. Root was a clever boxer, and for eleven rounds he sidestepped the awkward charges and parried the telegraphed punches of Hart. But Root was 40 pounds lighter than his opponent, and as the fight wore on he tired under Reno's desert heat. In the twelfth round Hart landed a solid punch and knocked out Root. Jeffries raised his hand and, technically speaking, Hart became the new heavyweight champion.[17]

Nobody cared. Only 5,000 spectators saw the fight, and the purse was a meager $5,000. The new champion was something less than inspiring. Next to Sullivan, Corbett, Fitzsimmons, and Jeffries—around whom legends had grown—Hart was boring. In fact, Hart was boring even when compared to most of the fighters of his day. In the ring he was strong but awkward, and outside the ring he was slow of mouth and mind. So insipid was his personality that he was probably the only heavyweight champion who was never given a nickname. Sullivan was the Boston Strong Boy, Corbett was Gentleman Jim, Fitzsimmons was Ruby Robert, Jeffries was the Boilermaker, and Marvin Hart was Marvin Hart. He did not have even a middle initial to brighten his name. He was the Millard Fillmore of the boxing world.

Of course, when Jeffries named the contenders for the crown, he ignored Jack Johnson and other leading black heavyweights. Jeffries justified his choice because Hart held a victory over Johnson, but everyone realized that Johnson's exclusion was based on race. Had Johnson been white, he would have fought for the title years before. Instead, he was forced to fight meaningless matches in Philadelphia and other Eastern cities. Upset by his loss to Hart, he was further enraged by the subsequent course of events.[18]

In the ring Johnson's frustrations surfaced like sweat. Against white boxers his loose defensive style was tinged by a shade of cruelty. He carried opponents in order to deal out more punishment. In June, the month after Jeffries retired, Johnson fought Jack Monroe, a rugged former miner who had once battled Jeffries for the title. As Johnson moved about the ring, the smile was still on his face, but he used his talent to hurt Monroe rather than end the fight. Monroe was brave, but he suffered terribly. By the end of the six-round fight, he was bleeding from numerous facial cuts and his body was covered with welts. Surveying the damage Johnson inflicted, a reporter for the *Philadelphia Inquirer* described Monroe as "a mass of palpitating gelatine."[19]

This dark mood continued. In early July he fought Morris Harris and Black Bill, both black boxers, on the same night. He fought in a carefree manner and often passed up opportunities to hurt his opponents; he appeared more interested in putting on a good show than hurting anyone. But when five days later he fought Sandy Ferguson, a white boxer, his object was more serious. For seven rounds he hit Ferguson with sharp, cutting punches. Ferguson, who had a year before fought several nonviolent matches with Johnson, was obviously confused and more than a little angry. Finally he had enough of the pain and humiliation, and with calculated fury he hit Johnson in the groin with a hard left hook. Johnson sank to the floor but was awarded the fight on a foul.[20]

Within a week Johnson had recovered sufficiently to fight again, this time against the legendary Joe Grim. Saverio Giannone was born in Italy, but when he came to America and became a fighter he took the name Joe Grim. The name fitted. Between 1902 and 1913 he had more than 300 fights and officially won only ten of them. His fame rested on his abnormal ability to withstand punishment, and though usually defeated he was capable of great panache. After being thoroughly beaten—but not knocked out—he liked to announce, "I am Joe Grim! I fear no man on earth!" He was a white fighter seemingly made for Johnson's mood. The betting on the fight was brisk and centered on whether or not Johnson could knock out Grim, something no man had yet done. Johnson tried. In the first round he knocked down Grim six times, and before the end of the bout Grim was punched to the canvas fifteen to twenty times more. Boxing historian Nat Fleischer wrote that the ring's floor was spotted with Grim's blood and the Italian's face looked like a "hamburger steak." Still, Grim refused to stay down, and though on the floor at the final bell, he was not out.[21]

In his last three bouts for 1905 Johnson battled smaller black boxers. Twice he fought Joe Jeannette; the first Johnson lost on a foul and the second was a six-round "no decision" (Pennsylvania law prohibited fights to a decision). However, in both fights Johnson displayed superior ability. His other match was a twelve-round decision over Young Peter Jackson, who was over 50 pounds lighter than Johnson. Jackson was guaranteed 75 percent of the purse if he lasted the entire fight, his only object being to avoid punches. Actually, Johnson did not try too hard; he was content to impress the Baltimore audience with his own footwork and speed. Talking good-naturedly to Jackson throughout the fight, Johnson again showed a reluctance to hurt boxers of his own race.[22]

A year after leaving San Francisco Johnson was still chronically short of money and unable to find a profitable match. And though he fought an occasional second-rate white fighter, most of his bouts were still against blacks. This pattern went unaltered in 1907. Five times that year he fought Joe Jeannette. They fought in New York and Baltimore; Portland, Maine; and Philadelphia. Everywhere they were applauded, but the matches were seldom more than spirited exhibitions. Touring together, fighting bouts scheduled for anywhere between three and fifteen rounds, the two knew each other's style so well that every move called forth the perfect counter-move. The two moved as synchronistically as a man and his shadow. Throughout the years the two grew to be good friends, and they fought each other ten times. But the matches were merely entertaining, never really competitive.

Actually, the racial forces that formed the Johnson-Jeannette team were fairly typical. The four or five very talented black heavyweights were forced by economic necessity to fight each other. No black fighter realized this grim fact more than Sam Langford, the great heavyweight from Nova Scotia. He fought Jeannette fourteen times, Sam McVey fifteen times, and, incredibly, Harry Wills twenty-three times. Langford fought the lesser black heavyweights Jim Barry twelve times and Jeff Clark eleven times.[23]

Langford fought Johnson only once. They met in Chelsea, Massachusetts, in late April 1906. Since they were the two great black boxers of the first quarter of the century, and since their only fight against each other was in an out-of-the-way location, myths about the match inevitably arose. Oral tradition—improved on by Langford's manager—holds that it was a close fight and that Langford dropped Johnson for a nine count. But the truth was that Johnson, who outweighed Langford by 35 pounds, won rather handily. Several times he knocked down Langford, as well as breaking his nose and cutting his lip. Nat Fleischer's father-in-law, A. D. Phillips, saw the fight and said Johnson was never in trouble. Always upset by the false legends, Johnson himself claimed that he could have knocked out Langford, but the management of the Pythian Rink asked him to prolong the fight. Conscious that good boxing was also good theater, Johnson agreed. The fight ended with Johnson easily winning the fifteen-round decision.[24]

Other than the Langford bout and the Jeannette series, 1906 was an uneventful year for Johnson. He again defeated Black Bill and Jim Jeffords, but neither fight attracted any interest. While training with Joe Walcott in the Boston area, Johnson accepted a match against Charlie Haghey, a second-rate white boxer. It was no contest; Johnson knocked him out in the first round. A few months later he fought a ten-round draw with Billy Dunning, but there were strong suspicions that Johnson had agreed to carry Dunning. The fight was held in Millinocket, Maine, and no doubt Johnson cared little about what boxing fans there thought of his ability. It was a simple case: allow the local boy to look good, collect the money, and leave town.[25]

Toward the end of 1906 Johnson's life changed. His world became decidedly whiter. First, he formed a partnership with Sam Fitzpatrick, a fine white manager. As his own manager, Johnson had been a failure; he simply did not have the right connections. Fitzpatrick, however, knew promoters on three continents. A short, thin man with a cynical smile, Fitzpatrick was a perceptive judge of talent and had an uncanny ability to arrange matches that other managers and promoters believed impossible. If any manager could pull down the color barrier, it was Fitzpatrick. For a black man of Johnson's ability Fitzpatrick was willing to work his magic. Though he did not like the style of Johnson's personal life, he was attracted to his gate potential.[26]

The other change in Johnson's life and one that Fitzpatrick found most unsettling, was his choice of female companions. For the first time he began to travel openly with white women. While in Boston training with Walcott, Johnson met and lived with a young white girl. When he returned to Philadelphia, she went along. For a while she stayed at a house of prostitution on Ellsworth Street that allowed the white girls to cater to black men. Johnson often visited her there. And though the relationship ended after several months, it was a clear indication that Johnson was attempting to extend the borders that circumscribed all black boxers. Not only was he more willing to punish white fighters severely—itself a violation of the unwritten code by which black boxers lived—but his taste in prostitutes changed from black to white.[27]

The reason for the change is uncertain. Johnson attributed it to the way he had been treated by black women: "The heartaches which Mary Austin and Clara Kerr had caused me, led me to forswear colored women and to determine that my lot henceforth would be cast only with white women." Friends of Johnson believed fame was the crucial factor. Charles Horner, a friend of Johnson's from this period, said that once Jack became widely known as a fighter he deserted Kerr for various white women. Of the two explanations, Horner's has the greater surface validity. In America black acceptance of a white criterion of beauty was deeply rooted, and a light skin color was a constant standard for feminine attractiveness. In Johnson's day many black leaders had light-skinned wives. The ultimate extension of this attitude was the possession of a white wife or mistress.[28]

In Johnson's case, however, the choice of white women as companions has more unsettling implications. Though not apparent to his friends, it is clear in retrospect that it was not coincidental that Johnson began visiting white prostitutes at the same time as he began angrily lashing out at white fighters. Disturbed by restriction both inside and outside the ring, Johnson had begun a personal rebellion. Bred more by frustration than conscious decision, it was a rebellion nevertheless, and in the years to come it would grow even more strident. The more white society attempted to push Johnson back into the circumscribed borders of the black boxer's world, the more he balked at any restrictions. In time this attitude would force a confrontation. But that time was still six years in the future.

In late 1906 Johnson's eyes were fixed less on his showdown with white society than on the heavyweight championship. As Johnson was fighting Jeannette and other boxers on the East Coast, the championship had again changed hands. In his first defense of his newly won crown Marvin Hart fought a small Canadian heavyweight named Tommy Burns. Although only 5 feet, 7 inches tall, Burns, whose real name was Noah Brusso, was a rugged boxer with a deceptively hard punch. His fight with Hart was a dull affair that attracted little public interest. Burns won, but from the newspaper coverage of the fight it was difficult to say exactly what he won. Certainly he was the new heavyweight champion of the world, but the title by 1906 had reached its bargain-basement low. It appeared that the only people interested in the crown were a handful of undramatic contenders and a few Western promoters. The public and press showed no interest.

For Johnson, however, the lack of public concern was an advantage. It meant that Burns would be less concerned about the "color line," and if the price was right more willing to defend his title against a black boxer. Toward this end, Fitzpatrick took Johnson to Australia in early 1907 to build up his fighter's international reputation. Australia at that time was one of the world's boxing centers. In the 1890s the country had produced such notable fighters as Peter Jackson, Peter Slavin, Young Griffo, and Robert Fitzsimmons, and by 1900 it was an important stop on the itinerary of traveling boxers. Unlike the United States, Austrialia's largest cities welcomed prize-fighting. Bouts at the Gaiety Theatre in Sydney and the Cyclorama in Melbourne regularly drew large crowds and gates. But what Fitz-

patrick found most attractive was the current overrated crop of Aus-
trialian heavyweights. He believed Johnson could with little effort
become an international sensation.[29]

Fitzpatrick especially wanted to arrange a fight between Johnson and Bill Squires, the Australian champion. Negotiations began
and the public quickly became interested. But there were problems,
the most important of which was that Squires was about to leave for
America for a tour of his own. John Wren, his manager, was therefore reluctant to risk his fighter's reputation in a bout with Johnson.
Instead, Johnson had to be content to fight Peter Felix, the second-
best heavyweight in Australia. The bout was a mismatch. Johnson
knew it, Fitzpatrick knew it; as soon as the fight started, Felix and
the spectators knew it. Uncharacteristically impatient, Johnson
knocked out the black Australian in the first round.[30]

A week later Johnson fought Bill Lang, a white boxer. Held at
Melbourne's Richmond area, the fight drew more than 15,000 spectators, and as rain drenched the arena, they shouted racial insults at
Johnson. Some commented that his gaudy robe looked like a woman's dressing-gown; others laughed at his preening style. But the
amusement stopped once the fight began. After a few moments,
Johnson turned to his seconds and announced, "Dis is a joke." And
it was. Fighting without haste or concern, he carried Lang for the
first six rounds. Then, increasing the pace, he knocked Lang down
twice in the seventh and four times in the eighth. In the ninth round
he put his outclassed opponent down for the count.[31]

A sensation inside the ring, Johnson outside it also drew excited
comments. He was fined five pounds for pulling Fitzpatrick's nose
after being called "a black bastard" in a dispute over money. In a racially nervous country like Australia, such informality was hardly applauded. Blacks were not supposed to touch white men, regardless of
the provocation. But then again, blacks were not supposed to touch
white women either, and this too Johnson did. Stories circulated
about his affairs with theater ladies. There were rumors that he had
married a white woman in Sydney. One report linked Johnson with
Miss Lola Troy, a wealthy Sydney lady who was, so said a newspaper
man, as "white as her gold was yellow." These stories were as widely
followed as Johnson's ring activities.[32]

Then after a few days Johnson was mysteriously gone from Australia, almost as if he had never been there. Actually, Squires had left
for America and there were no serious contenders left down under.
The mystery of Johnson's disappearance was simply that he left with-

out prior notice. He soon enough reappeared in San Francisco, where he hoped to find Squires. Johnson discovered, however, that Squires had already signed a contract to meet Burns for the title. After a short stay on the West Coast, Johnson traveled back to Philadelphia. He had been gone for almost eight months, but the time had not been wasted. Now a boxer of international acclaim, Johnson had realistic hopes of bigger fights against leading white boxers.[33]

His optimism was justified. He signed to fight Robert Fitzsimmons in Philadelphia. In 1907 Fitzsimmons was forty-four years old, and his glory days were far in the past. In his prime he had defeated the very best and had won three world titles; he is still the only man ever to win the middleweight, light heavyweight, and heavyweight crowns. He had defeated James J. Corbett for the heavyweight title in a sensational fight held in Carson City. In that fight, he made the solar plexus punch famous. There followed two classics with Jeffries. Tall, thin, broad-shouldered, freckled—Ruby Robert, as he was called, was one of the giants of the Golden Age of boxing in the last decade of the nineteenth and the first decade of the twentieth century.[34]

Johnson fought the old boxer on a hot, rainy night in mid-July. Rumors circulated that Fitzsimmons took the fight only because he was broke and that Johnson had agreed to allow the white boxer to last the full six rounds. The first rumor was undoubtedly true; Fitzsimmons, who died in 1917 without a penny, was always chronically short of money. And for the first round it looked as if the second rumor might also be true. In a round a reporter for the *Philadelphia Inquirer* called "about as exciting as a crocheting match at an old ladies home," Johnson watched Fitzsimmons watch him. Any talk of a fix died in the second round. A right to the face sent Fitzsimmons to the canvas. When he got up, Johnson knocked him down again. It was pathetic. At the count of nine the old fighter tried to rise but lost his balance and tumbled back to the canvas. Rather than complete his count, the referee, in a merciful act unusual for that day, simply stopped the fight. If Johnson had not knocked out a good fighter, he had defeated a very big name.[35]

The victory increased Johnson's boldness outside the ring. Subconsciously, if not consciously, victories over white boxers stimulated Johnson's relationships with white women. He would celebrate every major victory in his career in the arms of one or more white females. After the Fitzsimmons fight Johnson met a white New York City prostitute named Hattie McClay. As Hattie later testified, she was living in a New York "call house," where she went "out on calls sporting." After she met Johnson, who knew her as simply "Mac," she began to travel with him. For the next four years they would be together often. When they were not together, Johnson would occasionally write or send a telegram to Hattie, usually telling her where to meet him. When their relationship ended in February 1911, Johnson paid her $500 for return of the telegrams and letters.[36]

Hattie was with Johnson in the fall of 1907 as he continued to build a reputation against white boxers. It was a satisfying season. In August he fought Kid Cutler, a protégé of the great John L. Sullivan. The former champion had a low opinion of Johnson. He believed Johnson as a fighter suffered from the general weakness he readily attributed to the black race. Sullivan was even more critical of Johnson's extrapugilistic activities. He was sure that Cutler could "chase Jack Johnson out of the ring." Upset by the remarks, Johnson agreed to fight Cutler in a small arena in Reading, Pennsylvania. In less than two minutes Johnson knocked out the former wrestler. Then, turning to the grim-faced Sullivan, Johnson called out, "How do you like that, Cap'n John?" It pleased Johnson to twit the white institution.[37]

After defeating Sailor Burke, another unmemorable fighter, Johnson returned to the West Coast. Obviously more sure of himself, he agreed to fight Fireman Jim Flynn in San Francisco. A good fighter, the pudgy Flynn had defeated such known boxers as George Gardner, Jack "Twin" Sullivan, Tony Ross, and Dave Barry. Confident that he would defeat Johnson, Flynn told reporters that after the victory he wanted a rematch with Burns. However, in the early rounds Flynn realized his mistake. Johnson dominated the boxing. Flynn countered Johnson's smooth style by clinching and butting. Frequently he had to be warned to fight fairly. Yet Johnson was unaffected. He continued punishing his white opponent until the eleventh round, when he knocked out Flynn with a right to the jaw.[38]

Johnson now wanted Burns. Sportswriters agreed that Johnson could no longer be ducked, that the color line was merely a flimsy cover for bigotry. As a writer for the St. Louis Post Dispatch commented, "Jack Johnson is a colored man, but we cannot get away from the fact that he is the greatest living exponent of the art of hit-and-getaway and as such, is the outstanding challenger for the title." Fair play, the editorialists insisted, demanded an equal chance for Johnson. That boxing had never been noted particularly for fair play or that Johnson had been treated most unfairly throughout his career did not seem to enter the picture. Americans—in theory—were committed to the idea of equal opportunity.[39]

Burns, however, was a Canadian and therefore immune to such arguments. While Johnson fought a rigged match against Burke (Johnson had agreed to allow his white opponent to go the distance), Burns left the country. Boxing had become unprofitable, and white challengers had become scarce in America. In the Old World he hoped to find some tame white boxers to fight. He was not disappointed. In London he knocked out Gunner Moir, whose terrible visage was deceiving. After his fight with Burns, Moir lost eight of his nine next fights, then switched to an acting career, where he had great success appearing in small parts in British films as an executioner. In Dublin Burns fought Jem Roche. The fight was held on St. Patrick's Day, and the Irish arrived at the stadium in droves to cheer on Roche. The celebrations were cut short, however, when Burns knocked out the Irishman in 1:28 of the first round. In Paris Burns twice more defended his title, knocking out both Jewey Smith and Bill Squires.[40]

Burns might have enjoyed himself if it had not been for Johnson, who arrived in England shortly after the champion. After another short bout against Jeannette, Johnson with Fitzpatrick and Hattie had boarded a steamer for England. Johnson claimed Hattie's father financed the trip, but that is doubtful. Certainly Hattie, who was a working woman, may have contributed something, but most of the bills were paid from a $5,000 loan Fitzpatrick acquired from George Considine and several other New York sportsmen.[41]

In England Johnson—as to a lesser extent was Burns—was viewed as something of a curiosity. The English sportsmen held American fighters in very low regard. Certainly they recognized the fighting ability of Americans, but they were generally disgusted by their American cousins' social deportment and physical appearance. Rising out of "polyglot slums" like some sort of prehistoric beast, American fighters looked as if they had "escaped from gaol or a museum of freaks." The English boxing expert E. B. Osborn said American boxers were grotesquely ugly: "round cast-iron head with no chin, ribs that almost meet across the stomach, the ape's curved, convulsive clutch, and a low nervous organization indifferent to pain." By contrast, English boxers like Billy Wells were pictured as "long-limbed, modest, good-looking youth[s]."[42]

Besides being ugly, American fighters had horrible reputations as social beings. In part this was because they "seldom [had] more

than a drop or two, if so much, of English blood in [their] veins."
Therefore, like the Jews in the early prize ring, the Americans lacked
the Englishman's "innate sense of fair play." Americans, Englishmen believed, would do anything to win; no trick was too low. One
American, it was reported, had a telegram sent shortly before a bout
to his opponent announcing the death of his ailing child. And they
would do anything to "get the goat" of an opponent: "A disgusting
taunt, a contemptuous smile, a refusal to shake hands, a preposterous bet, an elaborate wasting of time"—all these and more. Though
such methods often produced victories, they were hardly sportsmanlike. English fighters, who were "decent, well-conditioned citizen[s]," might lose, but they everywhere expressed the "decencies of
the English ring."[43]

Of all of the American boxers who visited England, Johnson
caused the most discussion. Nobody questioned his talent, and some
writers even believed that he was "not a bad sort of chap." The English boxing authority Fred Dartnell, who tended to see a noble savage in all black boxers, noted that "there was something childlike in
[Johnson's] inordinate vanity." And though Johnson was not as noble as Peter Jackson, who Dartnell described as "a real 'white'
man," the American was nonetheless intelligent and articulate on a
wide range of subjects. But Dartnell's opinion was decidedly the mi-
nority one. More often writers portrayed Johnson as dark and sinister, a living example of diseased racism. Bohun Lynch, who met
Johnson in England in 1908, said the black boxer was "regarded generally with the greatest possible dislike." Johnson, Lynch emphasized, did not know his place: "With money in his pocket and physical triumph over white men in his heart, he displayed all the gross and
overbearing insolence which makes what we call the buck nigger in-
sufferable. He was one of the comparatively few men of African
blood who, in a half-perceiving way, desire to make the white man
pay for the undoubted ill-treatment of his forbears."[44]

When Johnson could not get Burns into the ring, he accepted several
matches with inferior English fighters. After boxing a four-round exhibition with Al McNamara, he agreed to fight Ben Taylor, perhaps
the best British heavyweight of that time. Johnson was a good judge
of boxing talent, and he rightly judged that he had nothing to fear
from Taylor. Since arriving in England he had been drinking more
heavily than usual, and he saw no reason to alter this practice for Taylor. When he climbed into the ring in Plymouth, his naturally yellow-

ish eyes were inflamed and blurred. Yet even drunk, Johnson was far too good a boxer for Taylor. After allowing the British public time to gauge his ability, he knocked out Taylor. Though the fight was splendid exercise between his more serious bouts of drinking, Johnson did not avoid the real issue. He had come to England to fight Burns, not to drink or toy with English boxers.[45]

For a while it appeared as if the National Sporting Club in London would arrange the bout. Members of the club were from England's upper crust; the Earl of Lonsdale sat on its board of governors, and Sir William Eden, Anthony Eden's father, was a leading patron. These men believed Johnson, though black, was still entitled to some sort of an opportunity. They called Johnson and Fitzpatrick to their club and told them so or, more precisely, told the white manager so. Johnson had to wait outside on the street while Fitzpatrick heard the club's terms, for, after all, no respectable club admitted blacks. Though Johnson was offended by this affront, he was more upset by the National Sporting Club's terms. They agreed to pay the winner 500 pounds, but each side had to bear its own expenses. For once Johnson and Burns agreed. They were not ready for the club's idea for fair play.[46]

Through all the negotiations Burns had maintained that if the price was right he was willing, even eager, to erase the color line. For $30,000—win, lose, or draw—he would fight Johnson any time and anywhere. Actually, he told reporters, he hoped someone would arrange the fight. He did not like blacks and he particularly disliked Johnson. "All coons are yellow," he said. There were no exceptions. But the fight was not arranged in England, and Burns had run out of white challengers. So he departed for Australia. A few weeks later Johnson followed.[47]

4

The Days of Tamerlane

AFTERWARDS CONCERNED WHITES SAID it should never have taken place.
John L. Sullivan, who by 1908 had quit drinking and become a moral
crusader, said, "Shame on the money-mad Champion! Shame on the
man who upsets good American precedents because there are Dollars, Dollars, Dollars in it." A dejected sports columnist wrote,
"Never before in the history of the prize ring has such a crisis arisen
as that which faces the followers of the game tonight." The sadness
these men felt could only be expressed in superlatives—greatest tragedy, deepest gloom, saddest day, darkest night. The race war had
been fought. Armageddon was over. The Caucasian race had lost.
Twenty years after the event, and after a few more such Armaged-
dons, Alva Johnston tried to explain the mood of the day: "The mo-
rale of the Caucasian race had been at a low ebb long before the great
blow fell in 1908. The Kaiser had been growing hysterical over the
Yellow Peril. Africa was still celebrating the victory of Emperor
Menelik of Abyssinia over the Italians. Dixie was still in ferment because Booker T. Washington . . . had had a meal at the White
House. Then . . . Jack Johnson won the World Heavyweight Championship from Tommy Burns. The Nordics had not been so scared
since the days of Tamerlane."[1]

Black ghetto dwellers and sharecroppers rejoiced. In cities from
New York to Omaha, blacks smiled with delight. "Today is the zenith

of Negro sports," observed a *Colored American Magazine* editor. Other black publications felt such qualifications were too conservative. The *Richmond Planet* reported that "no event in forty years has given more genuine satisfaction to the colored people of this country than has the signal victory of Jack Johnson." Joy and pride spilled over into arrogance, or so some whites believed. The cotton-buying firm of Logan and Bryan predicted that Johnson's victory would encourage other blacks to enter boxing, thereby creating a shortage of field labor. Independent of Logan and Bryan's report, the black writer Jim Nasium counseled black youths to consider seriously a boxing career—where else could they face whites on an equal footing? In that last week of 1908 social change seemed close at hand. The implication of most reports was that Jack Johnson had started a revolution.[2]

How had it all come about? When Burns arrived in Perth in August 1908, the world did not seem in any immediate danger. He was treated like a conquering hero. From Perth to Sydney he was cheered and fêted. Mayors and members of Parliament courted Burns as if he were visiting royalty. When the train made its normal 6 A.M. stop at Abury, men stood shivering in the cold to greet Burns. And at Sydney, at a more civilized hour, more than 8,000 people cheered the champion. Speeches were made and applause modestly received. An Australian politician, Colonel Ryrie, extolled the virtues of boxing, telling the gathering that the sport produced sturdy young men needed for battle, "not those milksops who cry out against it."[3]

At these august occasions Burns was frequently asked about Johnson. Would he fight the black champion? If so, where? When? Burns patiently answered the questions like a saint repeating a litany. He would fight Johnson when the right purse was offered. The place was not important. In fact, Australia was as good as—if not better than—any other place. As Burns told a Melbourne reporter: "There are a lot of newspaper stories that I don't want to fight Johnson. I do want to fight him, but I want to give the white boys a chance first."[4] And since the early English settlers had exterminated the Tasmanians, there were a lot of white boys in Australia.

Listening to Burns was an ambitious promoter. Hugh D. "Huge Deal" McIntosh was an American success story with an Australian setting. As a boy he worked in the Broken Hill mines and as a rural laborer, but early in life he realized that a man could make more money using his brain than his back. His fortune was made as a pie salesman at Australian parks and sporting events, but his career included tours as a racing cyclist, a boxer, a waiter, a newspaper publisher, a member of parliament, a theatrical impresario, and other assorted jobs. All these stints equipped him with enough gab and gall to become a first-rate boxing promoter. It was McIntosh who had invited Burns to Australia to defend his title against Aussie boxers. A student of maps and calendars, he knew that when Teddy Roosevelt's Great White Fleet, then cruising about the Pacific, dropped anchor in Australia a heavyweight championship fight would prove a good draw. With this in mind, he rented a market garden at Rushcutter's Bay, on the outskirts of Sydney, and built an open-air stadium on it. By midsummer he was ready for Burns.[5]

In June he matched Burns against Bill Squires, whom the champion had already knocked out twice, once in the United States and once in France. In defense of Squires, however, it was noted by the press that in his second fight with Burns he had lasted eight rounds, seven longer than the first fight. On his home continent Squires did even better. He was not knocked out until the thirteenth round. Though the fight was not particularly good, the overflowing stadium pleased McIntosh mightily. More than 40,000 people showed up for the fight, including American sailors from the Great White Fleet, but only 15,000 could be seated in the stadium. The 25,000 others milled about outside, listening to the noise made by lucky spectators watching the fight.[6]

Less than two weeks later Burns again defended his title, this time against Bill Lang in Melbourne before 19,000 spectators. Like the stadium at Rushcutter's Bay, South Melbourne Stadium had been hurriedly constructed on McIntosh's orders—it was built in twelve days—and the result had been worth the effort. In the two fights Burns made more than $20,000 and McIntosh grossed about $100,000, half of which was clear profit. In addition, both fights had been filmed, and revenue from this pioneering effort was much greater than anticipated. Burns, McIntosh, and the Australian boxing public were all exceedingly pleased.[7]

In late October Johnson arrived, and the pulse of Australia picked up a beat. The fight had already been arranged. McIntosh guaranteed Burns $30,000. Before such a sum the color line faded. Therefore, when Johnson landed at Perth he was in an accommodating mood. "How does Burns want it? Does he want it fast and willing? I'm his man in that case. Does he want it flat footed? Goodness, if he does, why I'm his man again. Anything to suit; but fast or slow,

I'm going to win."[8] After eight years of trying Johnson was about to get his chance to fight for the heavyweight title.

Short of money, Johnson and Fitzpatrick set up their training quarters in the inexpensive Sir Joseph Banks Hotel in Botany, far less plush than the Hydro Majestic Hotel at Medlow Bath, where Burns trained. Yet Johnson, like Burns, trained in earnest. Johnson looked relaxed—he joked, smiled, made speeches, and played the double bass—but the men and women who watched him train failed to notice that he was also working very hard. Each morning he ran; each afternoon he exercised and sparred with Bill Lang, who imitated Burns's style. Johnson knew that Burns—short, inclined toward fatness, addicted to cigars and strong drink—was nonetheless a very good boxer. In Bohum Lynch's opinion, Burns was a "decidedly good boxer" who, though unorthodox, had a loose and easy style. And in the weeks before the fight Johnson showed by his training that he did not take Burns lightly.[9]

Nor did he disregard the power of Australian racism. He feared that in the emotionally charged atmosphere of an interracial championship fight he might not be given an even break. His concern was not unfounded. An editorial in Sydney's *Illustrated Sporting and Dramatic News* correctly indicated the racial temper of Australian boxing fans: "Citizens who have never prayed before are supplicating Providence to give the white man a strong right arm with which to belt the coon into oblivion." But of more concern to Johnson than white men's prayers were his suspicions of McIntosh as promoter and self-named referee. Several times the two quarreled in public, and they nearly came to blows when Johnson greeted the promoter with "How do, Mr. McIntosh? How do you drag yourself away from Tahmy?" McIntosh, a big, burly, muscular man, thereafter began carrying a lead pipe wrapped in sheet music. As he told his friend Norman Lindsay, it was in case "that black bastard" ever "tries any funny business."[10]

As the bout drew closer, the racial overtones destroyed the holiday atmosphere. It seemed as if all Australia were edgy. In the name of civilization, Protestant reformers spoke words that fell on deaf ears. The fight, said the Sydney Anglican Synod, with "its inherent brutality and dangerous nature" would surely "corrupt the moral tone of the community." But the community was worried less about being corrupted than about the implication of a Johnson victory. Lindsay, whom McIntosh hired to draw posters to advertise the fight, visually portrayed the great fear. Across Sydney could be seen his poster showing a towering black and a much smaller white. As Richard Broome has suggested, "This must have evoked the deepest feelings Australians held about the symbols of blackness and whiteness and evoked the emotiveness of a big man versus a small man and the populous coloured races versus the numerically smaller white race." Clearly, the *Australian Star* editors had this in mind when they printed a cartoon showing the fight being watched by representatives of the white and black races. Underneath was a letter that predicted that "this battle may in the future be looked back upon as the first great battle of an inevitable race war. . . . There is more in this fight to be considered than the mere title of pugilistic champion of the world."[11]

Racial tension was nothing new to Australia. Race had mattered since the colony's founding. Partly it was an English heritage, passed down from the conquerors of Ireland, Scotland, and Wales—an absolute belief in the inferiority of everything and everyone non-English. In Australia, however, it had developed its own unique characteristics. There common English prejudices had been carried to extremes, and when confronted with dark-skinned natives, the Australians did not shrink from the notion of genocide. The most shocking example of racial relations was the case of the small island of Tasmania off the southeast coast of Australia. When the English first settled the island there were perhaps a few thousand Tasmanians. Short but long-legged, these red-brown people were described as uncommonly friendly natives. But the friendliness soon died, as British colonists hunted, raped, enslaved, abducted, or killed the Tasmanians. Slowly the race died off, until in 1876 Truganini, the very last survivor, died. Her passing struck many Australians as sad—but inevitable. As a correspondent for the *Hobart Mercury* wrote, "I regret the death of the last of the Tasmanian aborigines, but I know that it is the result of the *fiat* that the black shall everywhere give place to the white."[12]

For Australia the problem was that other darker races had not given way fast enough in the generation after the death of Truganini. Though Social Darwinists preached the virtues of the light-skinned, by 1909 Australians felt threatened by the "lower" races. Increasingly after 1900 Australians demonstrated anxiety over their Oriental neighbors. Immigration restrictions aimed at keeping the country white were proposed and adopted. So bitter had the struggle become that in 1908, the year of the Johnson–Burns fight, the *Australia Bul-*

letin changed its banner from "Australia for Australians" to "Australia for the white men."[13]

Johnson and Burns became both an example of and a contribution to the fears of white Australians. Small, white Burns became the symbol of small, white Australia, nobly battling against the odds. Burns's defense was his brain and pluck, his desire to stave off defeat through intelligence and force of will. Johnson became the large, vulgar, corrupt, and sensual enemy. Reports said that he ignored training and instead wenched and drank. He had strength and size but lacked heart—in fact, he *should* win but probably would not. This last report gave rise to the rumor that the fight was fixed. Even the *New York Times* endorsed this view, as did the betting line that made Burns a 7 to 4 favorite.[14]

Cool rains washed Sydney on Christmas night, the eve of the fight. To allow filming, the fight was not scheduled to begin until 11 A.M., but by 6 A.M. an orderly crowd of more than 5,000 was waiting at the gate. The stadium would be filled to capacity; yet interest was much more widespread. Throughout Australia men milled around newspaper offices hoping to hear a word about the progress of the fight. Inside the stadium at Rushcutter's Bay all Christmas cheer had vanished. The mood and tone of the day, from the gray, overcast sky to the uneasy quiet of the spectators, was eulogistic.

Johnson entered the ring first. Despite his dull gray robe his mood was almost carefree. There were a few cheers—though not many—as he slipped under the upper strand of the ropes, but calls of "coon" and "nigger" were more common. He smiled, bowed grandly, and threw kisses in every direction. He liked to strut the stage, and the vicious insults did not outwardly affect him. If anything, his smile became broader as he was more abused. In a country exhilarated by the discovery of gold, Johnson's gold-toothed smile ironically attracted only hate. Satisfied that he was not the crowd's favorite, he retired to his corner, where Sam Fitzpatrick massaged his shoulders and whispered words of assurance into an unlistening ear.

By contrast, when Burns climbed into the ring, the stadium was filled with sound. Burns did not seem to notice. For a time it looked as if he had come into the ring expecting something other than a fight. He was dressed in a worn blue suit, more appropriate for a shoe salesman than the heavyweight champion. Methodically he removed the suit, folded it neatly, and put it in a battered wicker suitcase. Yet even in his short, tight boxing trunks he looked out of place. Jack London, covering the fight for the *New York Herald*, wrote that Burns looked "pale and sallow, as if he had not slept all night, or as if he had just pulled through a bout with fever." Pacing nervously in his corner, he avoided looking across the ring at Johnson.

Burns examined the bandages on Johnson's hands. He did this carefully, looking for hard tape or other unnatural objects. Satisfied, he returned to his corner. Johnson, however, was upset by the tape on Burns's elbows. He asked Burns to remove it. Burns refused. Johnson—suddenly serious—said he would not fight until the tape was removed. Still Burns refused. McIntosh tried to calm the two fighters. He was unsuccessful. The crowd, sensing an unexpected confrontation but not aware of the finer details, sided with Burns and used the moment as a pretext to shout more insults at Johnson, who smiled as if complimented on a new necktie but still refused to alter his protest. Finally, Burns removed the tape. Johnson nodded, satisfied.

McIntosh called the fighters to the center of the ring. He went over the do's and don'ts and the business of what punches would or would not be allowed. Then he announced that in the event that the police stopped the fight, he would render a decision based on who was winning at the time. The unpopular "no decision" verdict would not be given. Both Johnson and Burns had earlier agreed to this procedure. The fighters returned to their corners. A few moments later the bell rang. The color line in championship fights was erased.[15]

Watching films of Johnson boxing is like listening to a 1900 recording of Enrico Caruso played on a 1910 gramophone. When Johnson fought Burns, film was still in its early days, not yet capable of capturing the subtleties of movement. Nuance is lost in the furious and stilted actions of the figures, which move about the screen in a Chaplinesque manner, as if some drunken cutter had arbitrarily removed three of every four frames. When we watch fighters of Johnson's day on film, we wonder how they could have been considered even good. That some of them were champions strains credulity. They look like large children, wrestling and cuffing each other, but not actually fighting like real boxers, not at all like Ali captured in zoom-lensed, slow-motion, technological grace. But the film misleads.[16]

It was no Charlie Chaplin that shuffled out of his corner in round one to meet Tommy Burns. It was a great boxer who at age thirty was in his physical prime. No longer thin, Johnson was well-muscled, with a broad chest and thick arms and legs. His head was shaved in the style of the eighteenth-century bare-knuckle fighters, and his high cheekbones gave his face a rounded appearance. Although he had fought often, his superb defensive skills had kept his face largely unmarked. Like his mother he had a broad, flat nose and full lips, but his eyes were small and oddly Oriental when he smiled. He was famous for his clowning, but this stereotype of a black man obscured the more serious reality. He was often somber, and even when he smiled and acted like a black-faced minstrel, he could be serious. What he thought, he believed, was his own affair. His feelings could not be easily read on his face.

Both boxers began cautiously. Johnson flicked out a few probing jabs, designed more to test distance than to do any physical damage. Although Burns was much smaller than Johnson, he was considered a strong man with a powerful punch. Johnson clinched, tested Burns's strength, then shifted to long-range sparring. He allowed Burns to force the action, content to parry punches openhanded. Burns tried to hit Johnson with long left hooks, which fell short. Johnson feinted a long left of his own, but in the same motion he lowered his right shoulder, pivoted from the waist, stepped forward with his right foot, and delivered a perfect right uppercut. It was Johnson's finest weapon, and some ring authorities claim there never has been a fighter who could throw the punch as well as Johnson. Burns was caught flatfooted, leaning into the punch. His momentum was stopped and he fell backward. His head hit heavily on the floor. He lay still. The referee started to count.

"The fight," Jack London wrote only hours after it ended, "there was no fight. No Armenian massacre could compare with the hopeless slaughter that took place in the Sydney stadium today." From the opening seconds of the first round it was clear who would win. At least it was clear to London. It was a fight between a "colossus and a toy automaton," between a "playful Ethiopian and a small and futile white man," between a "grown man and a naughty child." And through it all, London and the 20,000 other white supporters of Burns watched in horror as their worst fears materialized.[17]

"Hit the coon in his stomach." Burns needed no reminder. After surviving the first-round knockdown, he shifted to a different strategy, one he had thought about before. In the days before the fight, when reporters asked about his battle plan, he had smiled knowingly at his white chroniclers and said he would move in close and hit the black fighter where all black fighters were weak—in the stomach. This theory was hardly novel; it had long been considered axiomatic that black boxers had weak stomachs and hard heads. So thoroughly was the view accepted that black boxers took it for granted that white fighters would attack the body. Peter Jackson once told Fred Dartnell, "They are all after my body. Hit a nigger in the stomach and you'll settle him, they say, but it never seems to occur to them that a white man might just as quickly be beaten by a wallop in the same region." Sam Langford agreed: blacks hated to be hit by a hard punch to the stomach, but so too did whites.[18]

Boxing was not immune to the scientific explanations of the day. Polygenists believed—and Darwinists did not deny—that the black race was an "incipient species." Therefore, whites maintained, physically blacks and whites were very different. Burns, for example, assumed that Johnson not only had a weak stomach but lacked physical endurance. So he believed that the longer the fight lasted the better were his chances. Behind these stereotypes rested the science of the day. Writing only a year before in the *North American Review*, Charles F. Woodruff claimed that athletes raised in Southern climates lacked endurance: "The excessive light prods the nervous system to do more than it should, and in time such constant stimulation is followed by irritability and finally by exhaustion." Only athletes from the colder Northern latitudes had enough stamina to remain strong during the course of a long boxing match. Therefore, Burns, a Canadian, had reason to remain hopeful. By contrast, Johnson, raised about as far south as one could travel in the United States and only a generation or two removed from Africa, had to win quickly or not at all. At least, this was what Burns and his white supporters hoped.[19]

Burns's strategy was thus founded on the racist belief that scientists, armed with physiological and climatological evidence, had proved that blacks were either inferior to whites, or—as in the case of harder heads—superior because of some greater physiological inferiority; that is to say, blacks had thicker skulls because they had smaller brains. Burns never questioned that his abdominal strength and his endurance were superior to Johnson's. Nor did he doubt that his white skin meant that his desire to win and willingness to accept pain were greater than Johnson's. But above all, he was convinced that as a white he could outthink Johnson, that he could solve the problems of defense and offense more quickly than his black opponent. Burns's faith, in short, rested ultimately on the color of his skin.

Burns forgot, however, that he was facing a boxer liberated from the myths of his day. Johnson's stomach was not weak, and, more important, he knew it was not. As the fight progressed, he exposed the fallacy of Burns's theory. He started to taunt Burns. "Go on, Tommy, hit me here," Johnson said pointing to his stomach. When Burns responded with a blow to Johnson's midsection, Jack laughed and said to try again. "Is that all the better you can do, Tommy?" Another punch. "Come on, Tommy, you can hit harder than that, can't you?" And so it continued; Johnson physically and verbally was destroying the white man's myths.[20]

Burns fought gamely, but without success. Johnson did not try for a knockout; he was content to allow the fight to last until the later rounds. Partly his decision was based on economics. The bout was being filmed, and few boxing fans in America would pay to watch pictures of pressmen, seconds, and other boxers for five minutes as a build-up for a fight that lasted only half a minute. But more important was Johnson's desire for revenge. He hated Burns and wanted to punish him. And he did. By the second round Burns's right eye was discolored and his mouth was bloody. By the middle rounds Burns was bleeding from a dozen minor facial cuts. Blood ran over his shoulders and stained the canvas ring. Before the white audience, Johnson badly punished Burns. And he enjoyed every second of it.[21]

But punishment was not enough. Johnson wanted also to humiliate Burns. He did this verbally. From the very first round Johnson insulted Burns, speaking with an affected English accent, so that "Tommy" became "Tahmy." Mostly what Johnson said was banal: "Poor little Tahmy, who told you you were a fighter?" Or, "Say, little Tahmy, you're not fighting. Can't you? I'll have to show you how." Occasionally, when Burns landed a punch, Johnson complimented him: "Good boy, Tommy; good boy, Tommy." In almost every taunt Johnson referred to Burns in the diminutive. It was always "Tommy Boy" or "little Tommy." And always a derisive smile accompanied the words.

Sometimes Johnson sought to emasculate Burns verbally. Referring to Burns's wife, Johnson said, "Poor little boy, Jewel won't know you when she gets you back from this fight." Once when Burns landed what looked to be an effective punch, Johnson laughed: "Poor, poor Tommy. Who taught you to hit? Your mother? You a woman?" Crude, often vulgar and mean, Johnson's verbal warfare was nevertheless effective.

Burns responded in kind. Bohum Lynch, who was a great fan of Burns, admitted that the champion's ring histrionics included baleful glaring, foot stomping, and mouth fighting. He often called Johnson a "cur" or a "big dog." At other times, when he was hurt or frus-

trated, he said, "Come on and fight, nigger. Fight like a white man."
Burns's comments, however, were self-defeating. When Johnson insulted Burns, the champion lost control and fought recklessly. But
Burns's taunts pleased Johnson, who responded by fighting in an
even more controlled way than before. Johnson gained particular
strength from Burns's racist statements. It was like playing the
Dozens, where accepting abuse with an even smile and concealing
one's true emotions were the sign of a sure winner.[22]

When Johnson was not insulting Burns, he was talking to ringsiders. Usually he just joked about how easy the fight was and what
he would do with the money he won from betting on the bout. That
the ringsiders hated Johnson and screamed racial insults did not seem
to bother him. Only rarely did Johnson show his disgust with the
white audience. Once as he moved from his corner at the start of a
round he spat a mouthful of water toward the press row, but such
actions were unusual. More common was the smile—wide, detached,
inscrutable. In describing the grin, Jack London came closest to the
truth: it was "the fight epitomized." It was the smile of a man who
has mastered the rules to a slightly absurd game.[23]

After a few rounds the only question that remained unanswered was
not who would win but how much punishment Burns could take. By
the middle rounds that too was evident—he could survive great
amounts of punishment. His eyes were bruised and discolored, his
mouth hung open, his jaw was swollen and looked broken, and his
body was splotched with his own blood. In the corner between rounds
his seconds sponged his face with champagne, which was popularly
believed to help revive hurt fighters. It did not help Burns. Yet at the
bell he always arose to face more punishment and insults. For the
white spectators, Burns's fortitude was itself inspiring. As Bohum
Lynch wrote, "To take a beating any time, even from your best
friend, is hard work. But to take a beating from a man you abhor, belonging to a race you despise, to know that he is hurting you and hu-
miliating you with the closest attention to detail, and the coldest de-
liberation . . . this requires pluck."[24]

By the thirteenth round everyone but Burns and Johnson was
surfeited with the carnage. Spectators, left with nothing and nobody
to cheer, now yelled for the fight to be stopped. After the thirteenth
round police entered the ring. They talked with McIntosh, then with
Burns. The white champion refused to concede. He insisted that he
could win. But in the fourteenth Burns was again severely punished.

A hard right cross knocked him to the canvas. He arose at the count of eight but was wobbly. Again policemen climbed into the ring, only this time there was no talking. The fight was stopped, although Burns—dazed, covered with blood, but still game—screamed at the police to give him another chance.

Everywhere was a stunned silence as the spectators accepted that the inevitable was now the actual. It had happened. A black man now wore the crown that had once belonged to Sullivan, Corbett, and Jeffries. As far as Australia was concerned, an "archetypal darkness" had replaced sweetness and light; the barbarian had defeated the civilized man. As the *Daily Telegraph* observed in doggerel:

> And yet for all we know and feel,
> For Christ and Shakespeare, knowledge, love,
> We watch a white man bleeding reel,
> We cheer a black with bloodied glove.[25]

The imagery in which the fight was reported clearly reflects the white Australian attitude toward Johnson. He was portrayed as a destructive beast. *Fairplay*, the liquor trades weekly, called Johnson "a huge primordial ape," and the *Bulletin*'s cartoons likened him to a shaven-headed reptile. He was the discontented black and yellow masses that haunted the Australian mind. Journalist Randolph Bedford, perhaps the most unabashedly racist reporter at the fight, depicted it in ominous terms: "Yet the white beauty faced the black unloveliness, forcing the fight, bearing the punishment as if it were none . . . weight and reach were ebbing against intrepidity, intelligence and lightness. . . . His courage still shone in his eyes; his face was disfigured and swollen and bloodied. He was still beauty by contrast—beautiful but to be beaten; clean sunlight fighting darkness and losing."[26]

In America the fight was not viewed in quite so maudlin a manner. Certainly the white American press was not pleased by the result, but it generally tried to dismiss it in a light-hearted mood. Perhaps, reporters reasoned, all was not lost. "Br'er Johnson is an American anyway," commented a reporter for the *Omaha Sunday Bee*. Then, too, boxing had declined so much in recent years that some experts wondered if the fight meant anything at all. Though John L. Sullivan criticized Burns for fighting Johnson, he added that "present day bouts cannot truly be styled prize fights, but only boxing matches." A fine distinction, but Sullivan believed it was enough to invalidate Johnson's claim as heavyweight champion. And certainly even if

Johnson were the champion, reporters all agreed that he was far below the likes of Sullivan, Corbett, or Jeffries.[27]

Though the mood had not yet reached a crisis stage, the fight's
portent was still most unsettling to American whites. This was especially true about the manner in which blacks celebrated Johnson's
victory. It was reported that the Manassas Club, a Chicago organization of wealthy blacks who had white wives, hired white waiters to
serve the food at their banquet. And one of their members said that
"Johnson's victory demonstrates the physical superiority of the black
over the Caucasian. The basis of mental superiority in most men is
physical superiority. If the negro can raise his mental standard to his
physical eminence, some day he will be a leader among men." In
other parts of the country blacks were reported as acting rude to
whites and being swelled by false pride.[28]

Johnson's actions in Australia did little to calm Caucasian fears.
Turning against the sportsmanlike tradition of praising one's opponent, Johnson openly said that Burns was a worthless boxer: "He is
the easiest man I ever met. I could have put him away quicker, but I
wanted to punish him. I had my revenge." Nor was Johnson discreet
about the company with whom he was seen in public. Hattie McClay,
his companion who had remained in the background during the
weeks before the fight, was now prominently on display. Dressed in
silk and furs, she seemed as prized a possession of Johnson's as his
gold-capped teeth.[29]

Johnson now seemed more apt to emphasize racial issues that irritated whites. Interviewed during the days after the fight, he told
reporters that he had the greatest admiration for the aboriginal Australians. Commenting on their weapons, he said, "Your central Australian natives must have been men of genius to have turned out such
artistic and ideal weapons."[30] Nor, he hinted, was he any less a genius. He understood human nature: because he defeated Burns he
could expect to be hated by all whites. But, he added, he could find
solace in his favorite books—*Paradise Lost, Pilgrim's Progress* and
Titus Andronicus. His comments achieved their purpose; everywhere
white Australians snorted in disgust. But his choice of books certainly did not reflect his own attitude. Unlike Milton's Adam, Johnson did not practice the standard Christian virtues.

Burns left Australia soon after the fight. A richer man by some
$30,000, he nevertheless was bitter and filled with hatred. Johnson,
however, decided to stay for a while in Australia. His side of the

purse, a mere $5,000, was hardly enough to make the venture profitable. He hoped instead to capitalize on his fame by touring Australia as a vaudeville performer. It was common for any famous boxer to make such tours. In 1908 he had toured in America and Canada with the Reilly and Woods Big Show and had enjoyed the experience. He loved the limelight and, unlike other boxers, put on a good show. He demonstrated a few boxing moves, sang several songs, danced, and played the base fiddle. During his Australian tour he actually made more money than he had in his fight with Burns. Not until mid-February was he ready to go home.[31]

He had changed. The Johnson who left Australia in February was not the same man who had arrived in October. Inwardly, perhaps, he was much the same. But outwardly he was different. He was more open about his beliefs and his pleasures, less likely to follow the advice of white promoters and managers. Undoubtedly he believed the title of world champion set him apart from others of his race. And in this he was right. He would never be viewed as just another black boxer. But he was wrong in his assumption that the crown carried with it some sort of immunity against the dictates of whites and traditions of white society. Now more than ever Johnson was expected to conform. And now more than ever Johnson felt he did not have to. The collision course was set.

5

White Hopes and White Women

No. NOT UNDER ANY CIRCUMSTANCES, he said, would he return to the ring. Like every other follower of the sport, he had read Jack London's piece in the *New York Herald*, and like everyone else he had been struck by its ending: "But one thing now remains. Jim Jeffries must now emerge from his alfalfa farm and remove that golden smile from Jack Johnson's face. Jeff, it's up to you. The White Man must be rescued." Yet white race or no white race, Jeffries refused to alter his pleasant rustic life. He was retired. The issue was closed. Besides, one look at Jeffries showed he had not been secretly training for a comeback. The former champion was fat. Though he did not look as if he weighed 300 pounds, he did. That exceeded by more than 80 pounds what he weighed in his prime, and at thirty-five his prime was well behind him. Certainly he deplored the idea of a black champion, and he wished well to each and every white contender, but he was not himself a challenger. No, positively. At least not in 1909.[1]

Thus began the search for the Great White Hope. It was like the search for the origin of the Nile, full of false hopes, preposterous characters, tragic deaths, and excessive newspaper coverage. Indeed, it was a promoter's and manager's dream. All one had to do to build up a gate or a boxer was to mention the magic words, Great White Hope. After the search began, as John Lardner said, "well-muscled white boys more than six feet two inches were not safe out of their mother's sight." Not in America or anywhere else. Billy McCarney, a college-educated manager with a remarkable imagination, combed the nation's mines, farms, and saloons for a prospect. James J. Johnston, an English manager, imported White Hopes from his mother country and her dominions. And Walter "Good-Time Charlie" Friedman went to China looking for a person—presumably a Yellow Hope—who could defeat Johnson. Unfortunately for the hopeful white managers, few white fighters even had a hope against the new champion. Still the managers were persistent, and for the next six years the search continued unabated.[2]

In early 1909, as the call for White Hopes was sounded, Johnson returned to America, determined to live according to his own rules. As his smile suggested, his life was his own, he meant to enjoy it, and he did not give a damn what anyone else thought. Johnson had become, in the language of the day, a Bad Nigger, that is, a black man who chose a different attitude and station from the ones prescribed by white society. In black folklore the Bad Nigger was a recurrent character. When pronounced "ba-ad" the term became a badge of honor, and stories were told and songs sung about these folk heroes. They were men who through their reckless life-styles openly courted destruction and therefore represented the ultimate in the emancipated black male. In style their lives were similar. They dressed well, had an insatiable love of a good time and an unquenchable sexual appetite, but most important had an utter disregard for death and danger.[3]

In the songs of Leadbelly and Jelly Roll Morton the Bad Nigger acquired immortality. There was Railroad Bill, a figure based on Morris Slater, a black turpentine worker who in 1893 shot and killed a white policemen in Escambia County, Alabama. There was Aaron Harris, who was said to have killed about twenty people, including his own sister. He was a New Orleans gambler and pimp who killed men who beat him in crap games and prostitutes who withheld money. Before witnesses he shot two policemen. There were Po' Lazarus, Snow James, Shootin' Bill, Slim Jim, Bad-Lan' Stone, Bad Lee Brown, Devil Winston, Dolomite, and Toledo Slim. But above all, there was Stagolee:

> Stagolee was a bully man, an' ev'y body knowed
> When dey seed Stagolee comin', to give Stagolee de road,
> O dat man, bad man, Stagolee done come.

The central event in Stagolee's life was when he shot Billy Lyons, who had won Stagolee's Stetson hat in a card game. Billy begged for mercy: "Boy please don't take ma life, For I got three little chillun, an' a poor little helpless wife." Stagolee's response was typical of the Bad Nigger:

> What do I care fo' yo' children, what do I care fo' yo' wife,
> You taken my new Stetson hat, an' I'm goin' to take yo' life.

When caught, Stagolee, in most versions of the ballad, is contemptuous and unrepentant:

> Judge, ninety-nine ain't no goddam time
> My father's in Sing Sing doing two-ninety nine.[4]

Starting in 1909 the American public began to see the Bad Nigger in Jack Johnson. They saw his flashy clothes and his brightly colored, fast automobiles. They saw the way in which he challenged white authority in his numerous brushes with the law. They heard stories of his night life, the lurid tales of his week-long drunks and parties. Tales of his sexual bouts were also told, and his shaved head came to symbolize the sexual virility of the black male. But most shocking of all were the times he appeared in public with white women.

Johnson was not pleased with the way the Australians treated him. After disembarking from the steamship *Hakora* in Honolulu in early March 1909, Johnson told reporters that he had been poorly received during his tour of Australia and looked forward to fairer treatment in America. He was bitterly disappointed. Arriving in Victoria, British Columbia, he was refused lodging at the prestigious St. Francis hotel. The manager said he was sorry, but rules were rules and the St. Francis, unlike Burns, did observe the color line. Johnson smiled and good-naturedly accepted the rebuff. The smile faded, however, when he was turned out of five other hotels and accepted only in a cheap, two-dollar-a-night fleabag.[5]

The smile hid the strain. Now champion, Johnson more than ever wanted to be his own boss. Fitzpatrick had been useful, but the two had never been friends. Fitzpatrick wanted to make all the deals and handle all the money; he viewed Johnson more as a highly trained circus animal than a partner. Johnson resented this. But the animosity was not just on Johnson's side. Fitzpatrick objected to Johnson's behavior with white women. In Victoria Fitzpatrick announced that he and Johnson would thereafter go their separate ways. The split, he hinted, had been caused by "Mrs. Johnson," who at that time was Hattie McClay.[6]

In Vancouver, Johnson agreed to fight an unknown boxer named Victor McLaglen. Though listed as a title defense, the fight was really nothing more than an exhibition designed to provide Johnson with spending money. McLaglen, a Tacoma heavyweight who was a last-minute replacement for Denver Ed Martin, was totally outclassed. The only serious punch Johnson threw was his first. A left to the solar plexus dropped McLaglen, and he arose not at all sure he wanted to continue. For the rest of the fight Johnson just toyed with his white opponent. He had fun, joking with ringsiders and standing rather than sitting in his corner between rounds. McLaglen tried but was helpless and more than a little foolish-looking. After the fight McLaglen seemed grateful that Johnson had not treated him more rudely. Obviously not a fighter, he thereafter channeled his talents into less violent arenas. Later as a movie star he won an Academy Award for his portrayal of Gyppo Nolan in *The Informer.* For his part, Johnson was pleased that he could earn a few thousand dollars in so easy a fashion.[7]

Although Johnson had not yet reentered the United States, his life-style was already being criticized. Specifically, the news had leaked out that Johnson had a white wife. A triumphant return to Galveston had been planned, and the port city had prepared for a parade and celebration. The news about Johnson's wife changed matters. If Johnson returned to Galveston with a white woman, a spokesman for the welcoming committee said, all celebrations were off. The committee had no wish to offend white Galvestonians. Johnson said the story was false. He was not married to a white woman. He claimed that his wife of two years was three-fourths black and had been born in the Black Belt of rural Mississippi. But, Johnson added, "I don't see where the outside world need concern itself with a man's private affairs." He had, if he chose, every right to marry whomever he wished.[8]

As it turned out, he decided to cancel his trip to Galveston. In mid-March he showed up in Chicago with neither a white nor a black wife, but with a desire to celebrate. In 1909 Chicago was a fine city for Johnson. His world revolved around prizefighting, saloons, and prostitutes. Chicago was short on the first but abounded in the other two. In recent years the growth of the city and its vice district had been spectacular. With a population just over 2,000,000, Chicago was the second largest city in America. It symbolized the achievements and the excesses of the nation. In the factories of Swift and Armour the poor of every ethnic and racial group worked. There the wealthy and the wretched might walk within feet of each other and breathe

the money stench of the stockyards. More than any other industrial city, Chicago offered limitless opportunities for her wealthy and great misery for her poor.

One of the opportunities that Chicago offered to both rich and poor was vice. Along Lake Michigan stretched the First Ward, the political and economic heart of the city, home of the great wharves of the Port of Chicago and the location of City Hall. There too was the Levee district, which could satisfy any desire of the flesh a male might have. One study of the region called it the Coney Island of the urban male id: "Along with an estimated two hundred brothels, it offered an untold number of barrelhouse saloons, gambling houses, peepshows, bucket shops, pawnshops, hop shops, voodoo doctors, and 'low' dance halls." Overseeing the whores, dope, and lesser vices were political bosses "Bathhouse" John Coughlin and Michael "Hinky Dink" Kenna, two Irishmen of the old school of urban corruption. Faithfully they delivered votes and money to the city's Democratic organization, and just as steadfastly the city refused to interfere with the activities of the Levee.[9]

George Little introduced Johnson to the Levee. A short but powerfully built man with dark hair, close-set eyes, and a full mustache, Little had once worked in the Levee for Kenna. He had failed at political infighting and had been shipped off to a saloon in Columbus, Ohio. Life in the provinces disagreed with Little, and in the managerless Johnson he saw his opportunity to return to Chicago in style. He courted Johnson royally. Nothing was beyond Little's— hence Johnson's—grasp, including the Everleigh Club, perhaps the finest whorehouse in America. The place was renowned. There in gilted splendor the very rich could drink, dine, dance, and enjoy whatever form of cogenial association with the employees they chose. They knew that their enjoyments would be kept confidential. Minna and Ada Everleigh prided themselves on discretion.[10]

One night toward the end of March Little took Johnson to the club. The Everleigh sisters, both Southerners born in Kentucky, objected to Johnson. Their club drew a color line money could not erase. But such was Little's influence that he "procured" three girls who were willing to leave with Johnson and himself. One of the Everleigh sisters tried but failed to talk the girls out of their folly. Off the five went to the hotel where Johnson was staying.[11]

One of the women who left with Johnson was Belle Schreiber. At twenty-three, she was in her prime as a prostitute, a profession in which the best years begin and end earlier than a boxer's. Until 1907 she had lived with her mother in Milwaukee; then she moved to Chicago and voluntarily became a prostitute, soon joining the prestigious Everleigh Club. Later she testified that she was trained as a stenographer and a typist, but she preferred the "sporting life." Though one person described her as "white, slender, with bleached hair, and very much painted," the photographer Frederick Gale said she was dark-complexioned, of medium height, weighed about 145 pounds, and—of course—was "painted." In truth, the color of her hair was subject to change, and like other prostitutes she did use cosmetics, but she was also a striking woman. Not surprisingly, Johnson was attracted to her.[12]

But then Johnson was attracted to other white women, both members and nonmembers of the Everleigh Club. Of the former, at least nine were dismissed from the club because of their relations with Johnson. These included Belle, "Jew Bertha" Morrison, Lillian St. Clair, and Virginia Bond, all of whom were later to provide evidence for the United States in its case against Johnson. But in 1909 they all must have enjoyed Johnson's company, for dismissal from the Everleigh Club could only mean a downward step in their profession. Johnson paid well, but not that well.[13]

Money alone can explain neither why Johnson sought out white prostitutes nor why they were attracted to him. The explanation runs deeper. The myth of black sexuality extends as far back as the sixteenth century, when the white Englishman and the black African first confronted each other. The English believed that centuries of life in the hot, often dank climate merely accelerated the African's natural tendencies toward lust and passion. Certainly Othello is portrayed in sexual terms, and Iago and others are quick to ascribe various acts of passion to the "lusty Moor."[14]

By Johnson's day the myth, buttressed by quasi-scientific evidence, had reached its fullest development. Frederick Hoffman's influential *Race Traits and Tendencies of the American Negro* (1896) argued that the major cause of disease among blacks was the "immense amount of immorality which is a race trait," and Joseph Tillinghast in *The Negro in Africa and America* (1902) agreed that blacks had a long history of sexual license. Physicians during the Progressive years added final "proof" of the sexual nature of the blacks. "Morality among these people is almost a joke," wrote Dr. Thomas W. Murrell, a lecturer on syphilis at the University College of Medicine at Richmond, Virginia. "A Negro man will not abstain from sexual intercourse if there is the opportunity and no mechanical obstruction," for "his sexual powers are those of a specialist in a chosen field." Indeed, some physicians said, the black male could not help himself; the *furor sexualis* he experienced resembled in intensity the sexual attacks in bulls and elephants. Dr. Daniel D. Quillian of Athens, Georgia, joked, "Virtue in the negro race is like 'angels' visits—few and far between." In his sixteen years of medical practice, he had never examined a black virgin over the age of fourteen.[15]

Consciously, Johnson exploited the myths. In cartoons his shaved head was sometimes pictured as the head of a snake, with all the sexual implications that reptile carried. In public he wore tight-fitting silk shirts and liked his companion of the hour to run her hands over his chest and back. Perhaps the most blatant exploitation of the myth was a practice he sometimes employed while training of wrapping his penis in gauze bandages, enhancing its size for all to see. In fact, everything Johnson did sharpened the image of his sexuality—the slightly lascivious smile; the speed with which he drove automobiles; the loose and easy boxing style; the inability to stay in any one place for very long; the attraction to prostitutes; the perpetually bloodshot eyes. Sexuality was the essence of Jack Johnson, the driving force behind his success, and this power was perceived by white females and males.[16]

Johnson's attraction to white prostitutes was more complex. Like other black males, he was a captive of the force of the dominant culture. White was the color of feminine beauty in America, and since the founding of the colonies wealthy women went to great extremes to preserve and even enhance their whiteness. They powdered their faces and shielded every part of their bodies from direct exposure to the sun. White was, then, the universal English color of purity, virginity, beauty, and innocence. White males accepted the implications of color, and to a great extent so too did black males. As James Weldon Johnson suspected, for the black man who had grown up in America the beauty of the black female was "a remote idea."[17]

At least on the surface this was Jack Johnson's attitude. Not only did he think that white women were more beautiful; he accepted the other stereotypes—that white women were kinder, gentler, more thoughtful, more loyal, and better companions. In later years Johnson explained his position to Ethel Waters, the black actress: "I could love a colored woman, but they never give me anything. Colored women don't play up to a man the way white girls do. No matter how colored women feel towards a man, they don't spoil him and pamper him and build up his ego. They don't try to make him feel like he's somebody." That white women treated him better than black women was a constant theme in any Johnson discussion of females. He told John Lardner that he did not believe he was too good for black women, but whites always treated him better. "I never had a colored girl that didn't two-time me."[18]

Beneath the surface, however, there were other impulses about which perhaps even Johnson was not fully conscious. He was not attracted to simply white women; he was drawn to white prostitutes, who could hardly be described as ideals of feminine virtue and innocence. Nor was Johnson himself particularly faithful. He enjoyed displaying his latest conquests—a word that best describes his attitude—even to his most steadfast companions. He openly flaunted his heroic infidelity. If there was love in his attitude toward white women, there was also hate. Capable of tenderness at one moment, he could be mean and cruel at the next. About all his relationships there was a pattern. He gave expensive gifts, then took them back. He made love to his white women, but he also beat them up. At once, he wished to elevate and defile them. They provided both a badge of his advanced status and reminder of his inferior position. To expect his attitude to be anything other than ambivalent would ignore the complexity of the man or the situation.

In Chicago Johnson began to court his own destruction. It was not just white women, though that was part of it. More than that, it was an attitude toward life: recklessness. Johnson was a victim ready to be claimed. He kept irregular hours, drinking often and sleeping little. He bought a car and quickly overturned it late one night driving from Chicago to South Bend. It was the first of many automobile accidents, but he never reduced his speed or, apparently, thought of safety. He was like his favorite car, the Thomas Flyer racing model, most comfortable when speeding past others. Perhaps more than boxing and women, he thought about cars and speed. Asked at his trial what concerned him, Johnson replied, "My mind is constantly on automobiles. If you ask me about that I can tell you." It was almost as if freedom could be found only on the borders of death.[19]

But speed and freedom took money. Therefore toward the end of March he left Chicago for New York City, where more than 1,000 blacks greeted him. Johnson was a hero, and parades were held in his honor. He told eager listeners that he would fight any man, that he would be a vaudeville star, that he would be champion for years to come. Stanley Ketchel, Al Kaufman, and Jim Jeffries—he was ready for them. In New York, amid the joy and celebration, he was believed, as well he should have been. He was a confident man with a great deal to be confident about.[20]

But talk was not money, and though he was well stocked in the former he was short on the latter. The only sure way to make money was to fight. The problem was that the mobilization of the Great White Hope corps had just started, and they were not yet ready to do battle. On little notice, the best that could be arranged was a match against Philadelphia Jack O'Brien, a former light heavyweight champion who seldom weighed over 160 pounds. O'Brien's career was almost over, but he was still a great draw. A dapper dresser and boxing stylist, he also claimed to be a major speaking talent. He once told a friend, "I have always loved to hear the verbiage that flows from an Englishman, whether he be an Oxfordian or otherwise." Certainly of all the White Hopes he was the most quotable. Explaining why he agreed to fight Stanley Ketchel, a boxer who knocked him out, O'Brien said, "I had heard that Ketchel's dynamic onslaught was such it could not be withstood, but I figured I could jab his puss off." And, as he told A. J. Liebling, he would have "put the bum away early" but his timing was a "fraction of an iota off."[21]

O'Brien accepted the fight with Johnson because he needed the money. He disliked Johnson and had a low opinion of the black race. Johnson knew this and used his champion's status to humiliate O'Brien. He forced O'Brien to come to Pittsburgh to sign for the match. Having to go to meet Johnson upset O'Brien, but the challenger was even more enraged by the place the champion picked for the signing. O'Brien had to travel to the "colored district" of Pittsburgh to meet Johnson. There in the back room of a saloon run by Frank Sutton, an old friend of Johnson's, they agreed to fight a six-round bout in Philadelphia. Disgusted by the entire affair, O'Brien left immediately after signing the contract. Johnson appeared totally satisfied with the confrontation. For the first time whites were forced to experience his world.[22]

There was nothing about the fight that Johnson took seriously. Reporters claimed he trained for the fight at Cole's gymnasium in Merchantville, but nobody actually ever saw him training. When asked about this, Johnson simply smiled. Sportswriters were annoyed by his haughty attitude. One said he had assumed an air of "exaggerated importance," which was to be expected from a member of a race "naturally fond of pomp and display." When asked about his opponent Johnson only smiled more. He would knock out O'Brien, he said.[23]

He did not. But then, he didn't really try. He entered the ring overweight and in poor condition. Rumors spread that he had been drinking the night before and on the day of the match. It was an uninspired fight. O'Brien's attack was timid and Johnson's defense and counterattack consisted mostly of laughter. He smiled, waved to the crowd, and made no attempt to hide the purpose of his presence. He was there for the $5,000 guarantee, for that and nothing else. Afterward Johnson said he stalled through the six rounds so as not to show Al Kaufman or Stanley Ketchel his true ability. If so, he succeeded admirably. But this offered small consolation to the spectators who paid money to see a fight.[24]

Criticized for his lackluster ring behavior, Johnson was also censured for his irresponsible financial dealings. Reporters remarked that although Johnson was paid splendidly for his boxing efforts, he was continually short of cash. The problem, they wrote, was that Johnson liked to spend his money. In a society rapidly shifting toward consumerism, the older belief that money was good only when it was saved or wisely invested still had a tenacious grip on the American consciousness. For example, with his winnings from the O'Brien fight, Johnson purchased a $3,000 roadster and a $1,800 diamond ring. This profligacy, though standard practice for boxers, was viewed as sinful in Johnson's case. John L. Sullivan was applauded for buying the house drinks. Robert Fitzsimmons, another free spender, was similarly cheered. But Johnson's behavior was stamped a racial character flaw. In this instance racial and class attitudes combined in an offensive against the champion.[25]

Johnson did not care. He had no use for the bourgeois values of thrift and respectability. That was not his world. Money was for spending, and at that exercise he was proficient. When he needed more cash, he agreed to fight another contender. Through Frank Sutton a bout was arranged against a fair Pittsburgh boxer named Tony Ross. Actually Ross's real name was Antonio Rossilano, but he believed that any good fighter had to have an Irish-sounding name. And the name was all he had in common with the great Irish fighters of the period. Though expecting little, more than 6,000 people turned up at the Duquesne Gardens to watch the fight. Again Johnson showed up tired and out of shape, and received a cool reception. In the first round he broke Ross's nose and split the white boxer's lip. Then, after knocking him down, Johnson slowed down and allowed Ross to finish the six-round bout. The spectators were unhappy. If the white fighter could not win, they had at least hoped to see more blood and faster action. Johnson, reporters complained, was not a very obliging champion.[26]

More serious boxers waited for Johnson in the West, but before meeting them the champion needed a rest. Along with a small group of friends he went to Cedar Lake, a quiet, pastoral village about 25 miles from Chicago. Sportswriters said he was training to meet Kaufman and Ketchel. In truth, he was attempting to slow down his frenzied pace of life. Since winning the title he had been constantly on the move. He had crossed southern Australia on a vaudeville tour, sailed across the Pacific, and raced about the Midwest and East in trains and cars. He had fought four exhibition-title fights; he drank almost every night and spent considerable time with various prostitutes. The strain was starting to show. He needed a tranquil period for recovery and regeneration.[27]

Johnson's companions at Cedar Lake were kindred spirits. There was George Little, a gambler, saloon keeper, and fringe member of the boxing world. Roy Jones was there. He was a black friend of Johnson's who had ties in politics, real estate, gambling, and prostitution. To help Johnson train was Yank Kenny, a 255-pound sparring partner who had a large, flat, crooked nose and cauliflower ears. When not sparring with better fighters, he was a full-time drunk. With these men—and others who turned up one day and were gone the next—was a wide assortment of women. Some were wives, some claimed to be wives, but most had no ambitions at all in that direction. Their backgrounds and lives were remarkably similar. The hazards they faced were also uniform. Violence, alcohol, drugs, and arrests punctuated their existence.[28]

Though Johnson tried, he had trouble relaxing. He liked Cedar Lake but was easily bored. He would stay a few days, become restless, and drive to Chicago. A few days later he would return and the cycle would start over again. His agitated behavior carried over into his sex life. Yank Kenny, whose room shared a wall with Johnson's, remembered that one night he was awakened by a woman's screams. In the next room he heard Belle cry out, "Don't beat me any more and I will do it, or do anything." The unusual aspect of this episode was not the blows. Johnson hit women before and after that night. It was Kenny's belief—and later the government's—that Johnson wanted Belle to perform some "unnatural" sex act. The nature of the act was never specified, and when Johnson later came to trial the affair, for reasons of propriety, was not disinterred. But it offers another intimation of Johnson's love-hate relationship with white women.[29]

As Johnson tried to relax, the West Coast prepared for his return. It had been over a year since he last fought there, and local promoters were eager to match him against a California boxer. But they were worried about his attitude. There were the reports that he no longer trained, that he loafed in the ring, and that he did not listen to his white advisers. Fitzpatrick had warned a San Francisco reporter that Johnson had changed: "Johnson was a different man" after the Burns fight. Before, Fitzpatrick continued, he would feed out of your hand, "but he is a hard man to handle now." The idea that Johnson was more independent, that he was no longer a domesticated animal, disturbed the local press. They much preferred the docile, slow-talking Johnson of 1902.[30]

But docile or not they still wanted him back. In early September he returned, scheduled to fight Al Kaufman in Colma. Promoted by "Sunshine Jim" Coffroth, the leader in that field in California, the match was greatly anticipated. Kaufman was no O'Brien or Ross. A former blacksmith, he was a big, strong, experienced heavyweight. In addition, the two knew and disliked each other. After some preliminary name-calling, Johnson had accepted Kaufman's challenge, and Coffroth expected a large gate. To ensure this the tickets were moderately priced. Bleacher seats sold for one dollar, and reserved seats cost two, three, and five dollars. At that time it cost fifty cents to sit in the bleachers at regular-season major league baseball games and one dollar for a reserved seat. Therefore, as a heavyweight championship fight, the Johnson-Kaufman match was a spectator's garage sale.[31]

As with most such bargains, the goods were a little shoddy. Kaufman trained hard and tried his best, but he was unable to hit the overweight and only modestly serious Johnson. E. D. Burrows, who covered the fight for the *San Francisco Bulletin*, estimated that Kaufman landed no more than a half-dozen clean punches, and those only stirred Johnson into action. For every punch he landed he was forced to pay a dear price. Burrows portrayed the bout as a jungle fight between a gorilla and a lion in which the cat was badly beaten. Johnson won, he wrote, without even trying. W. W. Naughton, the leading authority on boxing in the Bay Area, disagreed: "The trouble with Johnson is he does everything so easily that it looks as though he could accomplish a great deal more." The comment, although perceptive, was only half true. Johnson did make boxing look easy, but in most of his fights he *could* have done more. By the end of the bout Kaufman's face was smeared with blood and Johnson was clearly the victor. Beyond that the champion had nothing to prove.[32]

He really had nothing to prove. The fight was an interlude, a brief money-making adventure, between his more serious bouts with women and booze. During his trial Johnson was asked if he had made love with Hattie after the Kaufman contest. No, he replied, "After a man has a fight, he is not feeling like it." It was one of the few times during the early autumn that Johnson did not feel like sex or drinking. Between his fight with Kaufman on September 9 and his match with Ketchel on October 16, Johnson stayed in San Francisco at the picturesque Seal Rock Hotel. The weather was pleasant—a warm sun and a cool ocean breeze—and at the main house in Johnson's camp every day was a Roman holiday. One visitor to the "training quarters" wrote, "With the waning of the day the parlors blaze with electric lights, the wood leaps bright in the wide open fireplace, the entertainers play, the wine flows." Always in the center of the celebration were Johnson and his white women. On this occasion both Hattie and Belle lived with him, but he also spent occasional nights with locally recruited prostitutes.[33]

Reporters who interviewed Johnson discovered a confident, articulate champion who had opinions on a wide range of subjects. Miss Jacobson, a columnist for the *San Francisco Bulletin*, noted that "with the Simian slope of forehead and the thick African lips one is taken aback . . . by the brilliant flow of Johnson's conversation." He spoke with the erudition of a Harvard graduate, she said, except that his knowledge seemed "strutted," like Mark Twain's savage who, clothed in nothing but a silk plug hat, thought he had acquired civilized dress. He spoke about his appetites—about food and women and automobiles. "The female mind," he told Miss Jacobson, "is much slower than the man's. . . . The female mind naturally turns to dress." In this his views were akin to those of most men of the period.[34]

On the subject of automobiles, however, Johnson revealed something more personal, something perhaps James Weldon Johnson had seen in Johnson years before. In his autobiography the great black writer remembered spending quiet days with the boxer at his San

Francisco apartment. He remembered Johnson's face, "sad until he smiled," and the Texan's soft Southern speech and laughter. He recalled how Johnson would talk wistfully of being champion someday. Perhaps the Johnson of 1909 was not as wistful as the boxer of 1905, but he could become suddenly serious, even philosophical. Jacobson asked him what would happen if something went wrong with his car when he was speeding. " 'If' and 'suppose'—two small words, but nobody has ever been able to explain them. . . . One man falls out of bed and is killed. Another falls from a fifty-foot scaffold and lives. One man gets shot in the leg and is killed. Another gets a bullet in his brain and lives. . . . I always take a chance on my pleasures. We gets in this world what we're going to get."[35] It was this sense of fatalism that governed his life. "We gets what we're going to get." Johnson believed this. He was almost Calvinistic in his belief in predestination. His death was already written somewhere, and it would not come a day before or after it was scheduled. Tempting fate, therefore, presented no problems. He would continue to drive fast, sleep with white women, beat white boxers, and defy white authorities. They could not alter his preordained fate. "In New Jersey it was a slippery night. The car slid and climbed a tree. It cost $1,800 to have the machine repaired, but no one was hurt." Destiny, as James Weldon Johnson guessed, had always been a part of Jack Johnson.[36]

The weeks passed quickly. Decadence ruled the night. Johnson drank wine and dallied with white prostitutes. During the day he raced about the hills of the Bay Area in his automobile. He told one reporter that his only dream was to drive a car 200 miles per hour. When not speeding he submitted to light training, sparring with Young Peter Jackson and Bob Armstrong. Both were tough black fighters. Occasionally a white boxer would spar with Johnson. One day a skinny, rangy sailor, Gunboat Smith, came to the camp. Smith, who went on to be an outstanding heavyweight, remembered the classic style with which Johnson fought: "Johnson was a fellow that used to stand flat-footed and wait for you to come in. And when you come in, he'd rip the head off you with uppercuts, cut you all to pieces. That's the way he fought."[37]

The man he was scheduled to fight was much more aggressive. Stanley Ketchel, born Stanislaus Kiecal, had a reputation of being a very bad man. Philadelphia Jack O'Brien, whom Ketchel knocked out in June 1909, called him "a tumultuously ferocious person," and everyone who knew Ketchel agreed. At the age of twelve, Ketchel had found his father in a hayloft, his throat slit from ear to ear. A few months later his mother was discovered dead of "unnatural causes." Thereafter Ketchel roamed the country, lived in hobo jungles, and worked in lumber yards and mining camps from the Dakotas to Alaska. His reputation for meanness was well deserved, and he even looked the part, with thin, cruel lips; wild, staring eyes; broad, sloping forehead; and an oddly cut jaw. Wrote one sensationalistic piece on Ketchel, "A face like that cannot be manufactured by make-up artists. To find such a face—search the insane asylums, or the prison death house." Even a more balanced reporter like Dan Morgan became lurid when talking about Ketchel. As he told the biographer John D. McCallum, "Ketchel was an exception to the human race. He was a savage. He would pound and rip his opponent's eyes, nose and mouth in a clinch. He couldn't get *enough* blood. His nickname, 'The Assassin,' fit him like a glove." [38]

As an opponent for Johnson Ketchel's primary liability was his size. In 1909 he was only 5 feet, 9 inches tall and weighed no more than 160 pounds. Although he was middleweight champion of the world, and to some experts the greatest middleweight who ever lived, he had had little experience with bigger fighters and none at all with boxers of Johnson's size and ability. Still, Ketchel was the best White Hope that "Sunny Jim" Coffroth could find on short notice, and though Johnson was expected to win, the prospect of a great little man versus a great big man was appealing to the promoter.

Rumors have persisted that the fight was fixed. Asked at his trial if he knew beforehand that he would win the fight, Johnson replied, "I did." Johnson's lawyer objected to the line of questioning, stating that the government "wants to show that the fight was crooked or something like that." But before the court could rule on the objection, Johnson volunteered a cryptic, "They are all crooked." According to rumor Coffroth wanted to ensure that there would be no quick endings because the fight was to be filmed, and a fast knockout would kill the boxoffice potential. Therefore Johnson agreed not to knock out his lighter opponent. Such arrangements were not new to Johnson. Earlier in his career he had agreed to carry smaller or less talented white boxers. He viewed such actions as good business. Of course he knew he could defeat Ketchel. If by allowing the fight to go the full twenty rounds he could pocket a percentage of the film revenues, Johnson was only too happy to comply. Unlike Ketchel, blood and pain were not that important to him. [39]

It was the biggest fight Californians had seen in a long while. The stadium in Colma, just outside the city limits of San Francisco, was filled with sailors, Chinese, "fashionably attired ladies," and "men of almost every nation." High on the grassy top of a hill to the south of the arena dozens of "free-lookers" equipped with field glasses and telescopes had assembled. Most of the spectators wanted Ketchel to win, and this support was not lost on the usually unemotional fighter. In his dressing room before the fight Ketchel had sat coolly smoking a cigarette and telling a story. When his handlers told him it was time to leave for the ring, he had calmly finished the story and the cigarette. However, once in the ring the *sang froid* vanished. Hearing the swell of cheers when he was introduced, Ketchel was overcome by racial pride, and tears streamed down his face.[40]

Johnson wore his usual smiling mask. As in all of his fights, exactly what he felt or thought was difficult to say. Hissed at as he climbed into the ring, he coolly smiled. The spectators responded with a chorus of catcalls and groans. Not even the American flag he wore as a belt won him any popularity. As his handlers tied on his gloves, W. W. Naughton reported, Johnson "looked around over the sea of hostile faces with a half-grin on his face." This brief period was Ketchel's time, he knew, but once the bell rang the stage would be all his.[41]

The fight started like other Johnson matches. Bigger, stronger, and faster than his opponent, Johnson toyed with Ketchel through the early rounds. Sometimes Johnson displayed his mastery by hitting Ketchel, but more generally he showed it through his feints. So convincing were these deceptive moves that Ketchel began "whipping his gloves to and fro sidewise and blinking as though punches were coming from he knew not where." When this happened, Johnson would step back and laugh. He knew that a white fighter who withstood a brutal beating was heroic, but one who was made to look foolish fell considerably in the public's estimation. Naughton saw that Johnson allowed a number of openings to pass unnoticed, or "he may have noticed them at that, but he certainly did not avail himself to them." If the fight was fixed to go the distance, Johnson was cooperating fully. He rarely threw an uppercut, his best punch, or any other hard blow. Although Ketchel's mouth and nose bled freely, during the first eleven rounds he was not seriously hurt.[42]

Round twelve began like the rest. Johnson stepped briskly from his corner and met Ketchel's attack with a left jab. And another. Then someone in Ketchel's corner yelled, "Now then, Stanley," and the challenger threw a roundhouse right that seemed to curve around Johnson's neck. The punch landed on Johnson's mastoid process, the rear portion of the temporal bone located behind the ear. The champion fell clumsily to the canvas, partially stopping his fall with his right hand. On his face was a grin. He was up before the referee could begin a count. Ketchel, sensing the kill, rushed the champion and was caught by a volley of punches. Because Ketchel was moving forward, the power of the punches was increased. One punch, a right uppercut, landed on Ketchel's open mouth, and the leather of Johnson's glove was torn on the challengers teeth. Ketchel fell as if "shot through the heart," landing heavily on the canvas. "He was as lifeless as a log, and a look of concern spread over Johnson's face." After the referee completed his count, Ketchel's cornermen rushed into the ring and carried him to his corner. Johnson seemed worried but smiled with relief when Ketchel regained consciousness.[43]

Although the ending was dramatic—the film became a very hot item—the result was not surprising. A great heavyweight had defeated a great middleweight. Certainly Ketchel was not too upset. That night, Gunboat Smith remembered, Ketchel won $700 from Johnson in a crap game held at a gambling hall in Colma. It was the last fight Ketchel ever lost. One day short of a year later he was shot to death by Walter D. Dipley, the husband of a woman with whom Ketchel had been sleeping. The bullet, shot from a Springfield rifle, entered Ketchel's back and cleaved the main artery of his heart, and he died as fast and as violently as he lived.[44]

Ketchel, Kaufman, Ross, O'Brien, McLaglen—these were just preliminaries. In White Hope affairs, 1909 was, as John Lardner wrote, "the ace-in-the-hole period." Reporters were quick to concede that Johnson was a very slick fighter, but he was not a Jeffries. "There is but one man in all this world who can cause Jack Johnson to extend himself," wrote journalist H. W. Walker. "That man is Jim Jeffries." Another sportsman noted that "if Johnson shows no more class than he showed today, Jeffries with one-half his old-time form, can clean up the negro in jig time." About the call for Jeffries's comeback there was a smug confidence, a belief that the big, grizzly-strong white fighter would not disappoint his race. There would be no more grim pictures like the one taken with Ketchel spread out on the canvas while Johnson, one hand on hip, the other touching the upper rope, looked on. This photograph particularly disturbed whites because it showed that as the white spectators watched the scene in horror, one black spectator seemed to watch with quiet enjoyment. Once Jeffries returned, boxing enthusiasts assured each other, racial superiority would be restored.[45]

6

The Year of the Comet

"IT AMUSES ME TO HEAR this talk of Jeffries claiming the championship. Why, when a Mayor leaves office he's an ex-Mayor, isn't he? When a champion leaves the ring he's an ex-champion. Well, that is Jeffries; if he wants to try to get the championship back then I'm willing to take him on." Johnson was tired of hearing about Jeffries as if the former champion were still the title holder. In fact, that was just what many white Americans believed. They believed Johnson's claim lacked legitimacy, that if Jeffries had not retired, Johnson would not be champion—which was true, since Jeffries would never have broken the color barrier. At best, Johnson was viewed as a regent, a temporary ruler who would step aside once Jeffries decided to resume his reign. And throughout 1909, as Johnson humiliated one white pretender after another, the pressure mounted for Jeffries once again to raise high his scepter.[1]

Few if any fights in history generated as much interest as the 1910 Johnson-Jeffries match. The Johnson-Burns and Johnson-Ketchel affairs were mere warm-ups; the 1910 fight was for all the racial marbles. From the very first, it was advertised as a match of civilization and virtue against savagery and baseness. As early as April 1909 the *Chicago Tribune* realized what was at stake. It printed a picture of a cute young blond girl pointing a finger at the reader; underneath was the caption: "Please, Mr. Jeffries, are you going to fight Mr.

Johnson?''[2] Her call was as clear and her point as straight as Kitchener's in his famous Great War poster. Humanity needed Jeffries. He had inherited the White Man's Burden and he could not plead retirement to cloak his weariness.

The year 1910 was the center point of Johnson's life. It was a year that a Greek dramatist would have loved, for it saw both his greatest triumph and the actions that led inexorably to his fall. During those twelve months Johnson was engulfed by restless energy. He moved about like a caged lion, seldom spending more than a night or two in any one city before traveling to another town. Always calm and pleasant in public, in his private affairs he was often violent and mean. The speed of his life was becoming increasingly difficult to control, but he did not—or could not—take his foot off the accelerator.

Johnson left California a few days after his fight with Ketchel. Belle went with him, as did Little and a prostitute he was seeing named Lillian St. Clair, who had worked alongside Belle at the Everleigh Club. They rolled across the country in style, celebrating the entire way. Part of the way they traveled by train, sleeping and dining in the first-class cars. After Chicago they rode in Johnson's automobile, driven by his white chaffeur, Mervin Jacobowski. Parties were held in Johnson's honor in Chicago, Indianapolis, Pittsburgh, New York, and Philadelphia. It was a high time, and Johnson was the main attraction.[3]

The money, the success, the fame, the smile, the body—women now more than ever were attracted to Johnson. In New York he met Etta Terry Duryea, whom he would eventually marry. She was a sporting lady, though technically not a prostitute. Born in Hempstead, Long Island, and brought up in a fashionable section of Brooklyn, Etta had married Charles C. Duryea, an Eastern horse-racing patron. The marriage did not last long, but even after the two separated Etta continued to attend the races. One afternoon at the Coney Island track she met Johnson, and shortly thereafter the two began living together, Etta taking the unofficial title "Mrs. Jack Johnson." About her there was a certain sense of sadness. Her beauty was of a haunting sort—cold, distant, aloof. Her hair and eyes were dark, her chin pointed and dimpled. She had a beautifully shaped mouth, but one that appeared unused to smiling. In pictures her lips are always locked in a perpetual pout. But it was her eyes that registered the real sadness. They seemed to stare without seeing, as if they knew all too well that sight was not worth the effort of focus. It is difficult to look at pictures of Etta and still be surprised that she committed suicide.[4]

When Johnson left New York for Philadelphia, Etta went along. So too did Belle and Hattie. The two prostitutes were used to the arrangement, but Etta was not. There were several scenes, but nothing Johnson could not handle. The three stayed in separate hotels and waited for Johnson. That was his normal procedure when traveling with more than one woman. At any time in the day or night he might make a brief appearance for the purpose of intercourse, but he usually left after a short stay. Belle and Hattie, as prostitutes, were accustomed to such behavior. He treated Etta differently. She stayed at the hotel where he stayed. She was, it soon became clear, the number one Mrs. Jack Johnson.[5]

The changing nature of Johnson's fancy can be most easily traced through his gifts of jewelry. First the jewelry—mostly diamonds that Johnson treated like the Crown Jewels—was given to Hattie. When Johnson came to favor Belle, Hattie was forced to give the jewelry to her rival. Then came Etta, and once again the jewelry changed hands. Perhaps in an attempt to recapture Johnson's affections—and jewelry—toward the end of 1909 Belle announced that she was pregnant. This pleased Johnson. As Belle later testified, "He asked me to have this child and not to do anything to get rid of it." However, children were bad public relations in Belle's business, and the child—which she continually referred to as "it"—was never born. This did not seem to weigh heavily on Johnson's mind.[6]

But by 1910 Johnson's interest was elsewhere. The Ketchel fight had dramatically enhanced his reputation and he was sought after by several vaudeville agencies. In December 1909, while in New York, he signed for a tour with Barney Gerard's "Atlantic Carnival" show. For the tour, which was due to start in early 1910, Johnson was guaranteed $1,300 per week. It was a star's salary, and initially Johnson seemed satisfied. As he left to begin the tour, a reporter for the *Chicago Tribune* noted that Johnson was "his usual happy self." He was expected only to be himself, or what whites perceived was his true nature. He was told to dance about the stage, shadow box, sing a bit, and tell a few amusing stories.[7]

He was also supposed to accept the indignities that came with being a black performer. Even the top black vaudevillians were treated shamelessly. Bert Williams, one of vaudeville's greatest stars, was doomed to be a "funny nigger" despite his desire to give the white audience "both sides of the shiftless darky—the pathos as well as the fun." The star on stage, when the curtain fell Williams was just another Jim Crow black. His cubbyhole dressing room was separated from the other, better dressing rooms reserved for white performers. He was never supposed to mix socially with the white members of the tour, and a clause in his contract specified "that at no time would he be on the stage with any of the female members of the company." As the years of isolation and frustration lengthened, Williams's smile became bitter and his humor more biting. He once observed about the fate of a black vaudevillian, "It's no disgrace to be colored, but it's so inconvenient."[8]

Johnson was also expected to live with the inconveniences. Frank Calder, a stage manager, recalled working with Johnson at the Cleveland Star Theatre and the Indianapolis Empire Theater. Even though it was bitter cold, Johnson was not allowed in the heated dressing room that the other performers used. Rather he was forced to change clothes in the cellar. Unlike Williams, Johnson rebelled against such treatment. At the Fairland Theatre in Terre Haute, he refused to perform. It was too cold, he said, to go on stage in just boxing tights and gloves. An argument with the management followed, and Johnson angrily left town.[9]

As the novelty of the stage wore off, Johnson's irritability surfaced more often. For a while he traveled alone, but this made him angry, dissatisfied, and lonesome. He sent for Etta and Belle, but this too caused problems. Finding rooms for both women during the series of one-night stands proved a logistical nightmare, and the two women violently disliked each other. During one train trip the two accidentally met and, according to Gerard, the "fur flew." Thereafter the two women were sent home, and Gerard "lent" Johnson to Frank Rose for a one-week tour in Michigan. For the use of Johnson, Rose paid Gerard $2,500. A few weeks later Johnson learned of the deal and became enraged. He felt used and told Gerard so. They argued. Johnson said Gerard owed him $2,550. Gerard said he did not, but "upon threats of violence and seeing [his] life in danger," he paid the sum. Once back safely in New York, he discontinued the tour owing to Johnson's "arbitrary habits and ego." He also initiated legal proceedings to recoup the money Johnson had scared out of him.[10]

Johnson's anger and frustration were not confined to his theatrical dealings. In New York he got into an argument with a fellow black named Norman Pinder. It was a drinking dispute. Johnson said he drank only wine; Pinder remarked that he remembered when Johnson once drank beer from a bucket like a horse. Thereupon, Pinder claimed, Johnson knocked him down, kicked him in the ribs, threw a table and chair on him, and pulled out a gun. Pinder wisely stayed on the floor, and Johnson left the saloon. When Johnson was later arrested he told the police that his only regret was that he had not hit Pinder harder. A few weeks later, when Johnson was served with a $20,000 legal suit by Pinder's attorney, he threw the paper on the ground. For lawyers, theatrical promoters, and Pinderesque citizens he had only the deepest scorn. He would do and act as he wished.[11]

Money was no longer an immediate problem. Ahead of Johnson was a rainbow, and beyond it the pot of gold. The rainbow was Jeffries, the pot of gold their proposed match. Toward the end of 1909 Jeffries succumbed to the pressures of race and dollars. Hundreds of letters were sent to Jeffries with a single theme: it was incumbent upon him as a white man to shut Johnson's smiling mouth once and for all. White Americans doubted not that Jeffries was up to the task. They believed the Jeffries mythology—that he cured himself of pneumonia by drinking a case of whisky in two days, that with a broken leg he was still able to knock out a leading heavyweight contender, that upon inspection a physician told him that he was simply not human. Across America white bartenders told customers that if Jeffries fought Johnson, he would "probably kill the Negro." After more than a year of such stories Americans—and, more important, Jeffries—believed that he probably *would* kill Johnson.[12]

It was left to the business managers to work out the details. Sam Berger negotiated for Jeffries, George Little and Sig Hart for Johnson. They told reporters that the fight was open for bids and that the person who offered the most money could stage it. The leading promoters in America handed in their bids, which were supposed to be opened in public at the Hotel Albany in New York City. However, both boxing and the promotion of boxing matches were illegal in New York, and at the last minute the scene for the opening of the bids was shifted across the Hudson River to Meyer's Hotel in Hoboken, New Jersey. The greatest promoters of the day either were there or had sent representatives. "Tuxedo Eddie" Graney, short and "built somewhat on the spherical plan of a toy balloon," was there representing the Tuxedo Club of San Francisco. The Bay City's other leading promoter, "Sunny Jim" Coffroth, was represented by Jack Gleason. It was rumored that they already held Jeffries under contract.

"Uncle Tom" McCarey, who had promoted many of Johnson's early fights, hoped to get the bout for his Pacific Club in Los Angeles. Phil King, who represented Hugh McIntosh, wanted the fight to be staged in Australia. And a relatively new promoter, George Lewis "Tex" Rickard, said he was Johnson's personal favorite.[13]

The bids were opened. They were all attractive, but Rickard's was the best. He guaranteed the fighters $101,000 and two-thirds of the movie rights. In addition, he promised a cash bonus of $10,000 for each fighter upon signing. It was money unheard of in the boxing world, but it was not just talk. Rickard was backed by Thomas F. Cole, a Minnesota millionaire who owned silver and gold mines across the United States and Alaska.

In an age when a laborer still might earn only a dollar a day, the amount Jeffries and Johnson stood to make struck some observers as disgraceful. Not only would the winner get 75 percent of the $101,000 guarantee, and the loser, 25 percent, but additional revenues would be gained through their percentages of the film rights and vaudeville contracts. Edward R. Moss, sports editor for the *New York Evening Sun*, estimated that if Jeffries won, the white fighter would make $667,750 and Johnson would earn $358,250. If Johnson was victorious, the film rights would be worth less and he would make only $360,750 to Jeffries's $158,000. Either way the amounts were staggering. "A new era is at hand in pugilism," wrote Moss. "These horny-fisted survivals of the Stone Age are . . . the real moneymakers. Primitive Nature seems to reward her followers handsomely, despite civilization's boasted triumphs."[14]

Behind the new era and manipulating the million dollar match were Tex Rickard and Jack Gleason, who was brought in on the promotion to please Jeffries. Rickard was a new sort of promoter. He did not know much about boxing, and in 1910 he had few connections in the puglistic world. He did not even look like a fight promoter, who as a species were overweight, cigar-chewing, carnival shellmen. Rickard was sleek and clean. Bob Edgren of the *New York Evening World* said Rickard was "tall, lean and sinewy as a cowboy, dark-tanned from exposure to the sun and wind, and [had] a sharp eye, thin lips, straight-nosed countenance, and [was] as alert as an eagle." And he was. If he looked like the clean-living Western movie hero William S. Hart, his past was as checkered as that of a character from a Bret Harte story. Orphaned at the age of ten, Rickard had grown up on the bloody strip of land in Missouri along the Kansas border that composed Clay County during the years when the James brothers ruled there. As a teenager he moved to Texas and worked as a horse wrangler and later a frontier marshal. In 1895 his wife and baby died and he left Texas, drifting north to Alaska. It was a time for making money and getting rich, and Rickard panned for gold, tended bar, and gambled. He managed the Northern Saloon in Nome but lost everything he earned at the poker and roulette tables. Tired of Alaska, he drifted south, this time ending up in the gold fields of South Africa. Back in the United States, he opened the famous Northern Saloon in Goldfield, Nevada, where another gold rush was under way. There in the hot, dirty-rich town of Goldfield Rickard tried his hand at promoting boxing matches. He did it not for the love of boxing or even the love of money, but to draw the nation's attention to Goldfield. He matched Joe Gans, the magnificent black lightweight champion from Baltimore, against the rugged Battling Nelson, and for forty-two rounds the two men butted and kicked, sweated and bled, and occasionally punched until Nelson sank a left hook in Gans's groin and lost on a foul. But the scheme worked. Overnight Goldfield became famous and Rickard became a success as both a promoter and an advertiser.[15]

No advertising genius was needed to market the Johnson-Jeffries fight. The issues in this fight were literally black and white. Rickard felt no qualms about exploiting the race issue. Jeffries became the "Hope of the White Race" and Johnson the "Negroes' Deliverer." Seen as a battle for racial superiority everything about the fight was treated as having momentous importance. When San Francisco was chosen as the site for the bout, the world's attention focused upon the Bay Area. An editorialist for *Current Literature* observed the fight was "casting its shadow over a palpitating world. England and France, China and Japan, Australia and Hawaii, are even now starting their delegations toward the Golden Gate." In a cartoon in the *New York Globe* entitled "Relative News Values," Jeffries and "Masta Johnson" loomed over Roosevelt and Taft and completely dwarfed men like Charles Evans Hughes, House Speaker Cannon, and William Jennings Bryan. Every public move Johnson and Jeffries made was photographed and recorded. Quite conceivably there had never been a more important athletic event in American history.[16]

The fighters retired to their training camps. Jeffries went to the tiny village of Rowardennan in the Santa Cruz Mountains along the narrow San Lorenzo River. He worked hard because he had to. He was thirty-five years old and weighed over 300 pounds, and the effort it took to prepare for a forty-five-round fight was enormous. Never a gregarious man, Jeffries became sullen and grouchy. Writers accurately compared him to a grizzly bear: "He growls and snarls and grumbles like an old grizzly when strangers come around. . . . He has a bear's aversion to being disturbed—particularly when he eats. He doesn't like to mingle much with the other animals." There was a concerted journalistic attempt to soften Jeffries's image—stories were told that he was kind to his wife and sparring partners, and that his home life was "wholesome and clean"—but it was difficult to gloss over his irritable and unfriendly disposition. Eventually reporters stopped trying to get close to him and submitted fictional pieces about how friendly Jeffries might be if he were not so unfriendly. Writers following the Jeffries camp survived on inspiration.[17]

Rumors were more common than facts. It was said that Jeffries was having difficulty losing weight and still retaining his strength. Reports close to Jeffries's camp—but usually not in it—said the boxer was having trouble sweating, a sure sign that there was something wrong with his health. Other rumors were spread that he had syphilis and was a mere hollow shell, though at 300 pounds he was admittedly a heavy hollow shell. The most persistent report, however, was that the fight had been fixed, that Johnson had agreed to lose. In a day when fixed fights were common, the report was taken seriously. Early betting, which was usually done by the professional gamblers, favored Jeffries. And though the fight was not fixed, it is conceivable that during the early summer days Jeffries believed that it indeed was in the tank.[18]

Johnson trained as if he believed the fight was fixed. He arrived at the Seal Beach training quarters on April 30, but he did not begin to work out until much later. Reporters said that he was devoted to pleasure, refused to train, and spent his days relaxing on the beach. Or, even worse in Rickard's opinion, he left for day-long drives along the California roads and into the mountains. He was always good copy. One day he would entertain sportswriters by playing the bass viol and telling stories; the next day he would quarrel with Little. The relationship between Johnson and his manager was as stormy as a soap opera love affair. They would argue, tell reporters how cheap the other was, threaten lawsuits, then make up. A few days later the cycle was started anew. The only thing usual in the Johnson camp was the unusual, and through May and early June it provided the drama for the prefight buildup.[19]

That summer the old order seemed to be toppling. In Mexico the epic revolution had begun, and that next May Porfirio Diaz, the very symbol of order and authority, resigned as president and left the country to the quixotic Francisco Madero. Across the Atlantic in England militant suffragettes challenged the order of the sexes. They smashed the windows at 10 Downing Street and London's shopping districts, chained themselves to the railing at Parliament Square, poured acid into mail boxes, slashed pictures in public art galleries, and when arrested went on hunger strikes. On May 7 Edward VII, king of England and uncle of Europe, died, and with him perhaps the world's best hope for peace. Since the death of his mother, Queen Victoria, Edward had guided both Europe and fashion along traditional paths; he was the English representation of the Pax Britannica and the order of the nineteenth-century world. In late May, when Halley's Comet was spotted, America and Europe seemed far less stable than they had when the comet was last seen.

Many people opposed the change. In reform they sought to establish the world as they believed it once existed, a world of Christian morality and puritanical virtues. Opposed to the new immigrants coming to America and to alcohol, prostitution, and other vices, this group tried to persuade other Americans to adopt their beliefs. In the late nineteenth century they looked in pity and sympathy on drinkers and prostitutes and tried to help them help themselves. However, when persuasion failed, reformers turned to more forceful techniques to remake the world in their own image. They now viewed their opponents not with sympathy but with open hostility; they hoped to win the battle not by words but through legal restrictions. To fight the battle a wide range of rural-based reform groups sprang into action. Such organizations as the Law and Order Leagues, Committees of Public Decency, and Protective Societies stood for legislated morality.[20]

In Johnson and prizefighting these reformers saw the incarnation of everything they opposed, feared, and hated. They embraced traditional, rural, puritanical values, the values that at least in popular theory had accounted for everything pure and great about America. The world of prizefighting, they argued, was as alien to those values as an illiterate Jewish immigrant from Russia. Professional boxing was viewed as an immigrant sport that attracted Irish and Polish Catholics, Russian Jews, and other undesirable sorts, which in fact it did. It was also quite correctly seen as having close ties with saloon keepers and Democratic urban machine politics. And the epitome of the evil of the prizefighting world was Jack Johnson. He drank, supported prostitutes, and threatened the very social and racial order of America. He was not the type of man rural Anglo-Saxon Protestants felt comfortable with. Instead he was a constant reminder of the powerful threat to the traditional American order.

When the site of the Johnson-Jeffries fight was announced as San Francisco, reformers strapped on their swords. It was an affront to civilization, they said. In Cincinnati a million post cards were distributed among the faithful for signing and posting. They were addressed to the governor of California and contained the simple message: "STOP THE FIGHT. THIS IS THE 20TH CENTURY." Other protests were staged in California. Fifty ministers formed a prayer session on the capitol's steps in Sacramento. They prayed for Governor J. N. Gillett to see the light of civilization and reason. Finally Congressman William S. Bennett of New York, chairman of the House Committee on Foreign Relations and a good churchman, wired the president of the San Francisco Board of Trade that the "prospective fight" stood in the way of congressional efforts to secure the Panama-Pacific Exposition of 1913 for San Franscisco. This message was quickly relayed to Governor Gillett.[21]

Up until then Gillett had steadfastly supported the match, claiming that it in no way conflicted with the laws of California. The potential obstruction of the Panama-Pacific Exposition, however, made him reread the statutes. After some soul-searching he concluded that the Johnson-Jeffries contest would not be a boxing exhibition, which California law permitted, but a prizefight, which state statutes forbade. In an open letter to the attorney general of California Gillett claimed, "The whole business is demoralizing to the youth of our state, corrupts public morals, is offensive to the senses of the great majority of our citizens, and should be abated, as a public nuisance, and the offenders punished."[22]

Moral outrage and economic pressure had won for the reformers. Although Mayor Pat McCarthy opposed the governor's decision, the fight was pushed out of San Francisco. Moral reformers could not contain their glee. The Reverend H. R. Jamison of Cincinnati declared, "Within the last few days there has gone to the governor of California such a deluge of letters from all parts of the country that I believe he has come to a rightful appreciation of the fight question, and that he has seen through all this betting and 'fixing' business only a way to the pocketbooks of the people. I believe he has seen the light of a good life, and that it has called to him so earnestly by day and by night that he has decided that the Jeffries-Johnson fight must not come off.'' This smug and confident voice underlay a grim reality. Prizefighting, like liquor and prostitution, was seen as an evil trick to rob good people of their money and their virtue, and it was up to the morally anointed to use spiritual and economic suasion to protect their weaker brethren.[23]

The man most affected by Gillett's decision was Jeffries. The ex-champion, who suffered from ''constitutional peevishness,'' was bitter about the announcement. Walter Kelly, famous for his vaudeville character ''The Virginia Judge'' and uncle of yet unborn Grace Kelly, was with Jeffries when they heard the news. Visiting the camp to keep his friend Jeffries from becoming too morose, Kelly and the fighter were trout fishing when a messenger boy handed Jeffries the telegram. He became pale and angry. ''I should tell them all to go to hell and go back home. If it wasn't for Tex, that's just what I would do.'' Afterward Jeffries became increasingly gloomy, turning even more inward. ''In my soul,'' Kelly wrote, ''I believe that incident was the blow that whipped Jeff.''[24]

To Rickard fell the task of finding another city to stage the fight. He had already sold $133,000 worth of tickets and had invested between $30,000 and $50,000 in the stadium, licenses, and various political payoffs. Now he had only two weeks to find another city, build a stadium, and complete the many other arrangements. He received offers from Reno, Goldfield, and Salt Lake City. He chose Reno because of its superior railroad facilities and because the mayor of the town assured him that a 20,000-seat stadium could be constructed there within the two-week deadline. Further incentives were offered by Governor Denver S. Dickerson. He told the promoter that no reform movement had any power in Nevada and no amount of protest could force him to cancel the fight. Thus guaranteed, Rickard, Jeffries, Johnson, and everyone else involved in the match boarded a train for Reno.[25]

The confused series of events had no outward effect on Johnson. Estranged from Little and asserting his independence, the champion announced, ''I am my own manager and always have been.'' He thereupon made his own travel arrangements and left for Reno, where he arrived on June 26. He seemed totally relaxed, so unlike the dyspeptic Jeffries. Reporters could not understand Johnson's calm. Though ''sharp as a razor in a sort of undeveloped way,'' wrote one journalist, Johnson seemed oblivious to the seriousness of his task.

"He fiddles away on his bull fiddle, swaps jokes with ready wit, shoots craps, plays baseball, listens dreamily to classic love songs on the phonograph," apparently unconcerned about his upcoming fight with Jeffries. San Francisco, Reno, Sydney, or London—it made no difference to Johnson.[26]

For American reformers, however, the site was important. They wanted to prevent the match from being staged anywhere in the United States. With this goal in mind, they turned their collective zeal on Reno and Governor Dickerson. On Sunday, June 26, Reverend L. H. Burwell, pastor of Reno's Methodist church, delivered a sermon on "Reno's Disgrace." He told his congregation that the fight would demoralize the community and bring "riffraff" and the "offscouring of the country" into Reno. In Cincinnati Methodist ministers passed a resolution calling on Dickerson to follow Gillett's noble example. Across the nation protest was intense, and in the end useless. Dickerson refused to budge. For many godfearing Americans, Reno became a national disgrace. The city deserved the "reproaches of the whole country," wrote a columnist for the *Independent* magazine. "But we tell Nevada that this is its last time thus to serve the devil. . . . Just as universal condemnation and disgust compelled Mormonism to get a new revelation on polygamy, so will Nevada be plagued into decency." And the Reverend M. P. Boynton, a Chicago Baptist minister, suggested, "There should be some way by which our nation could recall the charter of a state that has become a desert and a moral menace. Nevada has no right to remain a part of our nation."[27]

This strident tone of the reformers' protests revealed their true objectives. To be sure, they opposed boxing matches in the past and would do so again. But their opposition had never been so angry and forceful. The difference between the Johnson-Jeffries match and the other prizefights they opposed was the problem of race. The Reno fight was not simply another brutal and demoralizing prizefight; it was a battle that was widely perceived as a struggle for racial supremacy. Both black and white journalists understood this. Jackson Stovall of the black *Chicago Defender*, wrote that "on the arid plains of the Sage Brush State, the white man and the Negro will settle the mooted question of supremacy." Similarly, Max Balthazar, a white writer for the *Omaha Daily News*, asserted that the crucial question to be answered in Reno was whether "the huge white man, the California grizzly, [could] beat down the wonderful black and restore to the Caucasians the crown of elemental greatness as measured by strength of brow, power of heart and lung, and withal, that cunning or keenness that denotes mental as well as physical superiority."[28]

It was this answer, and not just the fight, that white reformers wished to suppress. Just to allow the fight to take place was to admit a sort of equality. It implied that blacks had an equal chance to excel in at least one arena of American life. The black journalist A. G. F. Sims realized this and criticized white reformers for attempting to prevent it: "Just because the Negro has an equal chance, that in itself, in their opinion, is enough to constitute a national disgrace." He hoped that Johnson would soundly defeat Jeffries, "just to make it a good national disgrace."[29] White reformers, therefore, considered the fight a no-win proposition. Win or lose, if the fight took place Johnson would achieve a symbolic victory for his race.

And in that victory whites saw disturbing possibilities. They were sure that if Johnson won, the result would be race war. "If the black man wins," a *New York Times* editorialist noted, "thousands and thousands of his ignorant brothers will misinterpret his victory as justifying claims to much more than mere physical equality with their white neighbors." The use of "brothers" and "neighbors" to designate blacks and whites is significant; it implies the two groups are in no way related, and that a Johnson victory would literally turn neighbor against neighbor. This prediction was echoed throughout the United States, especially in the South. Southern congressmen "talked freely of the danger of the negroes having their heads turned" by a Johnson victory. One Southern official, incensed by the very idea of the fight, remarked, "Why, some of these young negroes are now so proud that it is hard to get along with them, but if Jeffries should be beaten by Johnson they will be crowding white women off the sidewalks and there are plenty of towns where such action as that would cause deplorable troubles." Again, the words of the warning are important. Southerners believed a Johnson victory would increase the possibility of physical contact between young, proud blacks and white women. This haunting specter led naturally to thoughts of racial warfare.[30]

Whites were not alone in predicting that the fight would beget violence. Conservative blacks feared the same possibility. Black admirers of Booker T. Washington had never felt comfortable about the implications of Jack Johnson. As early as March 1909 Emmett Jay Scott, Washington's personal secretary, wrote J. Frank Wheaton, a successful black New York lawyer, about the need for Johnson to be more humble in public. Scott, and by extension Washington, hoped that Johnson would grant as few interviews as possible and would "refrain from anything resembling boastfulness." They feared that Johnson challenged an order they wished to placate and that his emancipated life-style eventually would cause a violent white reaction. In this vein E. L. Blackshear, principal of the State Normal and Industrial College in Prairie View, Texas, and a disciple of Washington, warned that if Johnson defeated Jeffries, "the anti-negro sentiment will quickly and dangerously collect itself ready to strike back at any undue exhibitions of rejoicing on the part of negroes." Like the white reformers with whom he had much in common, Blackshear wished that the fight could be prevented.[31]

Yet by July that was no longer a realistic hope. The fight was going to be staged, and Reno was giddy with anticipation. In the days before the fight the little mining town became famous. Visitors to Reno discovered a beautiful backdrop for an epic fight. One reporter described it as "a bright green little oasis, ten or fifteen miles across, set in a sort of dish of bare enclosing mountains—brown mountains with patches of yellow and olive-green and exquisite veils of mauve and amethyst, and at their tops, blazing white through the clear air, patches of austere snow." Situated in the Truckee Valley, along the route that the ill-fated Donner party had followed more than a half-century before, Reno was a town of "delicious morning and evening freshness" and intense afternoon heat. The fertile valley appeared more lush because of the bare white desert that surrounded it, just as the town's wealth seemed somehow greater when juxtaposed to its muddy streets and grimy buildings. Indeed Reno was, as Harris Morton Lyon wrote, "a broad-shouldered, tancheeked, slouch-hatted, youthful town. A town that believed in red neckties and fireman's suspenders."[32]

For many Americans Reno was a moral as well as a physical desert. They assumed that most of the town's population of 15,000 was to some degree associated with vice and sin. There was the gambling—not normal secretive gambling, conducted behind locked doors and pulled blinds, but illuminated, unbashed gambling. In Reno gambling was legal. As Lyon's New York sporting friend delightedly explained, "Gambling. Wide open. Walk right in off the street. See a swinging door and push it open. Right inside you'll find roulette and faro and—and—I never was so tickled in my life." And there was the drinking. In a four- or five-block area there were more than fifty saloons, most with bare board floors and bare wooden walls and names like Jim May's Palace, Lacey's Louvre, the Casino, the Oberon, and the Mecca. Most notoriously of all, there were the divorcees. Reno even then was the divorce capital of America. "Shoutin' the battle cry of freedom, I'm on my way to Reno," went the popular song about a suffragette traveling to Nevada to obtain a divorce. Lawyers in Reno even advertised their ability to obtain speedy settlements. Reno's indulgent attitude toward gambling, drinking, and divorce, wrote an English visitor, H. Hamilton Fyle, "tends to attract a class of visitors which cannot be said to shed any luster" upon the town.[33]

According to most observers the more than 20,000 people who traveled to Reno for the fight did nothing to upgrade the town's reputation. It was a sporting crowd—boxers, ex-boxers, prostitutes, saloon owners, gamblers, pickpockets, hoboes, profligate sons of the wealthy, and high rollers of every kind. They came to drink, spin the roulette wheel, and talk about the upcoming fight. They talked and dressed loud. Bright plaid vests, thick black cigars, and large diamond rings were the order of the day. There were sporting men from England, France, Germany, Italy, Australia, and all over the United States. There were black sports as well as white sports. It was an atmosphere rife with tall tales, hard luck stories, big dreams, and grandiose plans.[34]

Perhaps at no time before had so many reporters descended upon so small a town. Upwards of 500 correspondents were present to report the town's celebrations. Every day in the week before the fight between 100,000 and 150,000 words about the fight—enough for two popular novels—were sent out from Reno. Some of the reporters were leading writers. Jack London, Rex Beach, and Alfred Henry Lewis, three of the leading writers *cum* Sports, detailed the activities. But far more famous were the boxers and wrestlers *cum* reporters. Covering the fight for various newspapers were John L. Sullivan, James J. Corbett, Robert Fitzsimmons, Abe Attell, Battling Nelson, Tommy Burns, Frank Gotch, William Muldoon, and a host of others. Reviewing the list of correspondents, Rex Beach regretted that there were not more writers *cum* pugilists. "I lament at the absence of 'Walloping' Dean Howells of New England. He may not possess the literary style of a Joe Choynski or an Abe Attell, but he has a certain following nevertheless. And 'Battling' Howey James, the

Devonshire Demon. . . . His diction is stilted, perhaps, and lacking in the fluent ease and grace of 'Philadelphia Jack' O'Brien's, but he is entitled to be heard."[35]

Another faction well represented in Reno was the criminal class. Thieves of all types roamed about the town's streets, and "if a hand was not dipped into your pocket sooner or later it was almost a sign of disrespect." The small police force was timid and ineffectual. Hotel rooms, trunks, Pullman cars, and safes were all robbed with alarming frequency. Nor were all the criminals there to work. Some of the more famous and prosperous had come just to watch the fight and wager a few thousand dollars. The bank robber Cincinnati Slim was there, as was Won Let, the hatchet man for the New York branch of the Hip Sing Tong. It was rumored that he had killed between twenty and thirty Chinese. Even the notorious Sundance Kid was reported to be on his way to Reno.[36]

While Reno's police force was unable to contain the crime, the rest of the town's services were similarly taxed. People slept anywhere they could find an empty space—hotel rooms, Pullman cars, cots, billiard tables, hammocks, or park benches. They slept with their hands on their money belts. Good food was as difficult to find as a good night's rest. As Lyon recalled, "Meals you got generally any way you could get them." People ate in shifts, and it was not unusual to wait three or four hours for service. It was not a time to be choosy. When you got a chance to eat you ate what was being served, and you were thankful for it.[37]

Perhaps the only visitors who were guaranteed a place to sleep and enough to eat were Johnson and Jeffries. The champion's quarters was an armed camp. Cal McVey, a friend of Johnson's, carried a shotgun, and the champion himself slept with a gun. However, if Johnson felt particularly threatened, he did not show it. His mood, at least outwardly, was light and easy. Yet even his calm temperament was interpreted by white reporters as an indication of his inferiority. Jack London remarked that the champion's "happy-go-lucky" disposition resulted from Johnson's concern for the moment and his inability to plan for the future. Alfred Lewis agreed. As "essentially African," Johnson "feels no deeper than the moment, sees no farther than his nose [and is] incapable of anticipation. . . . The same cheerful indifference to coming events [has] marked others of the race even while standing in the very shadow of the gallows. Their stolid unconcern baffled all who beheld it. They were to be hanged; they knew it. But having no fancy, no imagination—they could not anticipate.''[38] Seen through white eyes, even bravery demonstrated the inferiority of blacks.

There were no displays of false cheerfulness in Jeffries's camp. At his roadhouse called Moana Springs, on the Truckee River, the atmosphere was heavy. Jeffries was even more restless and irritable than he had been in California. Every new story or rumor upset him. He was particularly angry at John L. Sullivan, the ex-champion who was perhaps the most popular fighter of all time. Sullivan, who was covering the bout for the *New York Times*, wrote (through his ghost writer) that the fight looked like a "frame-up." A few days later he went to Jeffries's quarters. He was greeted at the gate by Jim Corbett, who was helping out at the camp. It was Corbett who had taken the heavyweight title away from Sullivan, and the two men actively disliked one another. The slender Corbett asked, "What the hell do you want?" This was not the best way to say hello to Sullivan. Heated words were exchanged. John L. stared coldly at Corbett, and for a while it seemed as if the two were going to fight. Then Sullivan said, "If you're running the camp, I don't want to see him." As Walter Kelly remembered, "I had a lump in my throat as I watched John L. drive away. He was leaving the camp of a heavyweight champion without even the tribute of a handshake or a goodbye. For some reason, it just didn't seem right."[39]

It was not right. The fat, self-righteous, yet beloved Sullivan was deeply hurt by the incident. But it was typical of the mood of Jeffries's camp. He had taken all the talk about his duty to his race to heart, and the pressure showed. He prepared for the fight as if getting ready for a funeral. By the eve of the fight his friends feared that he was overwrought. He could not eat supper and retired early, but he could not sleep. William Muldoon, the famous trainer who was in Jeffries's camp, remembered that the old warhorse was heard pacing about. Mrs. Jeffries went to his door once and spoke to him, but he told her to return to her room and be quiet. Twelve hours later he came out of his room. He was ready to go to the fight.[40]

By the Fourth of July the entire nation was a bit nervous. Henry Wales of the *Chicago Tribune*, reviewing his long career as a reporter and an editor, said that no event so captured the public mind until the Lindberg flight seventeen years later. It was fitting that the fight was scheduled for the national holiday, for the celebration and the excitement were intense. Never had so illustrious a group of Sports gathered in one spot. From hoboes like Watertank Willie to bluebloods like Foxhall Keene, Payne Whitney, and Tom Shevlin, the famous Yale halfback who arrived in Reno wearing a dove-gray waistcoat and a straw hat with a club ribbon, it was the greatest holiday ever for that masculine subculture.[41]

And everyone had an opinion about who would win. The betting was ten to six or seven on Jeffries, but as Arthur Ruhl wrote, the talk was 1,000 to 1 in favor of the white fighter: "You couldn't hurt him—Fitzsimmons had landed enough times to kill an ordinary man in the first few rounds, and Jeffries had only shaken his head like a bull and bored in. The negro might be a clever boxer, but he has never been up against a real fighter before. He has a yellow streak, there was nothing to it, and anyway, 'let's hope he kills the coon.' " Indeed most white Americans found themselves agreeing with the Chicago White Sox, who were polled on the fight. Fred Olmstead, a Southerner, hoped Jeffries would kill Johnson, and Manager Duffy said only, "I can't go against my race."[42]

Most boxers and intellectuals also predicted a Jeffries victory. John L. Sullivan, James J. Corbett, Robert Fitzsimmons, Tommy Burns, Abe Attell, Battling Nelson—the list is extensive. They all favored Jeffries. Even black boxers like Sam Langford and Joe Jeannette picked the white. Perhaps Jeannette, who had fought Johnson more than any other man, spoke for them all: "Why, Jeffries can lose half of his strength, have his endurance cut in two, carry a ton of extra weight and still whip Johnson. He has the 'head' and the 'heart' to do it." The head and the heart: it was a common theme among intellectuals too. A psychologist writing for the London *Lancet* remarked that Jeffries's brain should be the deciding factor, and Rex Beach predicted that Jeffries's education would be too much for Johnson. "The difference," wrote Beach, "is in both breeding and education. Jeffries realizes his responsibility all the time. When Johnson steps into the ring with him, his bubbling confidence will bubble away."[43]

Even America's churches were not immune to the excitement. In Hutchinson, Kansas, the Colored Holiness Church announced that it would hold special services during the fight to pray for Johnson. To counterbalance this plea for divine help a Midwestern white minister said he would pray for Jeffries. The Reverend H. E. Trials of the First Baptist Church in Omaha told his congregation, "Every man with red blood in his veins should see Jim Jeffries regain the heavyweight championship from Jack Johnson." Although some ministers disagreed with such statements, most did agree that there was something much greater at stake in Reno than a championship belt.[44]

On the Fourth of July the nation was ready. Every section of the country was connected electrically with Reno. At the wealthy Edgemore Club on Long Island, William Vanderbilt, Jr., Howard Gould, Lawrence Drake, and the rest of their crowd followed the action through a private bulletin service. Outside newspaper buildings in every major city crowds gathered to follow the progress of the fight. At Tuskegee Institute Booker T. Washington, who declined to cover the bout as a reporter, set aside a special assembly room to receive telegraphic reports from Reno. If the fight was a racial Armageddon as everywhere it was advertised, then the results would be known to everyone as soon as it concluded.[45]

"The day dawned spotlessly clear, one of those still crystalline mornings which come in the thin dry air of the mountain desert country." Because of the shabbiness of the event that was to follow, reporters in Reno remembered the beauty of the morning. They recalled the order with which the drunken mob, 15,000 to 20,000 strong, moved toward the stadium on the outskirts of Reno and checked their firearms at the gate; how they poured in through the four tunnel-like entrances into the huge eight-sided arena; how their voices rose strong and clear into the hot afternoon air; how a brass band climbed into the ring and played "All Coons Look Alike to Me" and other "patriotic" selections; and how the joy of anticipation seemed to affect everyone in the pinewood bleachers. It was a picture of boisterous American innocence, confident that Jeffries would triumph in the racial confrontation.[46]

Johnson was the first into the ring, wearing a gray silk robe and blue trunks with an American flag for his belt. A litany of racial slurs greeted him, but as always he seemed not to notice. Beach watched for some sign of fear, but Johnson merely "grinned and clapped his hands like a boy." Jeffries was greeted like an emperor. He looked nervous, chewing gum rapidly and glaring across the ring at Johnson. "If looks could have throttled, burned, and tore to pieces, Mr. Jack Arthur Johnson would have disappeared that instant into a few specks of inanimate dust." But Johnson did not look at Jeffries, and this was widely interpreted as a sure sign of fear. From the spectators came a wolfish hoot, "He darsen't look at him! O-o-o! Don't let him see him! Don't let him see him!" Johnson laughed and peeked at Jeffries from behind his white trainer.[47]

Jeffries looked big but also old and tired. A few days before Jeffries had told reporters, "I realize full well just what depends on me, and I am not going to disappoint the public. That portion of the white race that has been looking to me to defend its athletic superiority may feel assured that I am fit to do my very best." Now he looked as if he were not at all sure that his very best would be good enough. William Muldoon said that the orator who experiences stage fright knew what Jeffries felt. He believed he was "the center of all human attention. The mental pressure became unbearable. . . . His Caucasian mind, sensing this vast concentration of thought, was overwhelmed."[48]

Tex Rickard, who had named himself as referee, also felt the "vast concentration of thought," and he feared it might erupt into violence. In order to cool the heated racial feeling, Rickard called on William Muldoon to give a speech. Muldoon, the once great wrestler, was a pompous, humorless man who genuinely believed in such notions as honor and fair play. In a forceful voice he told the spectators so. It was necessary, he said, not to judge Johnson too harshly just because he was black, and regardless who won, the verdict must be accepted in a sense of fair play. Muldoon's speech and the lemonade, which was the only beverage served in the arena, seemed to sober the crowd.[49]

During the preliminary activities not all of the tradition of the prize ring was observed. Certainly all the ex-champions were introduced by the portly, stentorian Billy Jordan, who had been imported from San Francisco to handle such matters. Although the day was exceptionally hot, Jordan and the other ring luminaries wore stiff collars, watch-chained waistcoats, suits, and hats. This formality of dress was also traditional, part of the ritual and formal rules of the sport. However, by prearranged agreement Johnson and Jeffries did not shake hands before the fight. No detail more clearly illustrated the symbolic importance of the match. Not to observe such a fundamental ritual, the very expression of sportsmanship and fair play, indicated that this was not simply another championship fight.[50]

No fight could do justice to such an extended buildup. This one did not even come close. "It was not a great battle after all, save in its setting and significance," wrote Jack London. Johnson established the tempo of the fight in the first round—slow and painful. He waited for Jeffries to lead, then threw straight right and left counters. Both fighters showed a tendency to clinch, but even there Johnson had the advantage. For all the talk of Jeffries's grizzly strength, Johnson was by far the stronger of the two men. He tossed Jeffries around with alarming ease. At the bell ending the first round Jeffries winked to his cornerman, but the gesture lacked confidence. It was the brave front of a man who knows that the game is over and he has lost.[51]

In the second round Johnson started talking to Jeffries. "Don't rush, Jim," he said as he pushed Jeffries across the ring. "I can go on like this all afternoon," he exclaimed as he hit the challenger with a solid right hand lead. Jeffries's famous crouching, rushing, wild-swinging style was useless against the grace and economy of Johnson's defense. Jeffries tried to respond, but before he could throw a solid punch Johnson would connect with a left or right lead. Thereupon the two would clinch. During the clinches Johnson would talk to Jeffries or to the challenger's corner.

Jeffries had several good moments, but not many. In the fourth round a Jeffries's left drew blood from Johnson's lip, and the crowd yelled, "First blood for Jeffries'." But actually the cut was deceiving. Johnson's lip had been cut while training, and Jeffries had merely reopened the old wound. More often Jeffries was in pain, and he looked tired between rounds. In his corner he seldom spoke, but when he did it was to complain. Once he told his cornermen that his arms felt stiff and heavy. And he told Muldoon that his "head felt queer" and that he was having trouble judging distances. Both problems are indicative of tension. Jeffries was too tight even to fight normally.[52]

More interesting than the Johnson-Jeffries fight was what might be called the Johnson-Corbett match. Jim Corbett, who was acting as Jeffries's chief second, was the most vocal racist in Jeffries's corner. He hated all blacks, but Johnson more than the rest. And he had a theory that blacks became useless fighters when enraged. Therefore from the earliest rounds he screamed insults at Johnson. But they did not have the desired effect. Instead of making Johnson angry, the insults seemed to have a calming effect. When Corbett said something, Johnson replied politely and smiled. Arthur Ruhl, who covered the fight for *Collier's*, reported that Johnson's retorts were well-mannered, quiet, and generous; he had "the good sense or cleverness to keep the respectful ingratiating ways of the Southern darkey." This infuriated Corbett, who became increasinly irrational as the fight progressed. Finally, in round twelve, Johnson called to Corbett, "I thought you said you were going to have *me* wild." The irony was lost on Corbett.[53]

Most of the reporters believed that Johnson could have ended the fight in an early round. They said he did not because he was a good businessman and a vengeful person. Financially a quick fight would have been disastrous. It would have destroyed the potential of the film as a revenue source. But beyond the money question, reporters believed Johnson enjoyed watching Jeffries suffer. By round twelve Jeffries's mouth was cut inside and out; his nose was broken and bleeding; his face and eyes were bruised and smeared with blood. Even Johnson's chest and back were covered with Jeffries's blood. There was no reason for the fight to go on. But it did.

Jeffries came out for the thirteenth still chewing gum. He tried to clinch, but Johnson delivered a left to the body and a right uppercut to the chin. Johnson followed with two more lefts to the face and another right uppercut. He then grabbed Jeffries by the shoulder and hit him with three lefts to the face and still another uppercut. Jeffries, his eyes almost closed, swung wildly but was unable to solve Johnson's defense. More punishment followed. Corbett, struck with a sudden insight, yelled for Jeffries to "cover up." The bell sounded.

The fourteenth saw more of the same. Jeffries's arms were too tired either to throw an effective punch or to block one of Johnson's. "How do you feel, Jim?" Johnson asked as he hit Jeffries with hard lefts and rights. "How do you like it?" Jeffries did not answer. He was moving like a drunk on a shifting funhouse floor. He did not even try to fight back. He just chewed his gum and accepted the brutal punishment. "Does it hurt, Jim?" Johnson asked as Jeffries walked into three consecutive rights. "They don't hurt," answered Jeffries. The round ended.

In the fifteenth Jeffries's face was bleeding and swollen, and his movements were languid. But he continued to move toward Johnson. The round-by-round report accurately, if unemotionally, reflects the horror of the scene: "He shambled after the elusive negro, sometimes crouching low . . . and sometimes standing erect. Stooping or erect, he was a mark for Johnson's accurately driven blows. Johnson simply waited for the big white man to come in and chopped his face to pieces." Finally a combination of rights and lefts forced Jeffries onto the ropes. There Johnson landed fifteen or twenty punches to Jeffries's head and face. Jeffries fell to the canvas for the first time in his career. He was dazed, and Johnson stood over him until Rickard made the champion move back. At the count of nine Jeffries struggled to his feet. Johnson charged and landed another combination of punches. Again Jeffries fell to his knees. At the count of nine he once more arose. At this stage ringsiders shouted, "Stop it, stop it. Don't let him be knocked out." But the fight continued. Jeffries was helpless. A left-right-left combination knocked Jeffries into the ropes. He sprawled over the lower rope, hanging half outside the ring. Rickard picked up the timekeeper's count. At seven one of Jeffries's handlers rushed into the ring, and Rickard stopped the fight. The "fight of the century" was over.

Silence. Insults and cheers were few. The spectators accepted the end as they might the conclusion of a horse race where the favorite broke a leg and had to be destroyed. Johnson was clearly superior, so there was nothing to argue about. Jeffries was old and tired and should never have attempted a comeback. More than talking or yelling, the sad boxing fan wanted to leave the arena as quickly as possible and find a bar that served something stronger than lemonade. Across the nation thousands of other men who crowded around newspaper offices for news of the fight experienced similar reactions. And so they went to the saloons, and when they finished drinking and brooding about the fight they expressed their displeasure in spontaneous outbursts of violence. The emotions exposed by the Johnson-Jeffries fight were quite sincere and, once uncovered, were deadly.

7

The Demons of the
Hexenlehrling

IN GREENWOOD, SOUTH CAROLINA, close to the border of Georgia,
Benjamin E. Mays was almost 2,500 miles from Reno. Only fourteen
in 1910, the future educator remembered clearly how white men in his
town reacted to the news of Johnson's victory. They could not accept
the outcome. Because a black boxer defeated a white boxer in far-
away Nevada, whites in Greenwood beat up several blacks. Fear
swept through the black population, and in the presence of whites
they dared not discuss the fight. The match, which prompted random
violence and brutal deaths, touched every section of the country.
Compared with many cities, Mays's Greenwood was tame.[1]

Not far from Greenwood, in the small town of Uvalda, Georgia,
the postfight mood was even more raw. In the days before the bout,
blacks working in a construction camp on the outskirts of the town
had boasted that Johnson would kill his white opponent. Intoxicated
by Johnson's victory and considerable postfight celebration, the
blacks continued to sing paeans to the champion. Enraged, a gang of
whites approached the construction camp. What happened next was
uncertain. Shots were fired. Later whites claimed that they had been
fired upon, but none of them were hit. The black laborers were not so
fortunate. Three were killed and five wounded. Even when the blacks
tried to escape into the nearby woods, they were hunted down and
beaten. Throughout the night shots were heard, and several times

108

members of the white party had to return to Uvalda for additional ammunition.[2]

Elsewhere the rioting claimed other casualties. In Houston, Charles Williams openly celebrated Johnson's triumph, and a white man "slashed his throat from ear to ear"; in Little Rock, two blacks were killed by a group of whites after an argument about the fight on a streetcar; in Roanoke, Virginia, six blacks were critically beaten by a white mob; in Norfolk, Virginia, a gang of white sailors injured scores of blacks; in Wilmington, Delaware, a group of blacks attacked a white and whites retaliated with a "lynching bee"; in Atlanta a black ran amuck with a knife; in Washington, D.C., two whites were fatally stabbed by blacks; in New York City, one black was beaten to death and scores were injured; in Pueblo, Colorado, thirty people were injured in a race riot; in Shreveport, Louisiana, three blacks were killed by white assailants. Other murders or injuries were reported in New Orleans, Baltimore, Cincinnati, St. Joseph, Los Angeles, Chattanooga, and many other smaller cities and towns. The number of deaths and injuries is unknown. Different accounts give contradictory figures. But that the result of the fight was the triggering issue is not questioned.[3]

Many of the riots followed a similar pattern. They were started by blacks who, inspired by Johnson's example, refused to shuffle and briefly lifted their heads and raised their voices in pride. In New York City, Nelson Turner, a black, was almost lynched for yelling to a crowd of whites, "We blacks put one over on you whites, and we're going to do more." In Boston a black was bound and gagged when he publicly predicted the outcome of Johnson's next fight with a white challenger. In Cincinnati more than three hundred blacks, accompanied by a brass band, paraded through the streets of the black district. In St. Louis, where the *Post-Dispatch* reported that blacks "hired automobiles, drank freely, offered to do battle in imitation of Johnson and ran alongside street cars jeering at white passengers," one white lost his temper and stabbed a black who had boasted about Johnson's fighting ability.[4]

Participants in the riots also displayed similar traits. Most striking was the class element. The rioting largely saw lower-class whites attacking lower-class blacks, although occasionally a middle-class black might also be assaulted. Often white sailors or soldiers were to blame, as in the riots in Norfolk and Chattanooga. Just as common were attacks by white laborers on black laborers, as was the case in Uvalda. In larger cities organized gangs caused the most harm. In

New York City "roving bands of white hoodlums" like the Pearl Button Gang and the Hounds of Hell roamed through the city beating every black they could catch. In the districts known as the Black and Tan Belt and San Juan Hill, tenement houses inhabited by blacks were set ablaze and attempts were made to lock the tenants inside. The match, then, not only initiated widespread race warfare but also caused racially motivated class conflict. As an editor for the reform-minded *Independent* magazine wrote, "Like the *Hexenlehrling* these apostles of savagery have unchained demons of disorder whom they are powerless to lay."[5]

It was this theme—disorder—that was stressed by most commentators on the match. Editors warned that the result of the fight would disrupt traditional race relations: "In spite of occasional lynchings in the South, the social adjustment between the white and the black races was coming to a better status than ever before when along came the Jeffries and Johnson prize fight and put the conditions back at least forty years." Translated, such comments meant that race relations were most stable when blacks remained in their clearly defined, circumscribed place and when there was no nonsense about equality. Johnson's victory proved that in at least one arena blacks were not inferior. He demonstrated that, as a black editor for the *Baltimore Times* wrote, "any negro anywhere may reach eminence in peaceful ways by using the Johnson method in his particular trade or calling." Nowhere is the effect of Johnson's accomplishment on the psyche of the black community better expressed than in the folk ballad that was written after the match:

> Amaze an' Grace, how sweet it sounds,
> Jack Johnson knocked Jim Jeffries down.
> Jim Jeffries jumped up an' hit Jack on the chin.
> An' then Jack knocked him down agin.
>
> The Yankees hold the play,
> The White man pull the trigger;
> But it makes no difference what the white man say;
> The world champion's still a nigger.[6]

For whites, the fact that the world champion was black made a great deal of difference. It challenged the old notion of the blacks as an inferior race and raised once more the specter of black rebellion. A cartoon in *Life* magazine graphically portrayed white fears. In the middle of the page stands a large, apelike Johnson. He is smiling, and a halo circles his head. Beneath his right foot is Jeffries's head; he is pushing the white fighter's face into the dirt. No longer the respectful darky asking, hat in hand, for massa's permission, Johnson was seen as the prototype of the independent black who acted as he pleased and accepted no bar to his conduct. As such, Johnson was transformed into a racial symbol that threatened America's social order.[7]

Social critics rightly saw in the fight the glorification of disorder. The traditions of the nineteenth century were dying; the Johnson-Jeffries fight displayed disturbing signs of a slowly emerging new culture. For the brilliant English journalist, H. Hamilton Fyle, the fight showed that the cultured upper-class boxing patron had given way to barroom loafers, gamblers, and "creatures equally foul in . . . language and . . . thoughts." The brutalization of the sport reflected the more general condition of a society where, as Ibsen's Hedda Gabler said, everyone was anxious to witness something—anything— "frightfully thrilling." In modern industrialized society man did his fighting and lovemaking vicariously, through prizefighting and sensational novels. "To-day there is no time for contemplation, no widely spread delight in beauty. We are greedy of crude life. Rough slices, cut off anyhow, raw and bleeding, we gulp down with insatiable appetite. Imitations taste nearly as good as the real thing; we cannot distinguish between them." And for Fyle, the Johnson-Jeffries bout was a prime cut of sanguinary modern life."[8]

Disorder, sensationalism, shabbiness—such were the terms white observers used to describe the title bout. They doubted not what had taken place. But what was to be done? The most obvious solution was to prevent a repetition of the sordid affair. Their effort to do so, an attack on Johnson's world, was launched on two fronts. First, there was a widespread feeling that boxing should be abolished. Prominent magazines like *The Nation* denounced the "disgusting exhibition" and suggested that hereafter newspapers should refuse to cover such an uncivilized sport. This by itself was not unusual; genteel and reform journals had long been opposed to prizefighting. For the first time, however, they found support in surprising places. Ardent defenders of boxing like Theodore Roosevelt turned against the sport. In a classic Progressive appeal Roosevelt wrote, "I sincerely trust that public sentiment will be so aroused, and will make itself felt so effectively, as to guarantee that this is the last prize fight to take place in the United States."[9]

The abolition of prizefighting was the ultimate goal, but of more immediate concern was the film of the Johnson-Jeffries bout. "Decency and good order require that the public exhibition of these pictures should be prohibited," wrote an editorialist for the *Independent* magazine. Reformers believed that the film would pervert morals and incite riots in any community where it was shown. Led by such groups as the United Society of Christian Endeavor and the Methodist Epworth League, reformers urged state and city governments to ban the showing of the film. And from across America they received considerable support. In the South, where it was feared that the film would arouse large-scale uppitiness and violence among blacks, attempts to prevent its showing rapidly followed the fight. Governors of Alabama, South Carolina, and Arkansas quickly wired William Shaw, general secretary of the United Society of Christian Endeavor, that they would comply with his request to bar the film. They were joined by many Northern state governors. Where governors saw no legal way to ban the film, mayors often prohibited it in their cities. Governors and mayors alike agreed with Mayor E. S. Meals of Harrisburg, Pennsylvania, who said that his town had too "many colored people and . . . could not take any chances on disturbances."[10]

Throughout the statements of prohibition run a common theme: blacks were viewed as simple-minded children who could not distinguish between meaningless sport and reality. Therefore they tended to see in Johnson's victory a substantial racial gain. Mrs. James Crawford, vice president of the California Women's Club and self-proclaimed friend of the black race, said that "the negroes . . . are to some extent a childlike race, needing guidance, schooling and encouragement. We deny them this by encouraging them to believe that they have gained anything by having one of their race as a champion fighter. Race riots are inevitable, when we, a superior people, allow these people to be deluded and degraded by such false ideals."[11] For many whites, then, the goal was to destroy the visions of equality and tear down the false symbols of achievement. They saw Johnson as an apparition—only a specter of equality—whose example should not be held before other blacks. To display Johnson's victory over and over again in movie theaters would irreparably harm American race relations.

This clear picture of right and wrong, true and false, was clouded by other issues, the most important of which was censorship. As one editorialist wrote, "If the moving pictures of the fight are to be prohibited why not printed descriptions of the fight? And if prize fighting and representations thereof are to be thus censored why not football . . . ? Those [cities and states] that have taken action [to ban the film] may well hesitate lest they open the door too wide to the spirit of censorship.'' The point was well taken. Why, indeed, was there no talk of censorship of printed material about the fight before the result was known? As long as many whites believed that Jeffries would win, the fight was seen as an acceptable contest between the races. Now, with Jeffries bruised and defeated, the same white writers were saying that it was wrong to see any racial significance in the result. Why, too, would the Johnson-Jeffries fight film be banned when other prizefight films had not been outlawed? The fear of racial violence, which many proponents of prohibition espoused, was unfounded. The film was shown in Detroit, Hoboken, Jersey City, St. Louis, Kansas City, New York, and other places without incident. The hypocrisy of the issue was not overlooked. Mayor Brand Whitlock of Toledo commented that after months of building up the fight "as if it were of the last importance of humanity . . . now . . . we experience a recrudescence of Anglo-Saxon morality and suddenly wake up to the fact that all of this is brutal and likely to corrupt somebody.''[12]

It was this selected censorship that many blacks found particularly obnoxious. While newspapers editorially deplored the showing of the Johnson-Jeffries film, they ran advertisements for Thomas Dixon's *Clansman*, a play based on the famous novel that depicted a black man raping a white woman and glorified the Ku Klux Klan as the savior of civilization. If the first fueled racial animosities, why did not the second? This was the question that black journalists asked. "Never," wrote Julius F. Taylor, editor of the *Chicago Broad Ax*, "have [white journalists] cried out against such blood thirsty anarchists as Benjamin R. Tillman, James K. Vardaman, Rev. Thomas Dixon, Jr., and their broad rank of enemies to society, law, and order." Black writers criticized a society that protected white race baiters and lynchers but swelled with moral outrage at the prospect of the Johnson-Jeffries film.[13]

Although no federal law prohibiting the fight film was passed in 1910, the film was barred from most communities. For reformers, this indicated that all was not lost for civilization; people could still express outrage at uncivilized and disorderly behavior. But the riots and the film were only the sideshows. The main attraction was still Johnson himself. The *real* disorder of the riots and the *potential* disorder of the film were caused by Johnson, and to shut him out of public sight was impossible. Victory made Johnson bolder, quicker to challenge racial customs. Neither the voices of reformers nor Booker

T. Washington himself could persuade Johnson to soften his assault on white society.

In Chicago, as in every other city with a racially mixed population, opinion concerning Johnson was widely divergent. For whites, he was that "Smoke Nuisance." Usually they referred to him as "Little Arthur"—a diminutive as disparaging as the appellation "boy." Johnson was viewed as an overbearing, conceited, uppity black. Because of him, wrote an editor for the *Chicago Tribune*, "the white portions of the free republic are about to lose all interest in pugilism" and to turn instead to "intellectual enjoyments."[14]

But in Chicago's black community Johnson was a hero. There he was the black man's answer to Robin Hood, Paul Bunyan, and Santa Claus. Even before the fight the *Chicago Defender*, the city's leading black newspaper, had consciously tried to publicize Johnson as an authentic black hero. The paper printed stories about his love of his mother and his diligence in teaching a Sunday school class for black children; it recounted his heroic rescue of several victims of an automobile accident; it advertised an 18-inch statue "for the home of every negro" of "the first negro to be admitted the best man in the world." He was portrayed as a larger-than-life race savior who defeated white oppressors and gave freely to his black brothers. Even after his victory over Jeffries led to riots, his image was not tarnished. A correspondent named William Pickens wrote that it was better for Johnson to win and a few blacks be killed in body than for Johnson to lose and all blacks be killed in spirit. Pickens concluded his assessment of the impact of the match: "It is better for us to succeed, though some die, than for us to fail, though all live." It was as if the rioting, suffering, and death allowed all blacks to share more fully in Johnson's triumph. More completely than whites realized, the fight represented an authentic racial victory.[15]

When it was learned that Johnson had boarded the Overland Limited bound for Chicago, blacks in that city prepared a hero's welcome. Bob Mott, chairman of the reception committee, arranged for the Eighth Regiment Band to greet Johnson at the railway depot and organized a parade to accompany the champion to his mother's home at 3344 Wabash Avenue. On July 7 Mott's expectations materialized. The reception was friendly and loud. In the black belt and along Michigan Avenue automobile horns blared. It was a high time, one of genuine and open joy. The celebrations continued throughout the afternoon and into the evening, when all the speeches were made. Most of the talk centered on Johnson's great accomplishment, but

Jack Johnson in 1907, the year before he won the title. *(Gary Phillips Collection)*

In training at the Seal Rock House in San Francisco before his 1910 fight with Jim Jeffries. *(Gary Phillips Collection)*

Training at Ric's Resort in Reno for Jeffries fight, 1910. On the left of Johnson is his trainer, Doc Furey, and on his right is Kid Cotton, a sparring partner. *(Gary Phillips Collection)*

Johnson tests Jeffries's strength in their July 4, 1910, fight. *(Gary Phillips Collection)*

On a vaudeville tour in 1910. On Johnson's right is Etta Duryea. *(National Archives)*

Belle Schreiber in Atlantic City, where she went to meet Johnson in 1910. *(National Archives)*

Johnson marries Lucille Cameron in 1913. *(National Archives)*

Johnson at the wheel of one of his favorite racers. Doc Furey is with him. 1910. *(Library of Congress)*

Johnson after his release from prison, 1921. *(Library of Congress)*

Still active in his forties, ca. 1935. *(Library of Congress)*

the most important speech was delivered by the champion himself. Realizing that his victory had forged a temporary racial unity, he hoped that the improvement would not be fleeting. "I only hope the colored people of the world will not be like the French. History tells us that when Napoleon was winning all his victories the French were with him, but when he lost, the people turned against him. When Jack Johnson meets defeat, I want the colored people to like and love me the same as when I was the champion."[16]

In comparing himself to Napoleon, Johnson was dead serious. He was conscious that he symbolized success for millions of blacks, and that his advances were all the more important because he confronted rather than humored white authorities. He was hated by whites, arrested on various minor charges, and criticized by the press—but in one day in Nevada he had earned several hundred thousand dollars. And through all the abuse he received, some hidden reservoir of inner strength enabled him to flash his golden smile. This was success on his own terms. Knowing that his every movement was followed closely by his black admirers, Johnson wanted to be the center of attention even when he was in trouble. Arrested in Chicago for speeding in his scarlet racing car, he told the policeman, "Stand back, Mr. White Offisah, and let dem colored peoples hab a look at me."[17]

Though Johnson recognized his status in the black community, he did not attempt to alter his behavior to conform to accepted bourgeois standards. He did just as *he* pleased. After a few hectic days and sleepless nights in Chicago, Johnson left with Etta and several business associates for New York. Eager to cash in on his name while it was still on the front pages, he planned to return to the vaudeville stage. Judging from his reception in New York, Johnson had correctly gauged his popularity. Nat Fleischer, who traveled with the champion, remembered that holiday atmosphere: "Thousands of Negroes crowded the streets, parading, shouting, shooting off fireworks, and carrying on in hilarious fashion." Grand Central Station was packed with well-wishers, and the mob followed Johnson to the Baron Wilkes Hotel on Herald Square, where the party mood continued unabated for another night.[18]

For all of Johnson's talk of a vaudeville tour, nothing developed. White promoters said that Johnson was for the moment too controversial. Fearful that boycotts or even race riots might follow him, vaudeville managers told the champion to allow time for public emotion to cool. Take a vacation, they told him. In a month or two they might arrange a tour, but not in July or early August, when late summer heat shortened tempers.

Johnson found it hard to withdraw from the public eye even for a few weeks. He was unable or unwilling to harness his energy. He was always in a rush—to go places, to see people, to do things—though the where, who, and what were seldom identified. He gave reporters the impression of being a man possessed. He seemed driven by forces he could not control. Occasionally this restlessness got him into trouble. He was arrested for reckless driving at 42d Street and Seventh Avenue. A few days later he was again arrested, this time for obstructing traffic; in a hurry to get from his car to an "important meeting" he had parked 7 feet from the curb and totally blocked an intersection. These minor episodes, in themselves unimportant, contributed to the larger picture of a man losing his sense of proportion. At a time when he was becoming identified as a traveling representative of his race, he became increasingly egocentric. He drove fast, parked carelessly, and did not concern himself with the inconvenience or harm he might cause others. He was like a watch spring that was being wound tighter and tighter, forming a circle that was moving ever inward.[19]

Johnson's personal relationships were a source of turmoil. From San Francisco to New York he was faced with legal suits, ranging from breach of contract to extortion. These were problems Johnson could handle. Boxing was an extraordinarily litigious business, and most suits were never heard by a judge. More serious than his legal difficulties were his spats with Etta. The pace of Johnson's life strained an already troubled love affair. Etta, who was used to a more courtly world, had trouble adjusting to the role she played in Johnson's. She was the champion's lover, but because she was white she was forced to stay well in the background. Johnson was not particularly sensitive to her position. While staying in New York in mid-July, he invited Nat Fleischer to his room for an interview. Unaware of the invitation Etta, who was preparing for a party, emerged from the dressing room nude. She accused Johnson of bringing a white man into the room to embarrass her, and in a fit of pique she hit the champion in the back with a chair. Johnson left with Fleischer, and the argument ended, but the episode was indicative of a more general pattern of behavior. Johnson seemed not to care about Etta's feelings. To him she was a possession, useful and gratifying when needed, ignored when not. Gunboat Smith, who knew both Johnson and Etta, said "he treated her like a dog." Ironically, Johnson's attitude toward Etta was similar to that of a plantation owner toward a mulatto mistress. Perhaps this turnaround was what Johnson desired, either consciously or unconsciously.[20]

After spending a few weeks with Etta in New York, the champion was ready for a change in both women and location. If he had to take a vacation, he decided to do it right. In early August he headed for the sun and sand of Atlantic City. He sent word to Belle Schreiber, who was then working as a prostitute in Pittsburgh, to meet him there. Belle readily accepted Johnson's offer. Since starting to work at Miss Painter's establishment on Caldwell Street, a high-class house in a rundown area of Pittsburgh, Belle had not had a single vacation, and she had not seen Johnson since early March. But they had exchanged several letters and were on good terms. In fact, Belle was one of the first people Johnson wired after the Jeffries fight, which so pleased her that instead of working at her trade she spent the night drinking. Upon receiving Johnson's invitation, she made a flimsy excuse about a sick relation and rushed to Atlantic City.[21]

Belle had learned about Johnson's troubles with Etta and expected to have the champion to herself. Johnson had other plans, and as usual things went his way. Around him he gathered a bevy of prostitutes from various Eastern cities. With a regal air, the champion demanded command performances. Several women stayed with him at Allen's Hotel, "a negro joint" close to the Boardwalk, and others were sent for when wanted. Charles Horner, a friend and former sparring partner then living in Atlantic City, was employed to bring the women to Johnson. In jinriksha fashion, Horner would pull the women along the Boardwalk, entertaining them, and then would deliver them to Johnson. This system, satisfactory enough for the champion, was not particularly favored by Belle, who did not even rate a room in the same hotel as Johnson. But still she stayed, content to try to impress Horner or anyone else willing to listen with tales of her life with Johnson.[22]

As the impact of—or the furor over—Johnson's victory declined, the champion enjoyed a week in the sun. Atlantic City, like Coney Island, was a spot where traditional rules were discarded and manners became more casual. Men and women could sit for hours in a café or dally along the beach. Here Johnson felt at ease. With Sig Hart, his manager, and Barney Furey, his close friend, he drank tea laced with whisky at Fitzgerald's Café, played cards, and told stories. But after a few days Johnson became restless. He was anxious to start his vaudeville tour, eager to move on to other sights in other cities.[23]

By mid-August theatrical bookers believed enough time had passed for Johnson to be safely exhibited on the stage. For his engagements there was no need to rehearse old routines or practice new material; talent was not needed or even desired. Like the large-chested females on the end of the chorus line, Johnson was on stage only to be seen. His was the role of the freak, the curiosity, the man who was different from the rest. Although he was allowed to play a few selections on the bull fiddle, his dance numbers and other displays of talent were removed from his act. What the agents wanted—and what Johnson agreed to give—was a smiling, happy-go-lucky black champion who would strut his hour upon the stage and appear more comical than threatening. So well did Johnson perform his task that reporters speculated that he was not a fighter by nature: "He's too good natured . . . he'd rather grin than frown." That, of course, was precisely the stereotype that bookers wished to cultivate.[24]

Throughout the remainder of 1910 Johnson toured the northern part of the Midwest and East and a few Canadian cities. He traveled with several burlesque shows—"Wine, Women and Song," "The Rollickers," "Follies of the Day," and "Yankeedoodle Girls." He was used where the bookers believed he would draw the best crowds. And in most cities he was a great success, smiling broadly and telling amusing stories to all-white audiences. On stage the violence, frustration, and anxiety that were Johnson's usual companions were never displayed.

Away from the footlights it was a different story. Theater managers who had to deal with Johnson found nothing amusing in his manner. To them he was a loud, conceited, overbearing black man who did not know his place. Charles Bagg, manager of the Lafayette Theater in Buffalo, where Johnson played in late August, said the champion had to be puffed up constantly with encouragement and praise: "It was necessary to pet him and swell him up with his own importance before he would go on." Otherwise he would sulk and threaten not to perform. Worse still, the managers were disgusted by his advances toward white women. Regarding Etta and Belle, who followed Johnson about, the managers were powerless, but they tried to police their own ranks. R. E. Patton, who managed "The Jolly Girls" when the champion traveled with them, told investigators that Johnson would not leave his girls alone and that on several occasions he had had to dismiss girls for having sexual relations with the boxer. Reportedly a manager in Indianapolis threatened to kill Johnson for taking a white girl for a ride in his automobile. These managers and others believed that the fighter's "disgusting manner" toward white women outweighed his value as a star attraction.[25]

Johnson's state of mind was as agitated as the managers'. For all his success, he was not a happy man. His moods fluctuated violently. One day he might be pleasant and generous, the next sullen and violent. Early in September while performing in Toronto, Johnson gave Belle a $600 sealskin coat. A few weeks later the two were quarreling almost continuously. The spats climaxed in Boston during a dispute over a dog, when Johnson slapped Belle violently in the face, then tore off her corset and her underwear in the presence of Julia Allen, Belle's maid. After this scene, Belle returned to Pittsburgh and resumed her professional duties.[26]

Nor were Johnson's relations with Etta any more tranquil. Throughout the early part of the tour Etta stayed in the same hotel as Johnson, the two registering as man and wife, while Belle was forced to stay at a different hotel, waiting for a man who might or might not appear. Etta showed little appreciation for her favored position. Mrs. Rice, the landlady at the Munroe Hotel in Buffalo, remembered that she drank champagne day and night, "grieving considerably" about being married to a black man who was having affairs with other women. The two quarreled often. One spat was caused by one of Johnson's other lovers, who accused Etta of being "intimate with other men." Evidently the list of Etta's alleged paramours was extensive, because she spent an entire day sending and receiving telegrams to prove her innocence. Mrs. Rice estimated that she received replies from fifty men.[27]

After Belle returned to Pittsburgh, relations between Johnson and Etta became, if not better, at least less difficult. In part this was because the champion had less free time. While still appearing on stage every night, he began preparing for another match. Johnson, still intrigued by automobiles and speed, in early October challenged Barney Oldfield to a race. Oldfield, the fastest driver of the day, accepted the challenge, much to the dismay of members of the American Automobile Association, who said that if Oldfield went through with the race they would bar him from their organization.[28]

Through a wet October Johnson practiced for the race. During the day he drove around the track at Sheepshead Bay on Coney Island, then raced back to New York City, where he fulfilled his vaudeville commitments. Several times the race was delayed because of rain, but even in the mud Johnson continued his obsession with speed. Finally the weather cleared and the race was held. Oldfield drove a 60-horsepower Knox car, Johnson a bright red, 90-horsepower Thompson Flyer. As in Johnson's boxing matches with whites, the racial implications of the event were prominent in the minds of many of the 5,000 spectators. Both drove products of white technology—one with reckless abandon, the other with skilled craftsmanship. The winner would be the man who could win two of three scheduled 5-mile heats. Oldfield won easily. In the first race he outmaneuvered Johnson on the turns and won by a half mile in the time of 4:44. In the second race Oldfield slowed down, finishing at 5:14 but still winning effortlessly. Like the Johnson-Jeffries fight, this contest was totally one-sided. Johnson, as countless speeding tickets proved, was a fast driver, but he was not a racer.[29]

The race had cut through the boredom of the tour. Afterward the monotonous and physically exhausting routine resumed. A night in Schenectady, a week in New York City, two nights in Atlantic City, a night each in Chester, New Haven, New Britain, and Lawrence, two days in Hayville, a night in Salem and one in Lowell, a few days in Portland, a night in Rumsford Falls, and one each in Bangor and Lewiston, a day in Boston, then back to New York. Johnson's life moved in a circle; he was always on the go, but he never got anywhere. Trapped in the world he had created, Johnson soon showed the strain. Professionally he was difficult. Because he did not use booking agents, there were constant changes and conflicts in his schedule, and his total independence made him "a hard man to handle." But his life-style was as hard on himself as on others. In Portland, Maine, depressed by the cold weather and snow, he refused to go on stage. He said he was ill, and Dr. Charles L. Cragin diagnosed his condition as "aggravated nerve exhaustion." He told Johnson to rest, and the champion said he would. But the next night he performed in Rumsford Falls. The tour continued.[30]

Wherever Johnson went there was trouble. Conflict seemed to supply the fuel of his existence. In New York City in late November he was arrested for assaulting a white woman. According to Henrietta Cooper, a burlesque dancer, Johnson propositioned her at the Gaiety Theatre, and when she "repulsed" him, he grabbed her wrists and hurt her. Bail was set at $300, whereupon Johnson pulled out a roll of banknotes "as round as a teacup," peeled off a thousand-dollar bill, tossed it on the desk, and said, "I guess that'll hold me for a

while." Although the case never went to court, the publicity it received reinforced Johnson's reputation. Such reports assured whites
that Johnson was a white-woman-chasing, big-spending, loud-
mouthed black.[31]

Consciously or unconsciously, the champion was courting disaster. Some white men believed Johnson should be killed. When Johnson was in Pittsburgh in mid-December, Brooks Buffington, described as a Southerner who hated blacks, told friends that he was
going to "fix" the black fighter. That night, drunk and armed with a
pistol, Buffington went after Johnson. He tried to gain admittance to
the Labor Temple, where Johnson was watching a boxing match, but
was refused. Later he approached a café where Johnson was holding
court, but he was unable to get through the crowd that surrounded
the champion. Discouraged, Buffington went to a bar and vulgarly
criticized Johnson. When Robert Mitchell defended the champion,
Buffington pulled out his gun and killed him. Buffington was arrested. Johnson went to Chicago.[32]

Waiting for Johnson in Chicago was Belle. Although the two
had quarreled and separated earlier in the year, they had kept in
touch. Belle had returned to Lillian Painter's house in Pittsburgh but
had not stayed long. Belle claimed that Estella Painter, Lillian's sister, discovered her relationship with Johnson and dismissed her.
Frank Sutton, a friend of both Belle's and Johnson's, said that Belle
had been "kicked out" of the Painter house because she had robbed a
client. Regardless of the reason, she had to leave Pittsburgh and
needed money. Johnson gladly helped out. He sent Belle $75 and told
her to meet him in Chicago.[33]

This was in October, before the Oldfield race and when Johnson
was on stage at the Gaiety Theatre in New York City. Even though he
was busy, he went to Chicago for a few days to help Belle get settled
in. Johnson later testified that he went on legal business, but he spent
most of his time with Belle. As he told her, she "was a sporting
[woman] and might as well make the money for [herself] as to make it
for others." With this in mind, he found an apartment for her in the
Levee District and furnished it with soft mattresses and other items
appropriate to her trade. Since other apartments at the Ridgewood
were rented to prostitutes, there were no objections when Belle asked
Lillian St. Clair and "Jew" Bertha, two old friends from her days at
the Everleigh Club, to live with her. Soon she was open for business.
She even contracted with Walter Mueller of the Heileman Brewing
Company to furnish beer, though when questioned about this Muel-

ler laughingly stated that he "did not think the books would show any cash transactions." In a few days Johnson returned to New York. He had spent several thousand dollars setting up Belle, but at no time was there any expectation that he would be paid back. He acted as an interested friend, not a banker or a pimp.[34]

Therefore when Johnson returned to Chicago in December Belle was ready to return his favors. That Etta was still with the champion did not worry Belle, or for that matter Johnson either, for he was soon calling on his old friend. Usually in a rush, Johnson seldom went up to Belle's fourth floor apartment; rather he would remain in his car, honking the horn until he attracted her attention. Other residents were upset by the noise, but again this did not concern him. He was the champion and, he believed, above ordinary etiquette.[35]

The week before Christmas was cold in the Midwest, but Johnson kept warm through sheer physical excess. Not only was he keeping two women, but he commuted daily from Chicago to Milwaukee, where he was performing at the Star Theatre. Sometimes he made the three-hour-and-fifteen-minute trip by train, but more often he drove. Most of each day he spent in Chicago; he went to Milwaukee just to perform and left as soon as his act was over. Sometimes he slept for a few hours on the trains, but more often than not he passed the time playing cards and telling stories. He ate only when he was hungry and there was food nearby. As the days passed his nerves frayed.[36]

Though Johnson appeared calm in public, his hectic personal life and frantic pace had their effect. Etta often complained about Belle. Arguments became more frequent and heated. Finally, on a cold, snowy Christmas Sunday, Johnson released his frustration in the only way he knew—violently. He beat Etta so severely about the face and stomach that she required hospitalization. Nurse Edna Walton, who was on duty the day Etta was admitted to Chicago's Washington Park Hospital, later recalled Etta's blackened and swollen face, the result of an "accident" suffered while boarding a streetcar.[37]

Shortly after Johnson beat Etta, he and Belle left for Milwaukee, but he was visibly shaken. On that day they traveled by automobile, with friend and trainer Barney Furey doing the driving. Johnson and Belle sat in the back, the champion complaining that he was cold and ill. Furey stopped in Libertyville, a small suburb of Chicago, and bought Johnson a bottle of brandy, but it did not help. At one point Johnson became sick; Furey stopped the car on a bridge while Johnson vomited and urinated blood. That night he was too upset to perform his usual routine at the Star Theatre. Instead he just talked to the audience, looking ill but otherwise confident.[38]

His looks were deceiving. Emotionally he was not at all sound. Troubled by Belle and Etta, he tried both intimidation and diplomacy to solve his problems. First he sent Roy Jones, another friend who was particularly close to Etta, to the hospital on a peace mission. Johnson, afraid Etta might file charges, hoped Jones could calm the beaten lover. He did. Next Johnson dealt with Belle. In the past he had hit her often enough to emphasize his seriousness, but this time he only relied on example. Accompanying her to Washington Park Hospital, he showed her Etta's injuries. Belle understood. For a time their arguments stopped.[39]

By January 1, 1911, Etta was well enough to leave the hospital. It was the season for resolutions; Etta and Johnson attempted to mend their tattered relationship by setting out on a vacation together. Evidently the surface—if not the deeper—wounds that they had inflicted upon each other healed quickly, for less than three weeks later in Pittsburgh they were married in an unpublicized ceremony. It was Johnson's first marriage and Etta's second, and almost from the start it was a tragic mistake.[40]

8

A Brunette in a Blond Town

THE ONLY WORLD LEFT to conquer was himself. Certainly there were no serious white contenders in sight. The only outstanding heavyweights—Sam Langford, Joe Jeannette, and Sam McVey—were black, and Johnson, like most other champions, drew the color line where the title was concerned. He rightly believed a fight with another black would entail a high risk for little gain. There was more to be made on the burlesque stage, and there was nothing risky about sparring behind the bright stage lights. For the time, he was an actor. When an attractive White Hope emerged from the current depressed crop, Johnson would give up the greasepaint.

Yet even the stage life was fraught with risks and temptations. For Johnson, the constant movement, lack of sleep, and excessive drinking took a physical and mental toll. There were rumors that he suffered a nervous breakdown, and in truth he was in a highly agitated state, subject to swift and dramatic changes in temperament. The bitter cold of the Midwestern winter did not improve his emotional condition. Talking with a reporter in Chicago, he said, "Can't drive my automobiles in this snow. Me for the part of the country where it is warm and where I can drive those wagons of mine a mile a minute." He longed to escape the commitments of the burlesque circuit and to enjoy the money he had earned. The thought of the mild California climate, the sun and the freedom, grew too strong to resist.[1]

He asked Belle to go along, saying that the rumors of his marriage were false. But she knew the truth and declined the invitation. Undaunted, Johnson left with a group of close friends, including his wife, a sparring partner, his brother, and several women. They traveled first class, and they traveled loudly. Pullman porter T. D. Culleny recalled that they drank a great deal, quarreled often, and "caused lots of disturbance." The trip to California set the tone for the rest of the vacation.[2]

The party rented a beach house on the outskirts of San Francisco, but there was little time to enjoy it. There were constant trips to the German Hospital, where Jack's brother Charles was suffering from an eye problem that caused temporary blindness. When Johnson was not at the hospital, there were more brushes with the law. J. T. Moran had Johnson's car attached for a nine-year-old, twenty-five-dollar bill. Angered, Johnson attempted to take his automobile by force, but Officer Bustin threatened to shoot the champion if he did. "All right, white man, I'll be good!" Johnson said. But he was not. Less than a week later he was arrested for racing through Golden Gate Park against J. M. Burg, an automobile demonstrator. The two were clocked at 62 mph.[3]

Such arrests had become common with Johnson, who normally paid his fines and quickly returned to his old ways. However, acting Police Judge A. B. Treadwell was determined that this time Johnson must pay more dearly for his violation. "It is absolutely unsafe," Treadwell said, "for women and children to venture off the sidewalks of this city simply on account of the wild, reckless racing of this defendant." Thereupon Treadwell shocked Johnson by sentencing him to twenty-five days in the county jail. Johnson's lawyers appealed the verdict but were unsuccessful in getting it overturned. By late March 1911 he was in jail under the watchful eye of Sheriff Thomas Finn. And there he stayed for twenty-five days. He was not treated badly; indeed, he was allowed to spend time with his wife, visit his brother, and send out for his meals. But still, it *was* jail, and he did not enjoy the time. It was not the vacation he had planned, and by April 23, when he was released, he was ready to return to work.[4]

Disgusted with the West Coast, Johnson traveled to the Eastern Seaboard. But he continued to be harassed by white authorities, often for minor offenses. In New York City he was arrested for having a Chicago instead of a New York license plate on his automobile. At the time of his arrest he had been slowly cruising down Broadway. Questioned about the violation, he angrily replied, "I goes fast they arrests me, and now it seems like if I go slow they does the same.

White man, what's the trouble now? Next thing somebody'll arrest me for bein' a brunette in a blond town."[5]

Other brushes with the law were not so petty, and Johnson was not so innocent. A sculptor sued Johnson to collect for the work he had done on a bust of the champion. Johnson claimed it was a poor likeness and, besides, he had never agreed to pay for it. The court found in the artist's favor. Even more serious were his relations with white women. While playing with a burlesque company in Philadelphia he had a brief affair with a sixteen-year-old white girl from Camden. Although he tried to pass her off as the sister of his trainer, the halfhearted excuse was unsuccessful. Each such affair brought him closer to his ultimate confrontation with white authority.[6]

That clash was still more than a year away. In the meantime white boxers were battling each other for the right to fight him. Together they formed a motley and uninspiring crew, but in order to separate the wheat from the chaff the New York promoter Tom O'Rourke staged a White Hope Tourney in May 1911 at the old National Sporting Club on West 44th Street. Twenty-three hopefuls entered, but only eleven showed up on fight day. They came in all shapes and sizes—from several behemoths who weighed about 300 pounds to a slender, 165-pound middleweight—and from five states and Canada, but in only one color. For a day they fought each other, inept boxer against inept boxer, with the least inept winning. Finally, late at night, Al Palzer of New York won a four-round decision over Sailor White of New Jersey and was proclaimed the World White Hope Champion. The event that was supposed to uncover the golden kernel turned up only chaff.[7]

Johnson was present at ringside for the circus. At one point a sportswriter asked him, "Learning anything, Jack?" Laughing heartily, he replied, "I'm learning plenty." And he was. He learned that if he was to find a suitable contender, he'd best try another country. With that in mind, a week after the tournament he sailed for England aboard the North German Lloyd liner *Kronprinz Wilhelm*. With Johnson went his wife, his chauffeur, two sparring partners, twenty trunks, two automobiles, and a small safe containing his money and his wife's jewels. He told reporters that he would play the Oxford Music Hall, attend the scheduled coronation of King George, and "take a run" to Monte Carlo. But if Bombardier Wells, the noted English heavyweight, or any other European fighter put up a $30,000 guarantee, he would change his plans.[8]

He took London by storm. When he appeared at the Oxford Music Hall a *Times* editorialist noted that he was not as much of a "flash nigger" as reports from America had indicated. Certainly, the journalist commented, Johnson was a "lover of many-jointed words" and displayed a weak stomach when sparring—two weaknesses that were seen as racially linked—but otherwise he was a "far more pleasant person to meet in a room than any of the white champions of complicated ancestry whom America exports from time to time to these unwilling shores." Johnson's stage debut was greeted with enthusiasm and sportsmanship—a quality English writers viewed as uniquely English—and he was cheered roundly when seen on the streets. Indeed, so great was his popularity that "in the eyes of the world" his visit dwarfed the coronation of King George. He became a social lion, fêted and sought after by royalty. Even ex-King Manuel of Portugal visited Earl's Court, where the champion was training, just to shake hands with him.[9]

Perhaps all the attention and talk of fair play turned Johnson's head. He told reporters that he felt at home in England, that he believed the island was "inhabited by a race of sportsmen." Unfortunately for Johnson, on the issue of race England was surprisingly similar to America. After the Johnson-Jeffries fight, a number of ministers and reformers attempted to have the film of the match prohibited in England. Reverend F. Luke Wiseman of the Birmingham Wesleyan Central Mission said the film had "no redeeming artistic, scenic, educative, or social value. It is wholly brutal, disgusting, and demoralizing." And such high-minded reformers were outraged when it was proposed that Johnson fight a white contender in England.[10]

Interracial matches were nothing new in England. In fact, the first interracial heavyweight championship fight was held in East Grimstead, Sussex, in 1810. In that match, held on a wet December day, Tom Cribb, a white Englishman, knocked out Tom Molineaux, a black American. However, reformers in 1911 were quick to oppose the scheduled fight between Johnson and Bombardier Wells. The leader of the reformers was F. B. Meyer, who only a year before had been working to get "noxious literature" (which included the writings of Karl Marx and Henry George) banned in England. In the announced Johnson-Wells match, Meyer saw sin every bit as great as was to be found in the pages of *Das Kapital*. But he also sensed something else—a chance to breathe new life into the National Free Church Council, a political group that in recent years had suffered crippling setbacks. In the opposition to the Johnson-Wells match, Meyer saw a national issue around which the Free Church movement could unite. Since it was a safe, non-political issue, he expected that all Free Churchers could and would support his crusade. Ideally the battle against the sin of pugilism would revitalize his organization and enhance his own reputation.[11]

At first Meyer and his supporters said that their opposition was *not* a condemnation of the manly art of self-defense. Meyer, indeed, went to great lengths to overcome the effeminate aspects of his character and to prove that he was a "man's man." Instead, he opposed the fight because it would "attract a horde of profligate people," encourage gambling, and "gratify that craving for the sensational and the brutal which is inconsistent with the manhood that makes a great nation." There was no mention of race in Meyer's early statements, only a heartfelt horror of exposing the innocent masses to the corrupting influences of professional boxing.[12]

Within a few days, however, racial issues were incorporated into the Free Church position. Not that they were ever far from the public's mind. Even before Meyer's opening attack, the chairman of the London County Council had remarked that "the sight of a black man pounding a white man is far from attractive, and certainly cannot be considered as a public entertainment. . . . London is not Reno, and in sheer self-respect London cannot tolerate this bout." Other Englishmen's thoughts focused on larger territory than simply London. The Earl of Lonsdale, who headed the National Sporting Club, England's most prestigious boxing establishment, counseled Britons to consider "the special position of trusteeship for coloured subject peoples which the British Empire holds." Rhetorically he asked, "Is a 'scientific' sport . . . worth the least possible exacerbation of the relations between black and white?" Certainly not. But, as Meyer soon added, to allow the fight to take place would promote racial misunderstanding and arouse "the instinctive passion of the negro race."[13]

For many Englishmen, then, the real question was not professionalism or brutality or even morality—it was racial order. And on that lofty ground, the Free Church Council demanded that the fight be canceled. As the day of the big event approached, Meyer won influential converts for his crusade. Bishops, lords, members of Parliament, headmasters, and ministers of almost every denomination wrote letters to the *Times* in support of Meyer. Even Dr. Edward S. Talbot, Bishop of Winchester and a leader of the High Church, expressed concern about the racial implications of the fight: "There is no problem more anxious for the present and the future than that of colour; none about which there are more sinister features; none on which instinct, passion, and prejudice are more inflamed; none, therefore, on which it is more imperative that nothing should be done to inflame or excite."[14]

Eventually the entire affair was dropped on the desk of Home Secretary Winston Churchill. It was one instance in which Churchill did not want the limelight. At first he tried to avoid the controversy, retreating to Scotland and refusing to return to London to receive Meyer's deputations. But as antifight pressure mounted, Churchill, much against his natural inclination, acquiesced. On September 25 he announced that the proposed fight was illegal. Though the legality of boxing was never again questioned after 1911, Churchill's ruling effectively denied Johnson the right to engage in his profession in England.[15]

Johnson soon left England, but not before commenting on the British tradition of fair play. Called into court, he defended himself with great skill. "Mr. Johnson was never so brilliant as in his retreat from London," wrote an editorialist for the *New York Times*. "He stood alone against the Archbishop of Canterbury and the Home Secretary, and in open court dared to measure wits with the Solicitor General." Johnson was never more calm or articulate than when fighting or debating a white before other whites. It brought out the best within him, and he always welcomed the opportunity to engage in such battles. His exposure of British racism and hypocrisy at Bow Street was as eloquent and as convincing as his defeat of Jeffries in Reno. In both Johnson took inordinate satisfaction.[16]

With the cancellation of the match Johnson's normal restlessness returned. As long as there was a fight in prospect, he trained in England and appeared nightly on the stage. Without the prospect of a match he became directionless, traveling back and forth from London to Paris and often missing vaudeville engagements. Sometimes, instead of fulfilling his commitments in London, he stayed in Paris and gave exhibitions against the great French boxer Georges Carpentier. Soon the British were disgusted with his antics. Where before they commented on Johnson's grace and pleasant nature, now they called him flashy and pompous. According to one report, the British were anxious to see him leave England. As long as a black boxer was modest and obsequious the English sporting crowd treated him well, giving him "almost as much consideration as his white opponent." But they had no patience for blacks like Jack Johnson who had a habit of not conforming to their prized stereotypes.[17]

Thus the trip that had begun so well ended badly, with Johnson and England discovering that they did not much like each other. English ministers and authorities prevented Johnson from boxing, and he, as if in the form of compensation, left a list of unpaid bills, broken furniture, and cracked crockery. Aboard the Lloyd liner *Kronprinzessin Cecille* he returned to America. Arriving in New York City a few days before Christmas, he announced that he was ready once again to fight in the States. That is, if a challenger were prepared to put up a $30,000 advance.[18]

Challengers. There were by 1912 a few, though none were in Johnson's class. Because most white heavyweights lacked superior ability, they were forced to rely on some gimmick to attract attention. Some were over 6 feet 2, which made them, as far as newspapermen, managers, and promoters were concerned, as good as giants. There was Jess Willard, the Pottawatomie Giant; Jim Coffey, the Irish Giant; Carl Morris, the Sapulpa Giant; and Fred Fulton, the Giant of the North. Others had reputations won for bravery in foreign wars. James J. Johnston, a wily manager who occasionally fractured the truth, advertised his South African white hope, George "Boer" Rodel, as a hero of the Boer War, a stalwart of the siege of Ladysmith. That the siege occurred in 1899, when Rodel was only twelve, did not seem to have achieved as wide a circulation. Still others were just big, wholesome farm boys, products of America's great and fertile prairies. One such lad, Luther McCarty, was from Driftwood Creek, Wild Horse Canyon, Hitchcock County, Nebraska. McCarty, according to press releases, had the stuff to be a real American hero: "He is willing to learn and to take a few hard wallops while the learning is in process. His habits are almost those of an ascetic and he never has smoked or used tobacco or liquor." There was even a rich white hope. Around Newport, Rhode Island, it was said that if Colonel William Barbour, a wealthy New York thread merchant, would permit his son, W. Warren Barbour, to fight Johnson the title would be returned to the Caucasian race. But the colonel never consented.[19]

Of the group, perhaps Carl Morris received the gaudiest buildup. According to the Fourth Estate, in July 1910 Morris was a locomotive engineer on the Frisco Line. On July 4 he was in Sapulpa, Oklahoma, when he heard the result of the Johnson-Jeffries fight. Turning to the station telegrapher he said, "Then I'll quit this job right here. I'm going to be a fighter and whip the Negro sure." At 6 feet 4 and 240 pounds, he was an awesome sight. Describing Morris's hands, a journalist for the *New York Sun* wrote, "It is easy to imagine one of them the head of some giant's club. . . . It would be more pleasant to be kicked in the face by a cleated football boot than to be struck by that hand.'' In his first seven fights—all staged in Oklahoma—he won by knockouts. Not one opponent survived the fourth round. In early 1911 Morris invaded New York, and sportswriters extolled his physical and moral virtues. He had a ''mighty'' body, a ''pleasant'' face, and ''wise modesty.'' In September he was matched against Fireman Jim Flynn, an experienced heavyweight. The fight proved that Morris's modesty was indeed earned, for he was ''severely mangled'' by Flynn. Morris bled so freely that referee Charlie White had to change shirts halfway through the fight.[20]

There was just no way of making real white hopes in a year or two. Only a seasoned fighter was qualified for a match with the champion, but Johnson had already defeated most of them. In early 1912 perhaps the most logical contender was Flynn, a former firefighter in Pueblo who was born Andrew Chiariglione in Hoboken, New Jersey. Though short for a heavyweight, with a pudgy roundness about his face and midsection, Flynn was a tough, mean boxer who had a reputation for dirty fighting. In 1911 he had defeated white hopes Al Kaufman and Carl Morris, and he had fought many of the best fighters of the early twentieth century. Certainly he was not in the class of a Johnson or a Langford—both of whom had in fact knocked him out—but he was an able white heavyweight, and in 1912 that in itself was noteworthy.[21]

More important to Johnson, Flynn's backers did not disappear when the subject of money entered the conversation. Johnson wanted a $30,000 guarantee. Jack Curley, a promoter who also managed Flynn, offered Johnson what he wanted. The champion was satisfied. He allowed the location of the bout to be decided by Curley, which, since boxing was still illegal in almost every state, was a major detail. Such places as New York City; South Porcupine, Ontario; Wendover and Jawbridge, Nevada; Albuquerque, Santa Fe; Las Vegas, New Mexico; and Juarez, Mexico, were considered as possible sites. But when Charles O'Malley offered Curley $100,000 on behalf of Las Vegas, the decision was made. Johnson and Flynn would fight on July 4, 1912, in the heretofore peaceful New Mexico town.[22]

One of the reasons Las Vegas was chosen was that New Mexico, which had just recently been admitted as a state, had no laws against prizefighting, but as far as reformers were concerned that was an oversight that could be corrected. No sooner was the site announced than a raft of New Mexico reformers raised a hue and cry. They were led by their first state governor, William C. McDonald. The governor admitted that he was not generally opposed to properly conducted bouts, but, he added, "If I can stop it I will not permit a contest between a white man and a negro." In this McDonald found strong, if diverse, support. Methodist and Episcopalian groups roundly criticized the scheduled bout as "detrimental" to the best interests of Las Vegas and "a disgrace to the entire state." They petitioned the New Mexico Senate and House to declare such legal pastimes illegal. Such sinful activities, they believed, should be prohibited. Even the Indians at the Laguna Pueblo in Valencia County agreed that the fight would be most undesirable.[23]

In the state capital the petitions were greeted by other reformers. In early April State Senator A. J. Evans from Portales introduced a bill to outlaw prizefighting and to provide a penalty of from two to five years in prison for anyone engaged in such contests. The bill was quickly referred to the Committee on Judiciary and just as rapidly forgotten. The capital was not in a reforming mood, at least regarding public amusements. Soon even Governor McDonald had to concede defeat. After visiting Las Vegas on June 21 and talking with the promoters, he announced that as long as there was no gambling the fight could be held.[24]

While controversy raged in New Mexico, Johnson confined his own controversial behavior to the Midwest. Most of his unconventional activities were, for him, fairly normal. During a short burlesque tour he traveled with a white showgirl from Brooklyn, much to the dismay of the theater managers. And in Pittsburgh he was involved in an automobile accident. Rumors quickly spread that he was dead, or at least seriously injured. Actually, he only wrenched his back. Surprisingly, the accident was not even his fault; his car was hit in the rear by a truck belonging to a wholesale liquor firm. The crash did, however, end Johnson's burlesque tour.[25]

More serious was the champion's run-in with federal authorities. While Johnson was in England he purchased a diamond necklace worth $6,000 for his wife, but when he returned to the United States he failed to report it, hoping to escape the import duties. When Johnson's "oversight" was reported to the Treasury Department by several people close to the champion, federal authorities went into action. In order to avoid prosecution Johnson would have to pay a penalty of $9,600. Since the government appropriated the necklace, Johnson hoped that he could avoid the large penalty. It was, he said, just a "little oversight." Federal officials took a different view. On June 21, 1912, they indicted the champion and his wife for smuggling. They decided, however, to allow Johnson to fight Flynn before trying the case.[26]

By late May Johnson believed that New Mexico would be safer than Chicago. So with his wife and a group of friends he left for Las Vegas. He set up camp at the Forsythe Ranch, 6 miles northeast of the city. It was a quiet, peaceful, bucolic setting—entirely too quiet for Johnson. He soon moved his camp into Las Vegas proper. He told a local reporter, "No lonesome ranch life for me. . . . I'll train right here in the town where I can see people and where they can see me." At the Francisco Baca y Sandoval house he trained before large crowds, putting on a good show. For relaxation he drove about the dusty countryside and lounged in the pleasant small-town restaurants. His life with Etta was as quiet as it had been since they first met.[27]

The atmosphere was not so peaceful in Flynn's camp. At the age of thirty-three and after almost twelve years of professional fighting, Flynn had good reason to expect that this would be his only chance to win a championship. But he was also experienced enough to know that he could not defeat Johnson in a fair fight. He decided, therefore, to train for a foul one. By inclination a brutal man, in his preparation for his fight with Johnson he was more vicious than usual. He hired inexperienced local fighters as sparring partners and cruelly practiced his dirty tactics on them. It became so bad that his trainer, Tommy Ryan, quit and left camp. Ryan, a former middleweight champion and widely respected as a judge of fighters, told reporters that he was disgusted with Flynn. "He is hog fat and has no chance whatever with Johnson." Ryan said that Flynn fully planned to foul Johnson, and as a result the trainer predicted that Flynn would lose the fight on a foul.[28]

In New Mexico interest in the fight was keen. The Las Vegas police made plans to expel "all hoboes and persons with shady characters," and city officials watched over the construction of a 17,000-seat arena. Beyond the borders of the state, however, few boxing fans cared about the fight. Unlike Johnson's fight with Jeffries, this one stirred no widespread interest. Sportswriters correctly predicted that it was a mismatch and said that it was useless for whites to place any hope in Flynn. Assessing the prospects for the bout, a *New York Times* writer commented, "Those who take any interest in the affair may be classed as suspicious ones, who are wondering if everything is on the level. The rank and file of the sporting public refuse absolutely to take any notice of the long noticed and much advertised event."[29]

Of course, the *New York Times* only reflected white opinion. Throughout the black "sporting public" there was considerable interest in the bout. If the major newspapers largely ignored the contest, publications like the *Chicago Defender* printed long stories about the doings in New Mexico. Black writers looked forward to an easy Johnson victory, which they believed would be an advancement for their race. Once again Johnson would show that blacks were not inferior, that in the test of the fittest they would not be found wanting. In one report that waxed eloquent on this theme, a feature writer for the *Chicago Defender* called Flynn "the pugilistic *Titanic* of the Caucasian race." The phrase was loaded with meaning. Only two months before the *Titanic* had sunk, sending 1,522 people to their watery graves in the cold North Atlantic. The *Titanic*, the "practically unsinkable" ship, symbolized the height of Anglo-Saxon technological culture, and when it left on its maiden voyage it carried only whites. Its sinking, like Johnson's defeat of Jeffries, was a blow to the myth of Anglo-Saxon superiority. The two episodes, both fondly remembered in Afro-American culture, were joined together in a song written by the black blues singer Leadbelly:

> It was midnight on the sea,
> The band was playin' "Nearer, My God, to Thee."
> Cryin', "Fare thee, *Titanic*, fare thee well!"
>
> . . .
>
> Jack Johnson wanted to get on boa'd;
> Captain Smith hollered, "I ain' haulin' no coal."
> Cryin', "Fare thee, *Titanic*, fare thee well!"
>
> . . .
>
> Black man oughta shout for joy,
> Never lost a girl or either a boy.
> Cryin', "Fare thee, *Titanic*, fare thee well."*

Typically, the story of Jack Johnson and the *Titanic* ended with the champion celebrating, dancing the Eagle Rock on the end of the pier.[30]

Black newspapers were particularly interested in who would referee the bout. Johnson was similarly concerned, for an actively racist referee could present serious problems for the champion. Johnson vetoed a half-dozen referees who were "known as Negro haters." Indeed, one had declared that "the Negro has no business at the head

---

*DE TITANIC. Words and Music by Huddie Ledbetter. Collected and Adapted by John A. Lomax and Alan Lomax. TRO— © Copyright 1936 and renewed 1964 Folkways Music Publishers, Inc., New York, N.Y. Used by Permission.

of anything." Another man who was eliminated was Mark Levy, director of the New Mexico Athletic Club and choice of the *Albuquerque Morning Journal*. The elimination of Levy led to unanticipated problems. Upset by the selection of a Chicago journalist, the *Morning Journal*, which had previously supported the fight and praised Flynn's chances against Johnson, now began to criticize the match openly. In a fight already marred by promotional difficulties, this blow was crippling.[31]

By the day of the fight even the promoters expected that the bout would be a financial failure. They were right. Only between 3,000 and 5,000 people attended, and even they did not seem very interested. They paid about $35,000, of which Johnson was guaranteed $31,000. Promoter Curley lost at least $15,000 but the other losses were not disclosed. The magic of Reno was not in Las Vegas. The promoters' only hope was for a good fight, one that would allow them to recoup their losses with revenues from the film rights.[32]

Flynn seemed determined enough. He told reporters that he would rather die than lose, and in event that he did lose, he asked Curley to shoot him. No spectator could ask for a greater commitment than that. Johnson also expressed his readiness to fight, if not to die. When the two met in the center of the ring at approximately 2:45 in the afternoon, the cameras were already recording the action.[33]

The fight was hardly worth the film. It started badly when Johnson refused to shake Flynn's hand and immediately got worse. Johnson was heavier than usual; he weighed close to 230 pounds. But that did not matter. From the first round it was clear that Flynn was sadly outclassed. In the early rounds Johnson landed cutting blows whenever he chose. Flynn, bleeding from gashes above both eyes, was particularly bothered by a cut inside his mouth, which forced him to swallow his own blood. When the challenger tried to force the action, Johnson pulled him in close and punished him with uppercuts. The only punches Flynn landed were to Johnson's stomach, and he was successful there only because the champion "shoved out his stomach and invited Flynn to blaze away." As if this were not humiliation enough, Johnson talked to ringsiders while Flynn was ineffectually hitting his midsection. Indeed, often Johnson seemed more intent on his conversation with his wife and handlers than on the business in the ring.[34]

By the start of round six Flynn's face was badly bruised and cut. Blood ran down his chest and stained his trunks. But Johnson, except for a small cut in his mouth, was unmarked. This situation must have struck Flynn as inequitable, for in that round he started using foul tactics. Specifically, he attempted to maneuver his head under Johnson's chin and then leap forward and upward, butting the champion's chin and neck. In theory it was not a bad tactic—that is, if one was tolerant enough to overlook fouling, which, unfortunately for Flynn, referee Ed Smith was not. "Stop that butting," Smith yelled. "Stop it, or I will disqualify you." In an attempt at self-justification Flynn answered, "The nigger's holding me. He's holding me all the time. He's holding me like this." Whereupon he attempted to hold Smith as Johnson was allegedly holding him. But Smith seemed particularly insensitive to that line of reasoning.

Nor did Johnson admire Flynn's innovations. In a flash of anger he lashed out with hard lefts and rights. But the anger quickly passed, and Johnson settled back into his slow but effective pattern. After all, Flynn's butts were dangerous only in theory. Try as he might, he was unable to land any. And he did try. As one *New York Times* reporter described the action, "Flynn's feet were both off the floor time and again with the energy he put into his bounces. Sometimes he seemed to leap two feet into the air in frantic plunges at the elusive jaw above him." In all, it was sad, almost as if the great El Córdobas were fighting an ambitious billygoat.

In the seventh and the eighth rounds Flynn continued to try to butt, and Smith kept telling him to stop. "One more time and I'll disqualify you," Smith would warn, whereupon Flynn would try again, and once more Smith would repeat, "One more time and I *will* disqualify you." Even with the added grammatical emphasis he was unable to make Flynn fight fairly. Finally in round nine a new twist was added to the farce. Flynn's "blond beam" lightly grazed Johnson's jaw. Smith did not seem sure what to do. However, Captain Fred Fornoff, who was representing Governor McDonald at the fight, had no such doubts. With a .44 six-gun strapped to his leg, he climbed into the ring and stopped the bout. The fight, he said, had become "a slaughter and a merely brutal exhibition." This said, he retired from the ring and Smith proclaimed Johnson the victor.

After it was over, newspaper writers argued over the finer points. Did Fornoff have the authority to stop it? Had he bet money that the fight would end before the tenth round? Had the fight been a mistake in the first place? There was a fair amount of talk of the Fourth being debased. "Hunger for gate money and the money of the weak-minded who have the betting habit was the only reason for the exhibition," wrote an editorialist for the *New York Times*. For money Flynn allowed Johnson to "disfigure his face and knock the breath out of his body." Like an old-maid schoolteacher, the editorialist scolded everyone who showed any interest in the match.[35]

In Washington, D.C., politicians believed that more than a reprimand was in order. There was still the question of the fight film and of the irreparable harm it might inflict upon young viewers. Unlike the Johnson-Jeffries film, the Johnson-Flynn film was of an unusually high quality and promised to be a great success. For antiboxing and anti-Johnson men in Congress, the only hope seemed to be a federal law to prohibit the interstate transportation of fight films. In fact, just such a law had been introduced into Congress in May and June 1912, sponsored by Representative Seaborn A. Roddenberry of Georgia and Senator Furnifold Simmons of North Carolina. Praising the bill, Senator Augustus Bacon of Georgia said that it was the "laudable desire on the part of the best people of the land that [prizefights] shall not be encouraged, and, that our young men and our young women . . . shall not be brutalized by the exhibition of such pictures." On July 1, 1912, Southern congressmen were restless; they wanted the bill passed before Johnson fought Flynn. But the lack of a quorum prevented the enactment of the law.[36]

After Johnson's victory the mood in Congress was even more earnest. Roddenberry, perhaps the most vocal critic of Johnson in Washington, reminded his fellow congressmen on July 19 that the time for debate and legal hair-splitting had passed. The fight, he said, "presented, perhaps, the grossest instance of base fraud and bogus effort at a fair fight between a Caucasian brute and an African biped beast that has ever taken place." Roddenberry's alliterative rhetoric proved effective. The House followed the Senate's lead and passed the law prohibiting the interstate transportation of fight films. In Congress America had found an authentic White Hope, one powerful enough to defeat Johnson. But the ban on fight films was only round one. There were more, many more, rounds left to fight.[37]

9

Trouble with the Mann

BEFORE THE TRAGEDY there were rumors that he was settling down. There was even some hard evidence. There was the house that he now called "home." It was a lovely dwelling on Wabash Avenue, well down on the South Side of Chicago. A big three-story house with all of the sharp angles and haunting gables of Victorian architecture, it had a full front porch and a neat lawn enclosed by a wrought-iron fence. Johnson bought the house in 1910 for his mother, and whenever he was in Chicago he stayed there. On the day he returned to Chicago after the Jeffries fight a crowd of about 10,000 blacks had followed his automobile to the Wabash Avenue house. The Eighth Regiment Band had played "There'll Be a Hot Time in the Old Town Tonight," and the Negro Knights of Pythias in full dress uniform of black and gold had paraded in his honor. But then it had been "his mother's house." By 1912 it was "his home." Not since he was a child in Galveston had he had such a sense of place.[1]

Then, too, there was the Café de Champion. Johnson opened this saloon in the week after the Flynn fight. An extension of his own ego, it conformed to Johnson's idea of class. The Café de Champion was located at 41 West 31st Street, immediately to the south of the Levee district, close to Chicago's vice center but not actually in it. Presumably, a man could bring a respectable date to Johnson's place, for it was a large establishment—five spacious rooms—that provided

138

separate rooms for drinking, dining, and dancing. The decor was ba-
roque. "Having traveled extensively," wrote Johnson, "I had gained
a comprehensive idea of decorative effects. . . . I also had collected
many fine works of art, curios and novelties. These I used in provid-
ing the attractive features for which my cabaret gained considerable
distinction." He claimed that he had hung a "few real Rembrandts"
and several paintings of Biblical scenes on the walls of his café, but
pictures of the place show that most of the art work concerned Johnson himself. There was a picture of Johnson in fighting togs, one of
Johnson and his wife, another of Johnson and his mother. In fur-
nishing, as in the paintings, he asserted that there was nothing
"gaudy nor vulgar." There were, however, silver cuspidors decorated
in gold and walls of red and gold damask.[2]

When the Café de Champion opened on July 11, 1912, white reporters laughed at the cuspidors and the many curios. They ridiculed
the obvious pleasure Johnson took in pointing out "dis and dat."
They belittled his accomplishment. Not so black journalists. The
Chicago Defender justifiably took pride in Johnson's success. It
praised the wine, food, and entertainment, but more than that, the
entrepreneurial spirit of Johnson himself. Here was a black going
into business for himself, showing other blacks that advancement was
possible. It did not matter that his business was a saloon or that the
interior was flashy. It mattered only that he was no longer dependent
upon whites.[3]

In 1912 blacks as successful as Johnson were uncommon. But
with the migration of Southern blacks into Chicago, many black
leaders felt it was important to have visible symbols of success. For
Robert S. Abbott, editor of the influential *Chicago Defender*, Johnson was such a symbol. Although Abbott never openly opposed
Booker T. Washington and was often critical of the elitism of
W. E. B. DuBois, he believed strongly in race pride and race solidarity. Editorials and news stories in the *Defender* portrayed Johnson as
the visible expression of Abbott's ideal. Blind to the insensitive side
of the champion, the *Defender*'s Johnson was a black who gave to
black charities, supported black businesses, and on Christmas played
Santa Claus for black children.[4]

The *Defender*'s Johnson was not necessarily bogus; he did support race pride. Where the *Defender* erred was on the side of omis-
sion. The stories about the new, settled Johnson deviated in the same
direction. Certainly there was the home on Wabash Avenue and the
Café de Champion, and true he was no longer eager for the life of

one-night burlesque stands, but the essential disorderliness of his life was unchanged. There were still no rules to which he admitted, no guidelines that he followed. Laws, customs, procedures, precedents—his supreme ego placed him, in his own mind, above them. His style was his own, and it represented an anarchism unfamiliar in American heroes. His was a style that many people in positions of authority viewed as threatening. One Jack Johnson could be easily handled, but a thousand Jack Johnsons, or ten thousand, in a city like Chicago with a swelling black population—that was a different matter entirely. For whites as well as blacks it was Jack Johnson as symbol, as potential, that was the hope and the problem.

Throughout the late summer, while Johnson spent most of his time at his café, the government collected evidence against him on smuggling charges. The prime government witness was Charles Brown, a former chauffeur of the champion. When Johnson discovered that Brown was telling everything he knew to the grand jury, he became furious. The matter became violent when Brown visited the Café de Champion on a sweltering day in July. Johnson demanded to know what Brown was telling the government, and upon finding out he hit his former driver in the face. Charges were pressed, and Johnson threw together a hasty cover-up that fooled no one.[5]

The assault was not unusual. When confronted with some difficulty he often lashed out with the weapons that had served him so faithfully in the ring, the one world where he had complete control. For him boxing was simple and even pleasurable, because he was the master of every situation. Outside the ring was another matter. When he was legally injured by a former friend who told the truth, he physically hurt that person. When a youth tried to steal a tire from his car, he beat up the boy. When Etta said or did something that particularly displeased him, he hit her also. His was a boxer's world, a physical world that demanded physical responses.[6]

For Etta it was a world of emotional as well as physical suffering. From the start of her relationship with Johnson she was aware of his heroic infidelity. Marriage had certainly not changed him. He had private rooms on the second floor of the Café de Champion, which he used to entertain his private guests. They were, of course, women, mostly white but not always. Some, like Ada Banks and Lucille Cameron, were listed as employees. Ada, a black, was a singer at the café, and Lucille, a white, was one of Johnson's private secretaries. But the jobs did not disguise their true positions, least of all from Etta.

Nor was Johnson's infidelity her only problem. There was also the loneliness, the sense of being an outcast both in Johnson's black world and her own white world. Often she complained about the treatment she received. As she told one of her maids, "I am a white woman and tired of being a social outcast. All my misery comes through marrying a black man. Even the negroes don't respect me. They hate me." This sense of desperate isolation increased when her father died in August. She had been close to him, and after his death she felt as if she had no one left who understood or cared about her. It deepened her ever present tendency toward melancholia.[7]

Increasingly Etta thought of suicide. According to Johnson she had already made two unsuccessful attempts on her life, once after the two quarreled in London and another time when they were traveling in the West. Both times Johnson, who was usually the hero of his own stories, saved his wife's life. On the night of September 11, however, Johnson was not around, and Etta was depressed. Below her, in the main bar of the Café de Champion, people were having fun; the cheerful sound of music and laughter drifted into her room. Perhaps the incongruity of the two worlds, separated by only a flight of stairs, was too much for Etta. In an almost businesslike fashion she made a few telephone calls, said goodby to several friends, and then, after asking that they pray for her, dismissed her two maids. Alone in her bedroom, she held one of Johnson's guns to her right temple and squeezed the trigger.[8]

Below, the laughter and the orchestra drowned out the report of the gun. Only the maids heard the shot. They knew what it signified and went downstairs to tell the bartender, Edward Hollard. Breaking open the locked door, he found the unconscious but still living Etta lying in a pool of blood, a hole above her right eye. She was taken to the Providence Hospital, where she died a few hours later.[9]

Ultimately, suicide is a great mystery, one whose answer can never be known. It is the ideal speculative arena. After Etta's suicide a number of explanations were given. Black editorialists tended to blame white society. The *Chicago Defender*, almost in an attempt of racial expiation, announced Etta's death with the headline, "MRS. JOHNSON WAS NOT HATED BY NEGROES." White editorialists commented upon the basic incompatibility of the races. Etta's suicide, wrote a Midwestern journalist, demonstrated "how sharp is the line that runs between the races." It showed "how limited was Jack Johnson's so-called 'conquest of the white race.' He whipped white competitors in the prize ring . . . but he could not extend the conquest to those achievements that lie in the province of sentiment and affection."[10]

Johnson took a more personal view of the tragedy; he did not see it as a subject for larger generalizations. When he learned of the event, he rushed to the hospital and was there when Etta died. He grieved publicly for all to see. In tearful statements, he told reporters that his wife suffered from "brain fever," that he tried everything to brighten her life. As proof that he had been a faithful husband—hence bore no responsibility for Etta's suicide—he gave his wife's last letter to the *Chicago Defender.* The letter was addressed to Etta's mother and would have served well as Johnson's nomination for canonization. Why the letter was never sent Johnson did not mention, but in it Etta reportedly wrote, "Jack has done all in his power to cure me but it is of no use. Since papa's death I have worried myself in [sic] my grave."[11]

Some reporters found Johnson's emotions touching. "Animal or not, he is not callous," wrote an editorialist for the *New York Times.* He was struck by Johnson's "apparently sincere grief," although he speculated that the "display of emotion may be racial." Undoubtedly his pain was real, but it was not great enough to absorb his essential egoism. In his first comments on his wife's death he emphasized his, not her, condition, almost as if he were afraid that her suicide would overshadow his own problems. Etta's "brain fever," he told reporters, was contracted while attending to his own "brain fever." He himself had been suicidal in the months after the Jeffries fight. He had even twice tried to strangle himself. Both times Etta had saved him. "My wife took care of me. She nursed me tenderly for hours. I wanted to go to a sanitarium. My wife would not let me. She insisted on nursing me. She did this night and day for a year, until finally she broke down herself." In this and similar statements of the champion's, "I" and "my" normally far outnumber "her" and "she."[12]

As Johnson grieved, Jack Curley, the fight promoter, looked after the funeral arrangements. Promoters, after all, were good at details. The fleshy, sad-eyed, full-lipped Curley did a fine job, though boxers and managers were given the important duty of pallbearers. A mixture of blacks and whites attended the services held in Johnson's Wabash Avenue home. It was terribly hot, and several women fainted. Afterward the mourners, and a large collection of curious onlookers, went to Graceland Cemetery. As a choir sang "Nearer, My God, to Thee"—the tune popularly believed to have been the last selection played aboard the *Titanic* a few months earlier—Etta was buried.[13]

The world belongs to the living. It had been Thomas Jefferson's philosophy and it was Jack Johnson's. Etta was dead and buried. He had cried. But he still had his duties at the Café de Champion, and there was still a bevy of other women who desired to console him. Etta was replaceable, and she was soon replaced. Johnson began to spend more time with Lucille Cameron, an attractive white woman but not nearly as photogenic as Etta. She had brown eyes, dark hair, and a figure that tended toward plumpness. But in 1912 a big bust, wide hips, and heavy thighs were much prized. Etta's beauty was cold and distant; she had the look of pain and the promise of unhappiness. Lucille in this respect was her opposite. When she smiled her eyes were happy and engaging, her lips warm and friendly. Lucille's face was open; it promised the sensuality and laughter of a good time.[14]

Lucille had moved to Chicago from Minneapolis in April 1912. Although only eighteen, she was an experienced prostitute, having worked in Fannie Simpson's house in Minneapolis. In Chicago she met Catherine Dorsey and Genevieve Grant, two prostitutes who acted as liaisons between Johnson and white "sporting women." On the night the champion returned to Chicago from Las Vegas, he was introduced to Lucille. For her part, it was an old story—the legendary love at first sight. Thereafter she went to the Café de Champion more frequently, and finally she went to work for Johnson, serving at least occasionally as a stenographer.[15]

Johnson later wrote that their relationship was "purely of a business nature and devoid of undue intimacy." Perhaps it was a business relationship, but Lucille's business was intimacy. Several waiters and a bartender at Johnson's saloon knew the real nature of the affair, and the champion did not try to hide anything. He was proud of his conquests among white women. He even told a few reporters that he could "get" all the white women he pleased. More than a month before Etta's suicide Johnson was sexually involved with Lucille. He took her to dinner several times at Curley's house, and on a few occasions they went for rides in Johnson's automobile and did not return until the next morning.[16]

Etta's death only intensified their affair. But its very visibility created problems, as did Johnson's intemperate remarks. There was talk of Lucille's youth and innocence, and even more talk of Johnson's blackness. Such a relationship, whites reasoned, could not be

natural. Johnson must in some dark and sinister way be forcing himself upon Lucille. Freed from his evil influence, she would certainly
see the error of her behavior. Following this reasoning, on October 18,
1912, Johnson was arrested on a charge of abduction. Mrs. F. Cameron-Falconet, Lucille's mother, pressed the charges, upon which
federal authorities gladly acted. The United States government had
begun its campaign against Jack Johnson.[17]

He had been in jail before, and he was not particularly frightened by the police. When he was arrested at noon he laughed, telling
reporters that he had too much money to remain long in jail. And indeed he was soon released on an $800 cash bond. But this time it was
different. The charge was not speeding or even smuggling. Those violations could be circumvented with enough cash. This time it was a
serious federal violation. From the first the Bureau of Investigation,
the predecessor of the Federal Bureau of Investigation, had decided
to press for a Mann Act conviction. Johnson had reached the point
where money was no longer the remedy for all ills.[18]

The White Slave Traffic Act, better known as the Mann Act, was as
serious as its sponsor. James Robert Mann was a Republican congressman known for his hatred of boodle and his strongly puritanical
attitudes. Though short and decidedly stocky, he believed that he
morally and intellectually towered over his fellow congressmen, and
he moved busily about his legislative rounds with a haughty sense of
superiority. When the Republicans held the majority he was an industrious, if a somewhat ideologically limited, reformer, but as the mi-
nority leader he pulled like a bulldog against what he considered un-
wise or loosely written Democratic legislation.

The Mann Act was similarly industrious and self-righteous. Traditionally, it has been regarded as a prime piece of Comstockery, an
act that allowed government to supervise America's sexual behavior.
Specifically it forbade the transportation of women in interstate or
foreign commerce "for the purpose of prostitution or debauchery, or
for any other immoral purpose." The implications of the act were
tremendous. In theory any man who took a woman other than his
wife across interstate lines and then had sexual intercourse with her
was in grave danger. And indeed since the 1920s the act has been
viewed as the very symbol of sexual repression and bluenoseism.[19]

In truth the act was not so forbidding. Like many other pieces of
legislation passed during the Progressive Era, it expressed the con-
cerns, fears, and hope of middle- and upper-class Americans. It

traded on the exaggerated belief that large numbers of foreign women were being smuggled into the United States for the purpose of prostitution, which in turn was destroying the moral fiber of American men. It was this sinister evil that the Mann Act sought to prohibit. The broad wording of the act was designed to prevent evasion of the law through some legal technicality. If the Mann Act had exempted noncommercial vice, offenders might have evaded the prohibitions by concealing evidence of money transactions. The inclusion of both commercial and voluntary vice was meant to be a safeguard, a hedge against the wily and devious minds of the true offenders and their lawyers. But as Attorney General George W. Wickersham claimed, the act was not intended to apply to cases in which profit was not the motive. He did not want federal courts to be turned into ordinary police courts. He was after the "real" white slavers, not the businessman who traveled from New York to New Jersey to have a fling with his secretary. Assessing the impact of the act, legal expert William Seagle has written that from the first "the United States attorneys have been under instructions to prosecute under the Mann Act only such noncommercial cases as those involving a fraudulent overreaching."[20]

Time and money prevented many abuses by the government of the loose wording to the Mann Act. Overseeing the implementation of the law was the Department of Justice, an agency chronically understaffed and strapped by a small budget. From 1910 till 1920 only 2,801 people were convicted for violations of the Mann Act, and of these the Department of Justice estimated that 98 percent involved commercialized sexual vice. In 1912 the Attorney General of the United States emphasized in his annual report, "In the enforcement of the act the Department has been careful to refrain from instituting technical or trivial cases, or cases which more properly belong to the state courts, and has restricted itself to the class of cases at which the act was primarily directed."[21]

For Jack Johnson the government was willing to make an exception. In Chicago, United States District Attorney James H. Wilkerson told reporters that Johnson had clearly violated the letter of the Mann Act. But in Washington, Attorney General Wickersham was not so certain. Wickersham was one of President Taft's most trusted advisers, and as a trained and experienced corporate lawyer he had a fine eye for detail as well as for the larger picture. He understood the desirability of locking Johnson away, but he was troubled by what

looked like trumped-up charges. Particularly, he did not want the
Mann Act to be used as an instrument of harassment and persecu-
tion. Although notoriously nervous in gait and speech, Wickersham
was usually blunt, even tactless, in his personal correspondence. So
that there would be no confusion as to where he stood, he wrote
Wilkerson the day after the boxer's arrest, suggesting the greatest
care in the Johnson investigation, "so as not to involve Federal authorities in [a] mere question of abduction or anything not within
[the] general scope of evils sought to be reached by [the] white slave
act." [22]

Caution was not one of Wilkerson's finer points. Besides, once
the government began its poorly planned case, it was not easy to admit its mistakes. The arrest of Jack Johnson was greeted by nearly
unanimous approval in white communities throughout America.
Once the government had spoken, it became almost a patriotic duty
to criticize or attack the black champion. The day after his arrest an
unidentified man threw an inkwell at Johnson from an upper story of
Chicago's First National Bank. Though it missed its target, its intent
was difficult to misinterpret, as was the meaning of effigies of the
champion burned in white sections of the city. Indeed, wherever
Johnson went he attracted angry mobs, which shouted "Lynch him!
Lynch the nigger." [23]

The sentiments of the mobs were seconded by a number of news-
paper editorialists. "The obnoxious stunts being featured by Jack
Johnson are not only worthy of but demand an overgrown dose of
Southern 'hospitality,' " wrote an editorialist for the *Beaumont*
(Texas) *Journal*. The sincere wish to hang Johnson for his antics was
fairly common in the South. As a writer for the *Fort Worth Citizen-
Star* speculated, "We bet we know one person that isn't singing 'I
Wish I Was in Dixie'." But the most bitter anti-Johnson tirades appeared in that barber shop staple the *Police Gazette*, whose sportswriter called Johnson "the vilest, most despicable creature that lives
. . . he has disgusted the American public by flaunting in their faces
an alliance as bold as it was offensive." [24]

Even black writers generally condemned the champion. A headline in the *Philadelphia Tribune* announced, "JACK JOHNSON,
DANGEROUSLY ILL, VICTIM OF WHITE FEVER." For many
proud blacks Johnson's preference for white women was interpreted
as an insult to their own females. A feature writer for the *Birmingham Exchange* declared that every "race-loving Negro, irrespective of
his intellectual development, must indefatigably denounce Johnson's

debased allegiance with the other race's women and only express our feeling [that] . . . he will get everything that is coming to him as far as the law is concerned."[25]

As Johnson assumed the role of the sinister black white slaver, Lucille was treated as an innocent victim. She was portrayed as the sweet girl who came to the big city in search of a good, honest job and was snared into a life of sin. Searching for an explanation, writers claimed that Lucille succumbed to Johnson's advances only after she became intoxicated. This story was embellished by Mrs. Cameron-Falconet and her attorney, Charles Erbstein. They told government investigators that Lucille had been lured from Minneapolis by Johnson and his associates in vice. Clearly, Erbstein said, the Mann Act had been shamelessly violated.[26]

It was expected that Lucille would aid the government's case with her testimony before the grand jury. But before that inquiry took place, the government felt it necessary to isolate Lucille from Johnson and what it believed was his Svengalian influence. When the Harrison Street Annex of the city jail proved insecure, Lucille was transferred to the Rockford, Illinois, jail, where she was closely watched. She was not allowed to communicate with either her friends or the press. Special agents for the Bureau of Investigation believed that the longer Lucille was isolated the more willing she would be to testify against her lover.[27]

On October 22 Lucille was brought before the grand jury. The government sought to provide evidence of an interstate prostitution ring run by Johnson and involving Fannie Simpson, Catherine Dorsey, and Genevieve Grant. Supposedly the three women scoured the Midwest in search of white girls who would service Johnson. Lucille denied this elaborate conspiracy theory as patently absurd. She admitted that she was a prostitute, which slightly contradicted an earlier claim that she was a virgin, but refused to implicate Johnson in her profession in any way. When the questioning became more specific, Lucille began to sob and fell into a "hysterical" fit. At that point the grand jury adjourned for the day, and Lucille was released into the custody of her mother.[28]

Unable to alter her story, government agents sent Lucille to Rockford for further meditation. The government's case against Johnson was beginning to fall apart even before it had been formed. By late October federal agents for the Bureau of Investigation realized that they had acted too swiftly, exciting the public when they had no evidence of a white slavery conspiracy. In his report to his superiors in Washington, Agent Bert Meyer noted that he had uncovered twenty-two witnesses who would testify that Johnson had paid Lucille to perform various sexual acts with him, but, alas, there was no evidence of any interstate violations. As for the elaborate network that allegedly brought Lucille fresh and innocent from Minneapolis to Johnson, it was established beyond doubt that she had been a prostitute in Chicago for three months before she even met the champion. Understating the government's case, Agent M. L. Lins reported that "the possibility that [Johnson] aided in any way in her transportation from Minneapolis to Chicago is very remote."[29]

If government authorities were beginning to lose hope, they were nevertheless ready to look for a new beginning. They knew Johnson was not guilty, but the public did not. Therefore they decided to keep Lucille locked away in Rockford while they considered other possibilities. Agent Lins met Assistant District Attorney Harry A. Parkin to explore the government's alternatives. Parkin agreed that the Minneapolis connection led only to a dead end and that Johnson had violated no laws in company with Lucille. In fact, as far as Parkin knew Johnson had been guilty of no crimes under the Mann Act. But he *might* have been. Somewhere in Johnson's sexually active and geographically mobile past he very well might have violated the letter if not the spirit of the Mann Act. Parkin therefore requested that the Bureau of Investigation "endeavor to secure evidence as to illegal transportation by Johnson of any other woman for an immoral purpose." Lins, who had once been the chief of detectives in the Canal Zone and thus no novice in imaginative detective work, assured Parkin that his department had been looking for such possibilities since the scandal broke.[30]

Washington officials agreed with the decision made in Chicago. Both A. Bruce Bielaski, acting chief of the Bureau of Investigation, and Attorney General Wickersham had by late October overcome their initial doubts about the case. Although the government's case had in no way improved, they had both decided that Johnson probably had committed some crime and deserved to be punished. To that end Wickersham informed Chicago District Attorney Wilkerson that the Department of Justice was at the command of the local federal officials.[31]

As the government worked on their own conspiracy and as their agents roamed through the "colored district and former haunts of Johnson's" gathering evidence for a yet unspecified case, the champion celebrated what he believed was another victory over his white challengers. The festivities, however, were short-lived. He was like the eye of a hurricane, the calm center around which all else was swirling confusion. If many blacks silently admired him, those who spoke publicly voiced severe condemnation. Even Booker T. Washington found it necessary to issue a statement on the case. He did not care to defend or condemn the champion, he said; that was the function of courts. But Washington deplored Johnson's self-centered lifestyle: "It shows the folly of those persons who think that they alone will be held responsible for the evil they do." Johnson's actions, Washington said, had injured his race; his personal rebellion would result in a more general racial repression. As Washington said a few days after his first comments on the case, "It goes to prove my contention that all men should be educated along mental and spiritual lines. . . . A man with muscle minus brains is a useless creature."[32]

When given the opportunity, Johnson ably defended himself. Speaking before a hundred prominent blacks at the Appomattox Club, the champion refused to consider himself a symbol. He was a man, a free man, this and nothing more. "I want to say that I am not a slave and that I have the right to choose who my mate shall be without the dictation of any man. I have eyes and I have a heart, and when they fail to tell me who I shall have for mine I want to be put away in a lunatic asylum." As for the statements of Booker T. Washington, Johnson announced, "I never got caught in the wrong flat. I never got beat up because I looked in the wrong keyhole." The champion was referring, of course, to the incident in 1911 when Washington was physically assaulted by Henry Ulrich for allegedly peeping through a keyhole at the latter's wife.[33]

The speech at the Appomattox Club was an exception. Since most people had already decided that the champion was guilty—of what did not seem to matter—there was no strong desire to hear Johnson defend himself. As often happened in such cases, public opinion moved much more swiftly toward conviction than the courts. No sooner was he charged than there were calls to boycott everything connected with the champion, from his saloon to his name. The Minneapolis Commercial Club, upset that the name of its fair city had been besmirched by the affair, proclaimed that because of Johnson's "defiance of the law, disregard of morals, and his other numerous crimes," it was "time suppression is made of his name." No publication should be allowed to print anything about him. If their effort failed to win support, other forms of suppression were successful. On

November 1 the Chicago City Collector refused to renew Johnson's
license for the Café de Champion, and the saloon was closed. Unable
to get his statements in print, denied the right to his livelihood, and
hounded by the press, Johnson, many felt, was still being treated too
well.[34]

One person even tried to kill the champion. Ada Banks, a black
former lover, attempted to shoot him in late October, or at least that
was the rumor printed in the Chicago dailies. Just where Johnson
was hit by Ada's bullet no one was sure. Some said the foot, others
the hip, but as he never went to the hospital it is fairly certain that he
was not shot at all. Ada, a singer and a prostitute who was married to
a pimp named "Dog" Davis, said that she had not wanted to kill
Johnson, that the daily papers "lied on me." But by then the press
was ready to believe anything about Johnson, particularly if it was
bad. As in the government's case against him, truth was becoming ir-
relevant and unnecessary—even undesirable.[35]

While Johnson moved about Chicago with a sense of uneasy
freedom and government agents searched for evidence that would rob
the champion of his liberty, Lucille remained in jail in Rockford. She
was useful only as a decoy to divert the public's attention away from
the fundamental weakness of the government's case. Unfortunately
for Lucille, the longer she stayed in jail the more attention and closer
inspection her past received. It was becoming clear that she was not
the artless innocent that the press had earlier portrayed. Though
young, she was an experienced prostitute, and any talk about Johnson's corrupting her was utter nonsense. "In the swift storm of modern life," wrote an editor for the *Chicago Defender*, "she lost her
footing." She knew the twists and turns of the prostitute's trade long
before she walked into the Café de Champion.[36]

At Lucille's expense the government constructed a new case. Although the Bureau of Investigation could not uncover any women
that Johnson had seriously corrupted—that is, "robbed" of their virginity—it could and did find a number of prostitutes with whom the
champion had had sex. Most important was Belle Schreiber. She was
discovered through a fine piece of detection by Agent Meyer. Searching for leads in Chicago's vice district, Meyer met James Duffy, an
"ex-post-office safe blower and all-round crook" who was familiar
with the underworld. Duffy told Meyer about Belle and how Johnson
had abused her. This was enough for the government. If Johnson had
sexually abused Belle and had traveled with her across interstate
lines, he had violated the Mann Act.[37]

Duffy led Meyer to Ollie Davis, who owned several "sporting houses" in Chicago. He too remembered that Belle had traveled with and serviced Johnson. He recalled that Johnson had taken Belle from the Everleigh Club, where she had previously been the favorite girl of Mortie Heyman, a leading vaudeville actor on the Western circuit. For a time, Davis said, Belle went everywhere with Johnson—New York, Canada, San Francisco, everywhere. And the champion had even set her up in business at the Ridgewood Apartments. But their affair was now over. Davis said that the last he had heard Belle was working in a house in Washington, D.C.[38]

Davis was right. Belle was working in the nation's capital in a house run by Grace Sinclair at 1229 D Street. On October 30, 1912, she agreed to go with Agent T. S. Marshall to Acting Chief Bielaski's office. There she told the long story of her life with Johnson. Her memory was superb. She recalled the cities they visited, the hotels where they stayed, the nights they made love. She remembered even the smallest details and names—the men Johnson knew in the different towns, the clothes she wore on various occasions. There was even a picture of her and Johnson that had appeared in a Boston newspaper with the caption: "Jack Johnson and His Pretty White Wife." The date of the picture and the date Belle said she was with the champion in Boston were the same. There was no doubt that in its essentials Belle's story was accurate.[39]

The government never doubted Belle's truthfulness. The only question was whether or not Johnson had violated any laws. Most of the time Belle and Johnson had spent together was before the passage of the Mann Act, and even after 1910 they had not traveled together *primarily* for immoral purposes. Belle had lived with Johnson more as a kept mistress than a paid prostitute, and the spirit of the Mann Act clearly distinguished between such niceties. As Bielaski wrote to his top agent in Chicago, Belle "did not engage in the business of prostitution" while she traveled with the champion. Their relationship was emotional and sexual—not commercial.[40]

Under normal circumstances the government's case would have ended here, for under normal circumstances the government would not have had a case. As later cases involving the Mann Act would demonstrate, the act does not prohibit illicit sexual relations, nor does it deny to those who engage in such activity the right to travel across interstate lines. An expert on the legal aspect of the act has written, "The crucial question in every Mann Act prosecution is thus the motive of the interstate journey. The courts have held that the existence of an incidental intent to engage in sexual immorality will not make criminal a trip that is entirely innocent in its motivation.'' Certainly, there is no violation of the Mann Act in continuing pre-existing sexual immoralities in the course of an interstate trip. Ironically, as William Seagle has observed, the men who are safest on interstate journeys are, paradoxically, ''those who are the most thoroughly immoral. The more consistently they have lived in sin prior to embarking on a grand tour, the less they have to fear that they will incur the pains and penalties of the Mann Act. The fact that their mistress[es] have accompanied them will be of no significance whatsoever, for it is patently absurd to contend that a man who has enjoyed the favors of a woman on innumerable occasions has taken her on a trip for the purpose of indulging his sexual passion.'' This relationship, immoral perhaps but certainly legal, was precisely the arrangement that Johnson enjoyed with Belle.[41]

Unfortunately for the champion, normal circumstances did not prevail and standard interpretations were not enforced. Most whites believed that Johnson had offended, and offended deeply. He had married a white woman and defeated white champions. He had, in the opinion of white authorities, refused to live the role society prescribed for him. As a rebellious black man he threatened America's social order. Bad Niggers clashed with the law. They shot white sheriffs or raped white women or in some other way legally placed themselves beyond the pale. When they did so they were punished. They were shot or lynched or burned. After death the more famous and notorious became black cultural heroes—men who fought and even won small battles over white society but ultimately paid for their transgressions with their lives. Contained within their lives was a single lesson: the price of total freedom was death. They were, as Lawrence Levine noted, ''hard men, but the world in which they lived, and perished, was harder.''[42]

The white response to the Bad Nigger was more visceral than intellectual. It was as close to an archetypal reaction as has developed in American culture. The Bureau of Investigation and the Department of Justice did not so much consciously conspire to get Johnson as express the more general attitude of white society toward blacks who threatened the social order. Johnson had unwillingly become a symbol of disorder and therefore a real threat. And if the intent of the Mann Act had to be perverted to restrict his freedom, the government was prepared to do just that. After learning about the interview with Belle, Acting Division Superintendent Lins of the Chicago Bureau of Investigation wrote his superior in Washington that "we are very much pleased with the prospects of making a case against Johnson." This was not simply another case. Lins, like the other government officials involved in the investigation, took the matter personally. They were determined to punish Johnson, and the Mann Act provided a useful whip.[43]

Armed with Belle, the government took its case to Chicago and the grand jury. While the public's attention was still focused on Lucille in Rockford, Belle was secretly brought into town. Fearful that Johnson's agents would discover her, federal officers kept her under close watch. On November 7 she told her story to the grand jury. Belle was a willing and convincing witness. For hours she told the sordid details of her life with Johnson—the clandestine meetings, the sexual encounters, the physical punishment. When she finished she was whisked out of town as rapidly as she had been brought in.[44]

After hearing Belle's testimony, the grand jury called for an indictment. Its decision was passed on to Judge Kennesaw Mountain Landis, the no-nonsense dispenser of justice, who promptly issued a bench warrant for Johnson's arrest. Specifically, the champion was charged with transporting Belle from Pittsburgh to Chicago on August 10, 1910, for the purpose of prostitution and debauchery. Both acts, according to the indictment, were crimes "against the peace and dignity of the . . . United States."[45]

Special Agent Meyer and several other detectives were sent after the champion. They first went to the Café de Champion but found it boarded and barred, a casualty of Johnson's condemned life-style. They found Johnson in room 21 of the Hotel Vendome on State Street. The police had to break down the door and force their way past Johnson's bodyguards to get to him. But after this initial confusion the arrest proceeded in an orderly way, and Johnson was allowed to call Sol Lewinsohn, a bondsman.[46]

Johnson admitted he knew Belle but said that he had broken no laws. "I met the Schreiber girl not only in Pittsburgh, but in New York and Brooklyn, where we appeared in vaudeville. But I never transported her anywhere." At first his mood was light, his attitude jocular, as if he knew he had done nothing wrong and fully expected that the government would find this case every bit as empty as the one involving Lucille. At the sight of the handcuffs, however, the champion became serious. As they snapped around his wrists, tears formed in his eyes. Tears brought not by fear or pain, but by humiliation. "You don't have to do this," he said. "I won't run away. I have too much property in town to run away."[47]

Around midnight he was freed on bail. His mother and a friend named Albert Jones arranged for a $30,000 bond. He did not even have to spend the night in jail. As far as he was concerned, it had been just another minor brush with the law. It was over now, and it would soon be forgotten. But this time it was different. Johnson's life was about to change radically, and he did not even realize it.

10

Love and Hate

THE WHITE-HAIRED JUDGE was angry. Although only in his forties, Kennesaw Mountain Landis looked and acted older, almost as if he were a throwback to the days of Judge Roy Bean. He cursed in a soft country accent, wore string ties, and was notoriously short-tempered. When his moral indignation was aroused—which was often—he tended to dispense justice like an Old Testament prophet. In 1907 he became outraged at the business tactics of Standard Oil. After forcing John D. Rockefeller to come into the courtroom to testify, a bold action for a young judge, he fined the company $29 million. On November 8, 1912, his hatchet face and cold eyes were turned toward Johnson and his associates.

Speaking to Johnson's attorney, Landis said, "Mr. Morris, you were not here earlier in the day. You presumably may not know there was attempted on me today something the like of which has never been tried before in my eight years' experience on the bench." The judge characterized the entire episode as "a disgusting and nasty piece of business." And, he was quick to add, "I cannot assume this happened without the knowledge of Johnson."[1]

Fraud. That was how Judge Landis described it. Johnson and his cohorts had tried to "put something over" on Landis and, by extension, on the United States government. Specifically, the judge discovered irregularities in Johnson's bond. The property Albert Jones put up as surety was not his. On the day Johnson was arrested, Jones assured Landis that he owned a four-story brick and stone residence on Michigan Avenue in Chicago and that the house was worth $35,000. It was his, he said, "clear of encumbrances." On this surety, Landis ordered Johnson released. But the next day it was shown that the house had been deeded to Jones's wife. Jones had perjured himself before both Landis and the clerk of the court. It was a mistake that would cost him twelve months in Joliet.[2]

That night the champion went back to jail. His mood was much more somber. It was a chilly night, a reminder that winter was close at hand. On the left sleeve of his coat Johnson wore a wide black badge of crepe in memory of Etta. As he walked into the Cook County jail, he was handcuffed to Deputy United States Marshal Northrop, and this only deepened Johnson's anger and embarrassment. When a photographer attempted to take Johnson's picture, Johnson became violent. With a cane he held in his free hand, he lashed out at the photographer's wrists. Northrop, who was being dragged about "like a palm leaf fan," tried to calm the champion. "Please don't, Jack. Be a gentleman."[3]

Johnson was not the only inmate in Cook County jail who did not always behave like a "gentleman." No sooner was the champion locked away in cell 506 than a volley of decidedly ungentlemanly complaints was let loose along the cellblock. "Get that nigger out of here" best summarized the position of the 530 white prisoners in the wing of the jail where Johnson was locked up. Finally, after the cries increased in volume, Johnson was removed from the all-white cellblock and quartered in the hospital section of the jail. The next day he was incarcerated in a cell with John Brown, who was accused of stabbing a fellow employee.[4]

As far as Johnson was concerned, the jailers were as ungentlemanly as his fellow prisoners. From his cell Johnson called out, "I want a dozen candles so I can have more light, a box of cigars, and a case of champagne." No highwayman brought to Newgate was more bold. He even requested that Assistant Jailer Tom Jordan remove his shoes. All these requests were refused, whereupon Johnson remarked that he was treated much better when jailed in San Francisco. "When I was in jail in California those gentlemen always treated me like a prince. And I am a prince. Ain't I?"[5]

After a few days in jail Johnson's attitude softened. The boldness and verve of his speech quieted. A reporter for the *Chicago Tribune* noted that the champion was "meek and submissive." On Sunday, November 10, he even attended two religious services, one offered by a Methodist mission group, the other by a Roman Catholic Sunday school. Although he still insisted on smoking fine cigars and refused to eat the regulation jail food, he was trying to appear as repentant as possible. But it was an unfamiliar role that he did not play well.[6]

After Johnson had spent a week in jail, his lawyers were finally able to arrange a bond acceptable to the court. Land owned by Matthew S. Baldwin, a real estate dealer, and by Tiny Johnson was used as surety. Johnson's lawyers assured Baldwin that his bond was safe, that the champion would not flee the country, but the land dealer insisted that a private detective be hired to trail Johnson. When, as later happened, the boxer did skip the country, Baldwin lost more than $15,000 in real estate, which, it was said, so upset him that he died a few months later.[7]

But in November Baldwin, if suspicious, was alive, and Johnson, much to the boxer's relief, was technically free. On the night he left jail he held a celebration and a banquet at his Wabash Avenue home. It was a wild affair attended by many of his friends, several of whom were white prostitutes also in trouble with the government. Johnson told friends that a little money, discreetly and quietly placed into the right hands, would end the affair. Prison seemed only a vague threat. Men with money did not end up there.[8]

The next day he drove downtown to talk to District Attorney James H. Wilkerson about the case. "My God," Johnson complained, "can't you allow me to plead guilty to this charge so I can be let off with a fine? . . . If I am prosecuted on these charges, then there are thousands of others who could be prosecuted on similar reasons." He was right, of course, but Wilkerson could not admit as much. And the district attorney refused even to consider plea bargaining. He told Johnson that the government would make no deals, and the champion left in a dejected mood.[9]

If Johnson was upset, Lucille was more so. Although she was no longer a material witness, the government insisted that she remain in the Rockford jail. More than anything else, they feared that if released she would return to Johnson. When Judge Landis sent Lucille back to jail on November 8, he did so to make sure she did not elope with the black boxer. But as her stay in jail lengthened, Lucille became a considerable embarrassment for the government. Journalists questioned the propriety—if not the legality—of incarcerating a woman simply to prevent her from making a foolish decision. Finally, and quietly, the government dismissed the abduction charges against Johnson and released Lucille.[10]

Once free, she did exactly what everyone expected. She went directly to Johnson's home. Within days rumors were heard that the two would marry. Some writers speculated that Johnson wished to marry Lucille to prevent her from testifying against him. Others held that Lucille used the threat of her testimony to force the champion to wed her. Few journalists considered that love might actually be involved. On the rainy afternoon of December 4 the rumors came true. The Reverend H. A. Roberts, a small, bent, gray-haired black preacher, married the two in a short ceremony held in Johnson's house. The entire service lasted less than three minutes, and judging from the smiles on Johnson's and Lucille's faces, it was just another happy marriage.[11]

Public reaction was swift and cruel. If Johnson sought to enrage white Americans at precisely the moment when his popularity was at its lowest, then his timing was perfect. A group of white Louisianians, in a typical Bible Belt reaction, inquired whether or not the citizens of Illinois knew what "seagrass ropes were made for." As had happened so often before, Johnson the individual was obscured by Johnson the symbol. The issue, as many whites saw it, was not a marriage between a black boxer and a white prostitute—it struck deeper, to the core of American society. Governor William Mann of Virginia called the marriage "a desecration of one of our most sacred rites." Governor John Dix of New York labeled it "a blot on our civilization." Addressing an annual conference of governors, Cole Blease, South Carolina's chief executive, asked, "If we cannot protect our white women from black fiends, where is our boasted civilization? . . . In the South we love our women, we hold them higher than all things else, and whenever anything steps between a Southern man and the defense and virtue of the women of his nation and his states, he will tear it down and walk over it in her defense."[12]

Even in Congress Johnson's actions were decried. Representative Seaborn A. Roddenberry of Georgia shed tears of indignation when he spoke on the central issue of the Johnson case. "No brutality, no infamy, no degradation in all the years of Southern slavery, possessed such a villainous character and such atrocious qualities as the provision of the laws of Illinois, New York, Massachusetts, and other states which allow the marriage of the negro, Jack Johnson, to a woman of Caucasian strain." As he spoke the packed gallery rewarded him with wild applause. Encouraged, he demanded a constitutional amendment that would prevent white women from being "corrupted by a strain of kinky-headed blood." A Northern representative interrupted Roddenberry's impassioned speech to remind his Southern colleague that Abraham Lincoln was also against interracial marriage. Exactly, Roddenberry continued, "Intermarriage between whites and blacks is repulsive and averse to every sentiment of pure American spirit. It is abhorrent and repugnant to the very principles of a pure Saxon government. It is subversive to social peace. It is destructive of moral supremacy, and ultimately this slavery of white women to black beasts will bring this nation to a conflict as fatal and as bloody as ever reddened the soil of Virginia or crimsoned the mountain paths of Pennsylvania." If the federal government allowed "sombre-hued, black-skinned, thick-lipped, bull-necked, brutal-hearted African" men to marry white women, then racial warfare would be the union's first offspring. Therefore, he concluded, "Let us uproot and exterminate now this debasing, ultrademoralizing, un-American, and inhuman leprosy."[13]

Sitting in the gallery and listening to Roddenberry rant about "no blacker incubus" and "no more voracious parasite," was James Trent, a black Howard University student. He turned to his mentor, the historian J. A. Rodgers, and said, "By God, I would like to put a bullet in his fanatical heart. If I only had a gun, that damned roughneck." But Roddenberry's rage sent more blacks fleeing for cover than searching for pistols. By marrying Lucille Cameron, Johnson had touched a sensitive nerve that enraged whites and frightened blacks. As W. E. B. DuBois suspected, whites found it difficult to be objective about the issue of interracial marriage. In the end it was always, "Do you want your sister to marry a Nigger?"[14]

Roddenberry and other Southern politicians made sure the issue stayed in the public spotlight. More than a month after Johnson's marriage, the Georgia representative was still reminding his colleagues that a constitutional amendment prohibiting interracial marriage was urgently needed. He cited a case in Michigan where a forty-two-year-old black man married a fifteen-year-old mentally retarded white girl. The man in the case, George Thompson, said that "if Jack Johnson could marry Lucille Cameron," then he could marry whomever he wanted. "In the name of girlhood and womanhood," Roddenberry begged his fellow congressmen to act before it was too late.[15]

Some states did act. In 1913 miscegenation bills were introduced in half of the twenty states that permitted interracial marriages. In Congress at least twenty-one similar bills were introduced. In Illinois, where Johnson had married Lucille, five bills were initiated. Remarkably, none of the bills was passed into law. Indeed, the historian Rayford Logan believed that the defeat of the bills was more important, more truly indicative of the national mood than their introduction.[16]

At the time, however, there were few indications that the episode would demonstrate that white America was becoming more liberal on the race question. In early 1913 there were only bitter feelings on both sides of the color line. Eventually liberal black leaders defended, if not Johnson's choice, his right to make that choice. The editor for the *Washington Bee*, a leading black newspaper, wrote, "we are unalterably opposed to intermarriages, but we are just as unalterably opposed to the enactment of any statute, state or national, to prohibit them." The most thoughtful editorial was written by DuBois, who also opposed both interracial marriages and legislation against them. To allow such laws, he argued, "would be publicly to acknowledge that black blood is a physical taint—a thing that no decent, self-respecting black man can be asked to admit."[17]

As if marrying a white woman was not enough, Johnson sought other ways to inflame white opinion. Without fear of the consequences, he moved forward in a revolutionary direction. He demanded real social equality. In late December 1912 he announced his intent to buy a house in an all-white neighborhood of Lake Geneva, the most exclusive summer colony of Chicago millionaires. The home Johnson wanted was next to the house owned by a director of the National Biscuit Company and not far from the summer cottage of the president of the Illinois Trust and Savings Bank. Johnson claimed that he would lead other wealthy blacks into the neighborhood.[18]

To no one's surprise, white residents of Lake Geneva complained. Mrs. John J. Mitchell, whose husband was the bank president, was "astounded" that the property was "sold to a negro." Mr. Mitchell was sure Johnson purchased the place through a third party. Actually, he never did buy it, and the entire affair might have been simply an elaborate scheme to inflate the price of the house. The real estate agent might have correctly believed that with Johnson as a possible bidder, the house would be sold to a white for considerably more than its true value. As Johnson's black attorney announced in a press conference, "When the house is put up for sale everybody will be on an equal footing. I and my friends will bid for it and the Lake Geneva people can also bid for it. . . . the people of Lake Geneva will be given an opportunity to show whether or not all this hue and cry they have raised against myself and my colleagues is on the square."[19]

Revolutionary or con man, Johnson was perceived as a threat to social order. It was now common for politicians and journalists to describe the champion as an instrument of chaos and disorder, a threat to civilization and Anglo-Saxon culture. Often opinions concerning just what Johnson represented lacked clarity, but the general impression that his deeds were a portent of doom seemed to seep from the pores of the press. It was a vague feeling of disquiet that many Americans hoped would soon pass. They yearned for the restoration of an absolute sense of racial order. And the government responded to these deeply felt desires. As Johnson sought to extend his conquest from white women to white neighborhoods, the government prepared its case.

By early 1913 the government's case against Johnson was completed. He was indicted on eleven counts, ranging from aiding prostitution and debauchery to unlawful sexual intercourse and crimes against nature. Most of the indictments dealt with the activities of Johnson and Belle during their many trips between Chicago and Milwaukee in late December 1910. As there was no question that the two had traveled together and had had frequent sexual relations, the government was confident that it could secure a conviction.[20]

District Attorney Wilkerson's only concern was the erratic behavior of their star witness, Belle Schreiber. Around her the government's case revolved. Without her there was no case at all. Therefore, as early as November, Wilkerson decided that it was "absolutely essential" that Belle be held in custody until the trial. In Washington, Attorney General Wickersham agreed. Belle was simply too capricious to be trusted on her own.[21]

The details of the custody were left to the acting chief of the Bureau of Investigation, A. Bruce Bielaski. A short, neat man with a weak chin and sharp eyes, Bielaski was considered a master at details. He was intelligent and efficient, and during World War I he would be America's premiere spy-catcher. In 1912 he had been in the Justice Department just five years. Through indefatigable effort he had risen to the top, but his boyish looks and bustling energy—manifested in long walks and gardening before breakfast and in boxing, baseball, running, and rowing after work—made him the target of office humor.[22]

However admirably suited Bielaski was for his job, his experience had not equipped him to deal with a woman like Belle. She was to be kept in custody, but where? Obviously in Chicago she would be too close to Johnson's influence. After talking with Belle, Bielaski decided New York would be the best place to keep her. Lodging was arranged at the Waverly Home, a house for "wayward women" at 238 West 10th Street. At first Belle was happy enough. She loved the center stage and never tired of telling her melodramatic story. In fact, she was almost a compulsive confessor, willing to talk to whoever would listen.[23]

She soon ran out of wayward women to tell her story to. No longer such a unique attraction but just another wayward woman herself, Belle became bored. She decided that Waverly Home was not nearly as good as the other houses where she had lived. In a letter to a friend she called the house a "regular prison—bars on the windows—no paper to read—no fire and cold indoors . . . food awful, retire at 9 P.M. and get up at 6:30 A.M.—what a life!" She wrote to her former employer in Washington that she was trying to escape. Special Agent William Offley, who was assigned to watch Belle, soon became apprehensive. Belle, he wrote to Bielaski, was "becoming very restless." She complained that she was addicted to dope and needed her daily absinthe. In Waverly Home she was not even allowed liquor. If she insisted upon leaving, Offley warned his chief, he had no authority to detain her.[24]

Offley tried to appease Belle. He took her to the cinema, which in itself acted like a drug on her, and out to dinner. When she was being entertained, she was satisfied, but as soon as she was alone at Waverly Home she began to complain. In addition, the enforced wholesome life-style of Waverly Home made her physically ill. Offley reported that she was "evidently suffering from the reaction following her inability to indulge in her usual amount of liquor." When the housekeeper refused to allow Belle the "medicine" required for her condition, the government's star witness became "rather peevish." It was clear that Bielaski would have to try something else.[25]

Bielaski tried to appeal to Belle's sense of drama. In a letter that reads like a fourth-rate detective thriller, Bielaski told Belle that of course she was free to go, but other girls in her position who had been left alone had been killed by white slavers. "Those girls unfortunately were not Government witnesses and hence were not afforded the protection they would have had from attack had they been such." And, Bielaski continued, it was the government's opinion that Johnson was a desperate man. Faced with a prison sentence, Johnson might even be capable of murder.[26]

The idea of being the heroine in such a fine drama seemed to satisfy Belle. Furthermore, Johnson's marriage increased Belle's desire to hurt her former lover. For its part, the government found Belle a more comfortable room at the New York Probation Society and entertained her nightly. But even with this renewed attention, Belle became bored within a few weeks. She wanted to work, but the government had doubts of the propriety of her practicing prostitution while under its custody. And with the Christmas season at hand, she longed to see her old friends.[27]

The crisis occurred on the night of December 14–15. Special Agents Rosen, Poulin, and Craft took Belle to dinner at Gonforcne's Café on Washington Square. After a good dinner and a few drinks, the troupe ventured up into Harlem in search of Belle's former boon companion, Lillian St. Clair. After midnight Belle became "absolutely obstinate and for a time obstreperous." She refused to return to the Probation Society and demanded to see Offley, who was the chief of the New York office of the Bureau of Investigation. When the agents tried to humor her, Belle created a scene, daring the officers to put her in jail. Finally they took Belle to see Offley, who was awakened at his residence in the Prince George Hotel. Offley called Bielaski, who decided to transfer Belle to Washington.[28]

Belle was in a decidedly bad mood. On the train to Washington she embarrassed Agents Rosen and Craft by accosting one Jerry Moore, one of her former patrons. She told Bielaski that she wanted to stay in D.C., close to her lover "Cal" Rosenthal and her friends. Bielaski said that Johnson's agents would surely find her there. A compromise was reached. Belle agreed to stay in Baltimore, where her friends could come to visit her.[29]

In Baltimore Belle's behavior was as erratic as ever. One day she would be pleasant and talkative, the next testy and abusive. This created problems in the houses where the government placed her, for even when Belle was agreeable she tended to talk about her days as a prostitute. Within a week of her arrival in Baltimore she was asked to leave the Florence Crittenton Home. The manager of the home told Special Agent Grgurevich that Belle was "not a friendly person." Life at a boarding house run by Mrs. Marie Kieth was a little better. Belle lasted more than two months there. But finally even the tolerant Mrs. Kieth had to admit defeat. She confided to Agent Grgurevich that Belle was not a "respectable woman." She would have to leave.[30]

The length of Belle's stay in Baltimore can be attributed to the admirable work of Agent J. J. Grgurevich. He took Belle everywhere she desired—shopping, the theater, dinner. Day after day he was Belle's full-time escort. At first Grgurevich refused to take Belle out alone. She was a very aggressive woman. But after a while Grgurevich agreed to be with her unchaperoned. It was, after all, his job. The diligence of Grgurevich's efforts even came to Bielaski's attention. In late December the chief of the Bureau told his agent to take Belle out less and not to spend so much of the government's money on her.[31]

During March and April 1913 Belle was moved about, both within Baltimore and between Baltimore and New York. They were difficult months. With the trial approaching, Belle became "extremely nervous and crotchety." Special Agent Pigniuola noted that she needed "constant humoring and pampering and if thwarted in the slightest wish, immediately 'went up in the air' " and threatened not to testify. It was with considerable relief, then, that Bielaski saw Belle put on a train bound for Chicago in early May. After more than half a year in custody, Belle was about to earn her keep.[32]

In early November, when Johnson was arrested for violating the Mann Act, the government had planned for an early trial. In December Bielaski wrote the head of the Chicago Bureau of Investigation, Lins, to push for a January date. However, Johnson's case was not tried until May. Judge George Carpenter, who was scheduled to hear the case, was partially to blame for the delay. He had grave reservations about the constitutionality of the act, and he did not want to hear Johnson's case until the Supreme Court ruled on the validity of the statute. Therefore, since Johnson was free on bond, Carpenter saw no reason to rush the case into trial.[33]

Nor was Johnson in any particular hurry. His position, in fact, was based on the hope that the case would never go to court. As soon as he was released from jail, he started working toward that end. His first—and most logical—plan involved persuading Belle not to testify. But first he had to find Belle. This problem was not insoluble, for Johnson had paid informants in the marshal's office. This justifiably concerned the government, though its reaction was unjustifiably strong. Any employee of the marshal's or the district attorney's office who was friendly with Johnson was immediately suspect. Llewelyn Smith, a black messenger for the district attorney's office, was seen visiting Johnson's home. Upon questioning he claimed he was visiting the champion's sister. Unsatisfied, District Attorney Wilkerson fired Smith. Next the hatchet fell on Marshal Edward Marsales, who had guarded Lucille when she was in Rockford. He had grown fond of her, and when she married Johnson, Marsales went to the Wabash Avenue home to congratulate the couple. When Attorney General Wickersham learned of Marsales's indiscretion, he ordered the marshal fired. Marsales complained that in eight years of service he had a perfect record for loyalty, that perhaps he had been foolish, but that he had not talked about the government's case with Johnson. Wickersham's decision remained final. The message was clear: for government employees, Johnson's friendship was a costly luxury.[34]

Johnson continued to believe in the power of money. He hired John Dannenberg, a former Bureau of Investigation agent and a nephew of Marsales, to find Belle. Dannenberg followed Belle's trail to New York but was unable to locate her. He did, however, spread the word that Johnson was offering a $10,000 reward for information concerning her whereabouts. This, even more than internal leaks, frightened the government. It also accounts for Bielaski's willingness to move Belle from city to city.[35]

Unable to find Belle, Johnson studied his contingency plans. By late December his initial *sang froid* had disappeared. Although he seemed happy at Christmas, playing Santa Claus for black children and giving expensive presents to his family, he was a worried man. Talks with Wilkerson and Bureau of Investigation agents convinced him that the government seriously wanted to see him in prison. The realization upset him, and his health began to fail. Throughout the winter he suffered from colds and what one doctor described as "nervous exhaustion."[36]

Under the circumstances escape became increasingly tempting. His saloon was closed, and he was prevented from boxing even in exhibitions. Johnson realized that he would have to leave the United States if he hoped to make any money. In the cold days of early January he made plans to flee the country. His valet, Joseph Levy, bought three first-class one-way tickets to Toronto and shipped two of Johnson's cars, a Chalmers limousine and an Austin racer, across the border. At 11:38 P.M. on the night of January 14 Johnson, Lucille, and Levy boarded train no. 6, Grand Trunk Railroad, bound for Battle Creek, Michigan, where it was scheduled to stop early the next morning. Then it would continue into Canada. They left quietly, and at 2:50 A.M. the train pulled into Battle Creek.[37]

In this game of cat and mouse, Johnson was no match for the Bureau of Investigation. From the start of the case they had expected just such an attempt, for Johnson's offense was nonextraditable. Therefore, Johnson was carefully watched. At 2:00 A.M. Chicago bureau chief DeWoody received a telephone call that Johnson had left. He quickly wired the police chief in Battle Creek to arrest the champion. That done, he sent his best agent, Bert Meyer, to bring the boxer back to Chicago. About 5:00 A.M. Meyer returned with Johnson, who spent the rest of the night in jail.[38]

The champion denied that he was fleeing the country. "I had no intention of jumping my bond or in any way breaking or evading the law," he said. "I was simply going to Toronto on a business trip." According to the champion, his only reason for crossing the border was to talk with fight promoter Tom Flanagan about arranging a title match in Paris against Al Palzer. As for the two cars, Johnson explained that he never traveled without them. On roads as well as tracks, he was a first-class traveler.[39]

DeWoody did not believe him. He wrote Bielaski that Johnson probably wanted to escape United States jurisdiction before the Supreme Court ruled on the constitutionality of the Mann Act. He also informed his superior that Judge Carpenter was being "exceedingly lenient" toward Johnson. The judge, noted DeWoody, believed the Mann Act would be ruled unconstitutional and therefore took Johnson's attempted flight casually. Surprisingly, however, DeWoody felt the best course of action might very well be to allow Johnson to escape. "I believe we all agree . . . on the advantage to the country if Johnson were to be exiled from it," DeWoody wrote Bielaski. In view of Johnson's subsequent escape, there is a prophetic quality to DeWoody's comment.[40]

Johnson's attempted escape only increased the government's vigilance. Not only was the champion carefully watched by Bureau agents; DeWoody also hired a friend of Johnson to serve as an informer. Ironically this man, Sig Hart, was a close confidant and former manager of the champion. Hart's concern, or so he said, was for Johnson's mother. If the champion fled the country, she would lose her home. From this high-minded position, he proceeded to file daily reports on Johnson's activities. However, since he usually reported that Johnson was about to escape at any moment, his usefulness as an informant was questionable.[41]

The government, not fully trusting Hart, also acquired the services of John Hawkins, a friend and neighbor of Johnson. Hawkins had previously helped the Bureau in a police graft investigation and, as DeWoody noted, was an "unusually intelligent" black man. The insult implied in DeWoody's observation was not lost on Hawkins. As a result, for four dollars a day he filed innocuous reports on the champion's inactivity. Johnson, noted Hawkins, played cards, visited saloons, and took lengthy drives about Chicago. Escape was never mentioned, at least not to Hawkins, who consistently told the government that Johnson would never leave Chicago.[42]

Thus, depending on the informer, the government was daily told that Johnson was carefully planning his next escape or that escape was the farthest thing from his thoughts. In reality, Johnson, for perhaps the first time in his life, had lost control of a situation. He waited for the Supreme Court to rule on the Mann Act, and he worried. As in the past, the mental tension made him physically ill. By mid-February Hawkins was reporting that Johnson was dangerously ill, perhaps with pneumonia. It was rumored that Johnson's temperature fluctuated between 101° and 104°, and that he was close to death.[43]

At first the government was suspicious. DeWoody believed the reports were a ruse, the initial move in an elaborate scheme to escape. He attributed Johnson's sudden illness to an unfavorable ruling by the Supreme Court and the champion's coming trial on smuggling charges. To gather firsthand information, he sent Agent Lins to Johnson's home. Lucille refused to allow Lins to see Johnson; she complained loudly that the government was to blame for her husband's condition. Everyone else in the house spoke in hushed tones, as if the champion were on his deathbed. Pulling Lins aside, Dr. R. W. Carter told the agent confidentially that Johnson was "critically ill." The champion, he said, was suffering from typhoid pneumonia and might not live.[44]

The next day Judge Carpenter postponed the smuggling trial indefinitely. A week later Johnson was well enough to leave his deathbed, but only for a very special purpose. A frank talk with DeWoody, he believed, was the only way out of this Mann Act business. He wanted to discuss the matter man-to-man with just DeWoody, but the chief Chicago agent insisted that Lins also be present. They met in DeWoody's office. Johnson said that of course he was technically guilty, but he had never "profited financially through his transactions with . . . prostitutes." In addition, because of his color he doubted if he would receive a fair trial. Johnson's solution was simple: he would plead guilty if the government would only "impose a substantial fine." No prison. DeWoody refused to bargain. Johnson, walking unsteadily, as if weak from illness, left the office in a "downcast mood."[45]

No deals. Appeals to government authorities from DeWoody to President Taft had no effect. Johnson, DeWoody noted, was an "undesirable American" who deserved no mercy from the courts. All this made Johnson nervous—and angry. His family suffered. His brother Charles, who was scheduled to testify against Jack in the smuggling trial, told Agent Meyer that he had received death threats. Charles was afraid to return home and wished to remain in police custody. Lucille also ran away, or at least that was what Charles said. Jack said she had just gone to see friends in Harrisburg, Pennsylvania. At any rate, Johnson's Wabash Avenue home was becoming a dangerous place to live.[46]

In late April the smuggling case was finally heard. Everyone realized that it was just a preview, a little something before the Mann Act fireworks in May. As such, it attracted little attention. Johnson plead *nolo contendere* and was fined $1,000, pocket money for the champion. Ben Bachrach, his lawyer, told reporters that the champion's plea should not be interpreted as an admission of guilt. It was just that he did not remember to declare the necklace. Johnson accepted the decision calmly, disturbed only by the court's ruling that he would also have to pay court costs. "What! $740 costs? That's a regular holdup." But he paid, for his eyes too were focused on the main event scheduled for May.[47]

11

A Fit of Blues

TOWARD THE END of April 1913 a cold rain swept across the Midwest. The weather was not at all to Johnson's liking. Nor was the list of people scheduled to testify against him. John Hawkins, still working under cover for the government, reported that the champion was deep in "a fit of blues." All his friends, or so he believed, were now his enemies. Belle, Hattie, Mervin Jacobowski, Yank Kenny, Julia Allen (Belle's former private maid), Roy Jones—Johnson had once been close to them all. He had once employed them all, and paid them well too. Now they were witnesses for the government. What was more, the grand jury had just returned two more counts against him. Both were for sexual perversions, legally known as crimes against nature. That made eleven counts all together. The realization that he was close to hearing the cold sound of a steel door slamming behind him was now fully upon the champion.[1]

DeWoody, expressing the government's position, was confident. Writing Bielaski, his superior in Washington, DeWoody commented, "If the attitude of the grand jury . . . can be taken as any criterion of the jury trial, there will be no difficulty in convicting Johnson." In all the months of preparation the government had not lost a major witness, a great achievement considering that most of their catches were of a decidedly transient nature. Pimps, prostitutes, and boxers normally did not lead settled lives. True, there were a few people the government never could find—prostitutes like Lillian St. Clair—but on the whole DeWoody was pleased with the efforts of his agency. There was no doubt in his mind that Johnson was going to prison.[2]

It was close to show time for Belle. Still in Baltimore on May Day, she was in the best of spirits and was looking forward to the trip to Chicago. She was scheduled to leave five or six days before the trial so that she would have enough time to confer with DeWoody and Assistant District Attorney Parkin. It was planned that her movements would be kept secret. They were not. A newspaperman named Morgan Royce discovered the government's plans and published them, much to the disgust of Bielaski. But no real harm was done. By May 3 Belle was safely locked away in a comfortable suite at the Great Northern Hotel, where for hours each day Parkin and DeWoody polished her story. As the star, she had to know her lines.[3]

Even the choice of the jury worked to the government's favor. Bureau of Investigation agent George Bragdon described a typical juror. William Ullrich, Bragdon reported, owned property, voted Republican, faithfully attended the Episcopal church, disliked sports, belonged to the Evanston Commercial Club, and was "strongly prejudiced against negroes." He was honest, hard-working, and abstemious—a no-nonsense man who could be trusted to find Johnson guilty as charged. As white male after white male was chosen to fill the jury box, the government's confidence soared.[4]

In fact, the government suffered only one setback, and it was a minor one. Through government parsimony, Yank Kenny was lost. DeWoody had uncovered the alcoholic former boxer in mid-April. At that time he requested the authority to give Kenny $25 to allow him to live in Chicago. Bielaski, who was a near-maniacal penny-pincher, refused to allow the expenditure. As a result Kenny drifted out of town and out of the case. This loss undermined the government's sexual perversion case against Johnson. It was Kenny who had heard Belle's screams on a spring night in 1909 at Cedar Lake. He had listened as Belle promised to "do it, or do anything" if Johnson would only stop beating her. This was the only evidence the government had that Johnson had committed crimes against nature. And now it had left town. If the government wished to press those counts, it would have to do it through Belle. And that was an embarrassment it was not ready to face.[5]

The messy Chicago trial was not the only government worry at that time. South of the border, white-bearded General Venustiano Carranza, a self-proclaimed constitutionalist, had gone into revolt against General Victoriano Huerta, the crafty, drunken "president" of Mexico. Carranza was encouraged by the implications of Woodrow Wilson's nonrecognition policy toward Mexico. Wilson, new in office and dedicated to moral leadership, wanted to unseat "that scoundrel Huerta," for in his opinion "butchers" had no business sitting in any president's chair, even Mexico's. With grim determination, Wilson pursued what he believed was the correct and orderly course. That he might be wrong never entered his Calvinistic mind.[6]

In Chicago it continued to rain. But that did not stop Wilson's government from restoring what it considered to be right and order at home. Johnson, the black threat, was perceived as every bit as dangerous to America's racial order as the Indian Huerta was to this country's sense of international order. Johnson's trial began on May 7, 1913. From the start Judge Carpenter demonstrated that it would be orderly. Johnson would receive a fair trial before being thrown into prison. To prevent his showcase of justice from being turned into a carnival, Carpenter announced that only relatives and reporters would be admitted to the courtroom of Chicago's Federal Building. The curious but technically disinterested were out of luck.[7]

Assistant District Attorney Harry Parkin opened the trial. He said the government would show a pattern to Johnson's behavior. Speaking barely above a whisper, Parkin claimed there was more to the trial than simply proving that Johnson "aided, assisted, caused and induced" Belle to go from Pittsburgh to Chicago for illegal and immoral purposes. Indeed, as far as the government was concerned, that was incontestable. The pattern Parkin spoke of involved thoroughly despicable behavior. Speaking louder at Carpenter's and the reporters' request, Parkin intoned, "Now, it will appear . . . that the defendant is a prize fighter; and in that connection it will be interesting . . . to see upon what victims he practiced the manly art of self-defense. It will appear that those women who he carried about the country with him were, very, very many times, when he either had a fit of anger, or when the girls refused to do some of the obscene things he demanded of them—that he practiced the manly art of self-defense upon them, blacking their eyes and sending them to hospitals." Here, then, Parkin was saying, was not a nice man, but one who beat, abused, and sodomized white women, and never mind that those women were prostitutes.[8]

Parkin's opening statement put Benjamin Bachrach, Johnson's lawyer, on the defensive. For Bachrach, Johnson's trade, his busi-

ness, justified his actions. What he did—and with whom he did it—
was hardly his fault. Women of a "certain class," sporting women,
were attracted by Johnson's feats of "physical prowess," and they
threw themselves at the champion. When Johnson met Belle, she was
an experienced prostitute who "consorted with a great number of negro men." That she and Johnson became lovers was an established
fact, and Bachrach did not contest it. But, he emphasized, they were
lovers and traveled together before the Mann Act went into effect on
July 1, 1910. "Prior to that time, however much . . . you might dep-
recate the idea of . . . a bachelor having intercourse with a woman
not his wife, it was no crime against the laws of the United States."
Nor was it a crime for Johnson to travel with Belle or "have intercourse with her on the train in the stateroom." And, Bachrach emphasized, since the passage of the Mann Act, Johnson had not taken
Belle across any interstate lines. He had broken no federal laws.[9]

With the two positions established, Parkin began his case. Witness after witness presented circumstantial evidence of Johnson's
guilt. Mervin Jacobowski, former chauffeur of the champion, told of
the many trips Johnson and Belle made together. Lillian Painter, the
madam of a Pittsburgh house where Belle worked, said that the
champion sent Belle money to return to Chicago. John Lewis, the
manager of the Ridgewood Apartments, presented evidence that
Johnson paid for the rooms where Belle practiced her profession.
Bertha Morrison admitted that she practiced prostitution alongside
Belle at the Ridgewood. Before Judge Carpenter and the jurors paraded painted and tired prostitutes and sleazy characters who seemed
to have leaped full-blooded from a Jack London novel. That Johnson
was even acquainted with such persons was enough to damn him in
the eyes of many of the jurors.[10]

For several days this 1913 version of Guys and Dolls continued.
Finally Parkin called Belle to the witness stand. She was calm and
well-groomed, both physically and mentally. The hours spent with
DeWoody and Parkin paid handsome dividends. The twenty-six-year-
old prostitute, who looked a decade or so older, surprised the courtroom with her detailed recall of her travels with Johnson. She remembered exact dates and locations, even the names of hotels where she
and Johnson had had sexual relations. In New York, for example,
Belle recalled meeting Johnson at the Wilkins, Bear and Wilkins Hotel on 35th Street: "It was called the Savoy Hotel. . . . It was, I believe, in the middle of May. . . . I was stopping at the Little Belmont,
on 45th Street. . . . I met him frequently in New York, and had sexual

intercourse with him." From the East to the West Coast, throughout the Midwest and into Canada, Belle and Johnson had traveled together as lovers. In a frank, almost emotionless voice, Belle recounted those days as if it had all been one long business trip, which, of course, it had been for her.

The cold reality of Belle's life surfaced throughout her testimony. Once she was questioned on the subject of love, a familiar but elusive word in her business. "Were you in love with him?" "I don't know." "What?" "I don't know." "Don't you know now—did you think you were then?" "I don't know what love is. . . . I don't believe I ever was in love." Another time, while recounting the little details of a trip, she remarked, "I was pregnant at the time." The sentence carried no feeling. She might as well have said, I was a few pounds overweight at the time, or I had a slight stomach ache at the time, or I had on a blue dress at the time. For Belle, pregnancy was merely an occupational hazard, much like a cut eye for a boxer. The only difference was that a cut lasted longer.

Parkin wanted Belle to be more specific about her sexual relations with Johnson, but defense counsel Bachrach refused to allow it. Early in her testimony Parkin began to explore the subject. Bachrach interrupted: "The admission is made here on record . . . that the relations between Johnson and Belle Schreiber were intimate carnal relations." Enough said, at least as far as Bachrach and Judge Carpenter were concerned. However, Parkin was able to bring out something of the extent of Johnson's carnal appetites. That Johnson often traveled with two or even three women was established, as were the champion's violent outbursts. But Carpenter tried to preserve decorum; he ruled out "all unsavory details" of Johnson's relations with the women.

If Belle's testimony was shortened by Bachrach's admissions, it was lengthened by his constant objections. He objected to questions concerning Johnson's life before the passage of the Mann Act, and he objected to questions that were not covered in the indictment. But most of all he objected to the Mann Act, which he believed was unconstitutional. To begin with, he said, the Mann Act was in clear violation of the Tenth Amendment: "All powers not delegated to the United States by the Constitution, nor prohibited by it to the States, are reserved to the States, respectively, or to the people." The Mann Act, in short, was an infringement of states' rights. In addition, the act violated the Fifth Amendment: "No person shall be deprived of life, liberty or property without due process of law." As if realizing he had stepped on unfirm ground, he quickly changed his argument. Conceding the power of Congress to regulate and legislate commerce between states, the basis of the Mann Act, what Johnson had done—if, indeed, he had done anything—had no commercial intent. Therefore, Johnson's case was "not within the spirit of the White Slave Traffic Act." Carpenter listened to Bachrach's scattershot objections, then overruled them. The trial continued.[11]

Parkin had several witnesses to corroborate Belle's story. Julia Allen was brought in from Pittsburgh to testify. Earlier, when questioned by the grand jury, she had favorably impressed DeWoody and Parkin. She was articulate and had a fine, clear memory. Particularly, she remembered Johnson wiring money for Belle to go from Pittsburgh to Chicago in October 1910. Since that was the primary charge against the champion, Julia's testimony was especially important. She also told the jury that Johnson paid for, furnished, and often frequented Belle's apartment at the Ridgewood, where Belle openly practiced prostitution. Julia had no doubts that Johnson significantly contributed to Belle's trade.[12]

Hattie Watson also supported Belle's story. Hattie had been shipped to Chicago from Astoria, Washington, where her husband ran the Stockholm Saloon and she practiced prostitution. Like Belle, Hattie had traveled with Johnson, but only before the passage of the Mann Act. Her testimony served more to confirm the pattern of Johnson's behavior than to prove he had violated any laws. That Johnson was even associated with such a woman was enough to harm him in the eyes of the churchgoing jurors. Decent men, they reasoned, did not know women like Hattie and Belle.[13]

Without getting too specific, Parkin believed he had demonstrated Johnson's guilt, having shown that the boxer had transported Belle from Pittsburgh to Chicago for base, immoral, and illegal purposes. He thereupon rested his case. No sooner was this said than Bachrach raised a new series of objections. First, he wanted the court to dismiss the two counts of crimes against nature with which Johnson was charged. In no way had they been proved. Judge Carpenter readily complied. He had no stomach for the "nauseating details" of Johnson's sex life. Nor did Parkin have any objections to dismissing the two counts. He had no wish to embarrass Belle—and himself—with such delicate questions. Bachrach also requested that the court dismiss all other charges against Johnson. The government's case, he said, lacked concrete evidence—railway tickets, telegrams, and, even more important, proof of Johnson's intent. Even if Johnson had furnished and rented a flat for Belle, and even if she practiced prostitution there, there was no evidence that the champion specifically gave her money to come to Chicago for that purpose. The government presented only circumstantial evidence, and the rule of such evidence emphasized that the "circumstances proved must exclude the theory of innocence—it is not sufficient that the circumstances proved be consistent with guilt." Once again Carpenter overruled Bachrach's objections.[14]

Bachrach's defense was less inspired than his objections. He was content to allow the basic facts of Belle's story to stand, while offering a different interpretation. The new slant, of course, was Johnson's. Yes, the champion admitted, he had sent Belle $75. She said she had lost her job and needed the stake. This, as a friend, he gladly gave her. She came to Chicago of her own volition, not at his request. Once in Chicago, Belle called Johnson and they met at the Hotel Vendome. "She told me that her sister was going to be sick, that she was pregnant, and that she wanted a place for her mother and her sister." Again, Johnson the loyal friend provided help. He rented and furnished a flat for Belle, her mother, and her sister. He also gave her $500 to live on until she got a job: "She told me she was going to work at stenography. She had done stenography work for me, lots of it." Johnson claimed he had no knowledge that Belle practiced prostitution at the Ridgewood.

As he spoke, Johnson became wholly absorbed in his story. At first he was visibly nervous. He spoke in a low voice, at times hesitatingly, sweat dripping off his forehead and trickling down his face. But after fifteen or twenty minutes he started to relax. His voice, no longer low, sounded a new confidence, and the touch of an English accent returned. No longer willing to stay on the defensive, he challenged Parkin, trying to outwit the government. And as if the verbal games were a boxing match, he tried to anger his white opponent. At one point Bachrach asked Johnson if he had sent Belle a telegram. Parkin objected. Johnson answered: "I never sent such a telegram in my life." Parkin: "I object. Wait a minute." Johnson: "Not in my life." Parkin: "Just a minute." Johnson: "Never in my life." Like the last punch, the last word was what the champion wanted.[15]

On the stand Johnson showed the most prized quality of the Bad Nigger—the ability to stand up to and outsmart white authority. In fact, for years any black who so challenged authority was dubbed "Jack Johnson." On the stand Johnson refused to be humiliated. He refused to lower his eyes and look humble. His gestures were those not of a contrite man who sought atonement but of one who believed he had done nothing wrong. To be sure, he made some concessions in order to win sympathy: his mother sat beside him every day, and Lucille never attended the trial. But he did not apologize for what he was or how he had lived. Unbendingly, defiantly he faced his white accusers.[16]

He spoke openly and frankly about his life and his profession. He admitted that he often traveled with prostitutes, but his account encouraged the idea that boxing itself was strikingly similar to prostitution. Before the trial Parkin had said he wished to expose several "faked" fights in which Johnson had engaged. Now, on the stand, the champion did not try to deny the allegation. Parkin: "You knew you were going to win [the Ketchel fight] before you went into it, didn't you?" Johnson: "I did." Judge Carpenter: "Now, you are going into the question of a man's self-confidence." Parkin: "No, no, not at all." Bachrach: "No, he wants to show that the fight was crooked or something like that." Without being asked, Johnson added, "They are all crooked." Bachrach objected, and the line of questioning was dropped. But the words—"They are all crooked"— had a haunting quality, as if he realized that for all the ballyhoo his profession lacked substance, that in the end they were all whores.[17]

After five days of testimony the show was almost over. When Johnson stepped off the stand it was late in the afternoon, but Judge Carpenter wanted to finish the trial. He therefore convened a night session. Before he sent the jury out, he gave a lengthy set of instructions that clearly indicated his position. Looking at the twelve men of the all-white jury, he told them that "a colored man in the courts of his country has equal rights with a white man, a man of your own color." The jury should remember that, Carpenter said. Similarly, they should consider the personalities of those who testified, especially Belle. She was an "abandoned woman," an "unfortunate creature," a "discarded mistress." Prostitutes, hangers-on, has-beens, "all sorts of unfortunate people"—they had all presented evidence. It was the jury's duty, Carpenter emphasized, "to sift all this evidence through and through to see where the truth lies."

As for Johnson, the jury was instructed to be open-minded. "You are not concerned with the defendant's morals save only as it may give you some information as to what his intention was" when he sent the money to Belle. And that was the soul of the issue—why did Johnson send the money to Belle? In Carpenter's pre-Freudian view, and in the eyes of the law, every normal person was presumed to intend the natural consequences—indeed, the inevitable consequences—of his own actions. It was this complicated question of intent that the jury had to decide. It did not matter that Belle was a prostitute: "The law does not apply solely to innocent girls. It is quite as much an offense against the Mann Act to transport a hardened, lost prostitute as it would be to transport a young girl, a virgin." It did not matter whether Johnson intended to make money from Belle's prostitution: the Mann Act was not concerned with pecuniary profit. Only Johnson's intentions mattered.[18]

Shortly after 10:00 P.M. the jury retired to consider a verdict. Of the eleven original indictments, four had been dropped—those involving crimes against nature and debauchery. What remained were the indictments charging Johnson with transporting Belle from Pittsburgh to Chicago for the purpose of prostitution and sexual intercourse.

Looking inside a man's heart—in this case a black man's—was not easy for the white jurors. The first vote was eight to four in favor of conviction. The second was the same. On the third ballot, two of those who favored acquittal changed their votes. On the fourth ballot there was unanimous agreement that Johnson was guilty as charged. They were, after all, looking into the heart of darkness. Even without hard evidence of guilt, the assumption must have been that for Johnson innocence was impossible. Fifteen minutes before midnight the jury foreman, James Bruce, stood up, cleared his throat, and announced, "We, the jury, find the defendant, John Arthur Johnson, guilty as charged in the indictment."[19]

When the jury returned, Johnson sat chatting with Bachrach. Outwardly he seemed calm, almost as if the trial did not really concern him. As the word "guilty" was pronounced, his smile faded and he sat solemnly in his seat. Bachrach demanded a poll of the jury. One by one, each juror was asked the same formal question: "How do you find the defendant?" Each answered the same: "Guilty as charged." Twelve white men faced the one black man: guilty.[20]

Parkin was not surprised. He knew that racial order was the real question. Earlier he had told the jurors, "If you should find this defendant not guilty . . . I do not see how any of you can go home and look squarely into the faces of those you respect and admire." Mothers, wives, daughters, all with white faces. Now, after the verdict, he was even more specific: "This verdict . . . will go around the world.

It is the forerunner of laws to be passed in these United States which
we may live to see—laws forbidding miscegenation. This negro, in the
eyes of many, has been persecuted. Perhaps as an individual he was.
But it was his misfortune to be the foremost example of the evil in
permitting the intermarriage of whites and blacks.''[21]

Race and sex were crucial aspects of Parkin's vision of social order, but they were not everything. In black advancement he saw ominous consequences. ''Five years ago [Johnson] was obscure, penniless, and happy. He beat down a man and became famous with a
blow. He beat down another and riches poured into his pockets.
Money and fame, such as it was, brought white women. One is a suicide, the others are pariahs. He has violated the law. Now it is his
function to teach others the law must be respected.'' For Parkin,
Johnson and blacks were better off ''penniless and happy''—like Uncle Remus's good slaves swapping stories in the shadow of the Big
House—than striving to advance. In his mind, black advancement
threatened American social, racial, and moral order.[22]

Journalists agreed with Parkin. Johnson the symbol had to be
punished, even if Johnson the man was technically innocent of violating the Mann Act. An editor for the *Indianapolis Freeman* acknowledged that to the champion was being ''meted out a terrible punishment for daring to exceed what is considered a Negro's circle of
activities.''[23] Certainly a boxer's proper circle of acquaintances included prostitutes. John L. Sullivan lived with a prostitute while he
was married. Sam Langford and Stanley Ketchel were constantly seen
with different ''lost women'' of their respective races. But Johnson
was the first boxer openly to shatter the color barrier with regard to
his paramours. He lived with, was seen with, and finally married
white women. In so doing, he violated social laws far more deeply
rooted than the Mann Act.

Sentencing was set for June 4. He faced a maximum penalty of five
years in the penitentiary or a fine of $10,000, or both. White sports-
writers and editorialists hoped Johnson would be put in prison for a
long time. Complimenting the new White Hope, Uncle Sam, one
Omaha journalist expressed the hope that the ''big black black-
guard'' would be forced to serve ten years behind bars. In bold head-
lines, the *Cleveland Daily News* announced, ''BLACK PUGILIST
WILL BE MADE AN EXAMPLE.'' The mood of the country demanded stern retribution.[24]

Some observers feared that Johnson would escape serious punishment. Bureau agent DeWoody was most concerned about Judge Carpenter, who had already expressed doubts about the case. Writing to his superior in Washington, DeWoody said the judge might only slap Johnson's wrist—six months in prison and a few thousand dollars' fine. All the government's efforts would then have been wasted.[25]

Indeed, Johnson acted as defiantly as ever. As his lawyers filed for a new trial, the champion raced about the streets of Chicago in his expensive automobiles. On one of these cars he had installed a "cut-out muffler," which was noted for its noise. He made no attempts to conceal his movements, and even when fined he refused to adjust his muffler. Fast and loud was the pattern of his life, the source of his fame and troubles, and he saw no reason to alter his style as long as he was free.[26]

On June 4, a fine summer day, he went to court to hear the sentence. Johnson looked confident, though just why is hard to imagine. It was not a good time to be other than white in America. A Southerner was in the White House, and he had ordered complete segregation on all federal jobs. In Congress the greatest flood of bills proposing discriminatory legislation against blacks was being debated. Even Japanese-Americans were experiencing the effects of the national temper. On June 4 Viscount Chinda, the Japanese Ambassador, met with Secretary of State William Jennings Bryan to lodge a formal complaint against the California Alien Land Law, which discriminated against Oriental Americans. Chinda's protest was useless. President Wilson supported the law.[27]

Interest in what Judge Carpenter would decide ran high, so high, in fact, that the proceedings were scheduled for late in the afternoon to avoid the overcrowding of the courtroom by curiosity seekers. Before sentencing Carpenter overruled Bachrach's motion for a new trial. He then turned toward the champion: "Does the defendant, Johnson, wish to say anything before sentence is pronounced?" Johnson rose slowly, hesitated for a moment, and replied, "No, nothing, your honor." Carpenter read a short prepared statement that condemned Johnson and violators of the Mann Act. But this case went beyond the individual, beyond the act: "This defendant is one of the best known men of his race, and his example has been far-reaching and the court is bound to consider the position he occupied among his people. In view of these facts, this is a case that calls for

more than a fine. Considering all circumstances in this case, therefore, the sentence of the court is that the defendant . . . be confined
in the penitentiary for one year and one day and be fined $1,000.''[28]

His days of freedom were now numbered. Carpenter granted
him two weeks to file a bill of error before the United States Circuit
Court of Appeals. But Johnson had lost faith in America's legal system. He knew that the appeals could only bring him a little time, that
they would not be successful. If he hoped to avoid prison, he would
have to go beyond the law. Freedom was no longer possible in the
United States, he reasoned. He would have to flee his country—forever.[29]

He planned his escape carefully. Each little detail was attended
to by Johnson and his resourceful lawyers. First, there was his bond.
Bachrach persuaded Carpenter to reduce the bond from $30,000 to
$15,000. This action made Matthew Baldwin the sole bondsman; it
released Tiny Johnson from any obligation. If her son jumped bail,
she would not lose her house. It was a small detail but a considerate
one.[30]

Of more importance was his escape route. His ultimate destination was Europe, where he planned to defend his title, box exhibitions, and go on stage. Obviously he could get there only via Canada.
However, he had to make sure that Canadian officials could not ex-
tradite him before he sailed for Europe. Violation of the Mann Act
was not covered under the extradition treaty between Canada and the
United States, so that presented no problems. His only concern was
that he might be deported back to the United States as an undesirable
immigrant. To circumvent this possibility, he purchased in Illinois a
ticket from Chicago to Le Havre via Montreal. This simple procedure
changed his Canadian status from an undesirable immigrant to an
alien traveling through the country. As such, he could not be deported.[31]

Such meticulous planning required the aid of lawyers, friends,
booking agents, and shipping agents. With informants close to the
champion, it was impossible for Johnson to keep his activities secret.
Almost two weeks before the boxer left the country, Agent X-102
(John Hawkins) reported that Johnson had shipped his two automobiles to Germany and was planning a tour of Europe. Johnson even
went to DeWoody's office to find out whether he could legally leave
the country. In the conversation that followed the champion admitted
that he had shipped the cars. There was no doubt in DeWoody's mind
that Johnson was about to flee the United States.[32]

This much of Johnson's planning is known. What is puzzling is why DeWoody and the other agents assigned to watch the champion failed to prevent the escape. Johnson had tried to escape before, and another attempt was clearly in the works; yet in mid-June, when he said he was going to Cedar Lake, Indiana, on a fishing trip, government agents relaxed their vigilance. The man whom they had watched for the past half-year was allowed to leave the country without opposition. Later Johnson said he had left Chicago disguised as a member of Rube Foster's baseball team. It is a flimsy tale. "The ball team was composed of strapping big players, many of them as large as myself. One of the players resembled me in stature and features and to him I gave my watch and ring, the latter having more than once served as an identification of me. . . . This was one of the ruses hit upon to serve in the event that officers . . . boarded the train en route in search of me." Playing on the white assumption that all blacks looked alike— indeed, could be distinguished only by height and rings and such— Johnson claimed he escaped. The tale, like so many others in his autobiography that have gained general acceptance, is ridiculous. It never happened.[33]

But he did escape using the simple and undramatic ruse of a fishing trip. The question remains: How and why were the government agents duped? Two, possibly three, answers can be offered. First, there was some question about the exact nature of Johnson's bond. It was unclear whether or not he could leave the jurisdiction of the court. After Johnson was safely in Montreal he wired DeWoody: "Am sailing Sunday morning for Russia. You don't need to worry. Will be back for trial." And Bachrach, Johnson's lawyer, told journalists that the bond the boxer was under "does not prevent him from leaving the state or the country. The only condition imposed by the bond is that Johnson shall appear in the United States Court of Appeals at the time his case is called there." Indeed, that was the precise view that Judge Carpenter took. Johnson had not and could not violate his bond until he failed to appear for his appeals hearing. In this view, the government was powerless to prevent his leaving.[34]

There is no indication, however, that the government shared Carpenter's opinion. DeWoody never told Johnson that he could leave the jurisdiction of his bond. In fact, DeWoody acted surprised when he discovered that Johnson was in Canada. Whether the surprise was genuine is the central question to the second explanation of Johnson's escape. There were rumors—and some evidence—that the champion purchased more than simply a ticket to France. Johnson's friends and relatives claimed his escape path was paved with generous bribes. This story became public on January 19, 1914, when the *Chicago Examiner* published an interview with Johnson. According to the champion, he bribed five government officials, including Parkin and DeWoody, with cash payments estimated as high as $50,000. Commenting on the episode, a *Chicago Examiner* editorialist wrote, "Unsupported the word of this beast is worthless, but corroborated to the extent that corroboration comes . . . it is at least sufficient to raise a doubt."[35]

In several telegrams from Paris Johnson confirmed the story. He gave $20,000 to Roy Jones and $30,000 to Sol Lewinsohn, both of whom acted as bag men for the Bureau of Investigation and the District Attorney's office. Lewinsohn, Johnson claimed, was the only honest man. The rest—DeWoody, Parkin, Jones—were "robbers," "blackmailers." He promised that very soon he would return to Chicago and present proof of his allegations.[36]

The charge was serious enough to warrant an investigation, especially after the *Chicago Examiner* published "facsimiles" of the checks made out to key government figures. Bielaski was understandably concerned and demanded to know if Johnson actually said what was attributed to him. An investigation of several telegraph companies showed that Johnson had made the statements. Next Bielaski inquired if the reports were true. Parkin said, "I never got a dollar from anyone except the United States government." DeWoody called the charge "absurd." Jones, a Levee district saloon owner, commented, "Jack is trying to get even with me for testifying against him." The other major actor, Sol Lewinsohn, was a fugitive from justice and could not be reached for comment.[37]

Friends and relatives of Johnson disagreed with Parkin and DeWoody. Tiny Johnson said her son paid large sums of money to DeWoody, and Mrs. Jennie Rhodes, the champion's sister, concurred. Jennie remembered going with her brother to Lewinsohn's office: "Jack and Lewinsohn discussed the payment of $5,000 to Harry A. Parkin . . . in return for which Parkin was to permit Jack to leave the country without hindrance. Jack and Lewinsohn agreed that the $5,000 was all that was left of a sum of $30,000 which Jack had turned over to Lewinsohn to be used in paying federal officials and protecting Jack's interests in various ways." Half an hour later, in front of Jennie, Parkin collected the money. She claimed her brother paid everyone from DeWoody and Parkin to Lucille's mother and Charles Erbstein. The government people were "bleeding him to death." Another woman, Mrs. M. Evalyn Kritzinger, who worked at the states attorney's office, confirmed the bribe reports. Her boss, State Attorney John Wayman, worked with DeWoody to extort money from Johnson. On one occasion he ordered dinner and drinks and said, "Have one on Jack Johnson." According to her story, even Benjamin Bachrach, Johnson's lawyer, was involved. He told her Johnson was paying everyone and, "We'll fleece that nigger before we get through with him."[38]

A grand jury probe was opened. It was, unfortunately, far less thorough than the investigation of Johnson's Mann Act violations. David Stansburg, who conducted the probe, did not search very deeply for evidence. As he saw the case, it was the word of Johnson and his crowd against the United States government. And even though private investigators questioned the honesty of several government agents, Stansburg had no doubt who was telling the truth. Stansburg and the grand jury were "entirely satisfied" with DeWoody's explanation of the affair, and they seriously doubted the "mental responsibility" of those who supported Johnson's story. As far as the government was concerned, the case was closed.[39]

In the next several years the press occasionally revived the case. Herbert Sims, a brother of Parkin, admitted that Lewinsohn and "loaned" him some money but denied that it was a bribe. Other government officials, when confronted with the cashed checks, gave the same story. Arrested in 1917, Lewinsohn himself confirmed the bribe stories. More significantly, in the same year DeWoody wrote a friendly but concerned letter to Harry Brolaski, a New York Bureau of Investigation agent. DeWoody, who was transferred to Cleveland after the Johnson trial, was worried that a man named Gregg would expose "a little secret" concerning the Johnson case. Gregg's threats were never carried out, and after 1917 no more was heard of the alleged bribes.[40]

For whatever reason, Johnson was allowed to leave the country. Nor did the government seem particularly unhappy about his departure. Publicly there was some bold talk. DeWoody told reporters that if Matthew Baldwin would appoint him deputy bondsman, he would go to Canada and bring Johnson home. And Secretary of State William Jennings Bryan asked Canadian officials to detain Johnson illegally. All that talk, however, was only for the press. Privately, the government had no wish to force Johnson's return. When District Attorney Wilkerson tried to get the government to act, the Attorney General told him that the government would not pursue the matter.

That America's problem would now become a European one did not concern the government. Johnson was gone, it was hoped, forever. Case closed.[41]

On June 29 Johnson sailed from Montreal bound for Le Havre. From there he planned to go to Russia. Asked how he expected to enter Russia, given his court record, the champion replied that that was "all fixed." Though he had his two cars and traveled first class, he needed money. The Mann Act trial, beside forcing him into exile, had drained his resources. All told, he claimed, it cost him $138,000. The Mann Act had been successful. As a writer to the *New York Call* cogently observed, "Johnson is black and has more money than is good for a black man. The Department of Justice must aid the 'white hopes' in taking away the superfluous cash of the stupidly brazen Negro pugilist. . . . Anglo-Saxon America is relieved of a most dangerous menace to the preservation of its color."[42]

12

The Hollow Crown

IN JULY 1913, at a public auction held in Chicago, the government sold the necklace Johnson had smuggled into the country several years before. It sold for only $2,160, more than one thousand dollars below its estimated value. At that moment Johnson was enjoying his freedom in Paris. Housed in a luxurious apartment in the Hotel Terminus, close to the St. Lazare railway station, he was unconcerned about his lost jewelry. In his mind, he still owned an ornament far more precious than a necklace. He still wore the championship crown he had won from Tommy Burns in 1908 and had defended successfully against Jim Jeffries in 1910. That piece of jewelry, he believed, was worth something, and it could not be confiscated by any government. In the next few years, however, Johnson discovered that his crown was hollow, worth not much more than the auctioned necklace.[1]

Paris, 1913: Something of the *belle époque* was still in the air. If La Goulue no longer did her frenzied high kicks and splits, no longer showed her silk stockings and underclothes, her free spirit lived on at the Moulin Rouge and the other cabarets of Montmartre and the Rue Pigalle. In theory, Paris allowed one to live an eccentric life without the least interference, and bourgeois conformity was seen as the only unpardonable deviation. Many American blacks believed it was a city without racism. When Johnson sailed for Le Havre, a writer for the

185

Chicago Defender said the champion was bound for a better life. It seemed that Johnson would finally settle in a city that suited his temperament.[2]

In public Johnson called Paris the city for him. He told reporters that he was collecting all books written about Napoleon and that he had read everything Alexandre Dumas ever wrote. It was reported that he moved about Paris like a prince, flashing thousand-dollar banknotes. In private Johnson was not at all happy, and Paris was a bitter disappointment. Racism existed there, just as it did in America. On his arrival he was refused rooms at the Grand Hotel, the Ritz, the Elysée Palace, the Excelsior, and the Hotel Neuilly before finding lodging at the Hotel Terminus. He could stay in Paris, but not at the best places.[3]

Johnson also discovered that although he could spend his money in Paris, he could not make much there. If he hoped to make money, he had to cross the Channel. In mid-August Henry Tozer, the head of a booking syndicate, engaged the champion to appear in the Euston and south London music halls as well as to tour the provinces. Johnson readily agreed. In Paris and Brussels his stage routine had been unsuccessful, and he looked forward to facing an audience that understood English.[4]

Many Englishmen were not looking forward to his appearance. No sooner was his booking announced than a groundswell of protest arose. It started with the performers themselves. The Executive Committee of the Variety Artists' Federation complained that the appearance of Jack Johnson on the London stage, where tradition was a source of pride, would overstep the bounds of "public decency." This was not a question of color, the committee said, but of morals. It was Johnson's "unsavoury notoriety acquired through the Law Courts" that was in question. Although the executive committee could not speak for the federation as a whole, it called upon the public and the licensing authorities to prohibit the boxer's appearance.[5]

Soon others joined the protest. Some thought of the consequences for Anglo-American relations if Johnson were allowed to earn money on the London stage. It would be a "public scandal," an "affront to the United States," wrote an editorialist for the *London Daily Mail*. The Reverend F. B. Meyer, who had so strongly crusaded against the proposed Johnson-Wells bout several years before, told reporters, "Jack Johnson is tabooed in the United States, where they know him well. Surely our variety stage will not stoop so low as to engage him. All that makes for national decency appeals to the variety managers to save us from the threatened disgrace.'' Many vocal Englishmen wished to touch hands symbolically with their American cousins and restrict the activities of Johnson, the black threat to order and decency.[6]

All this protest, as far as Tozer was concerned, was marvelous publicity. When Johnson crossed the Channel from Boulogne to Folkestone on August 24, he had every intention of fulfilling his contract. After driving to London he held a press conference in the West End house he was renting. He was in a good mood. Wearing a ''smartly cut'' gray frock coat and giving ''full display'' to his diamonds, he spoke confidently about the future. His conviction, he suggested, was a disgrace for America. The charges were ''trumped up,'' and the jury was a carefully picked collection of bluenoses, ''the sort of people to give you two years for drinking cider.'' His lawyer had told him, ''My boy, eleven of these men are for life conviction, and the other is for hanging before hearing the evidence.'' Asked about the protest over his London engagement, he attributed it to racism and, perhaps, jealousy over his £1,000-a-week salary. But this would pass when the actors realized that he was a ''loyal, true fellow.''[7]

His charm did not melt the cold anger of the protesters. Nor were the music hall managers anxious to upset the public and the licensing officials by employing such a controversial performer. It was best, the managers decided, to postpone Johnson's engagement until ''public opinion might be accurately gauged.'' With this bold move, Johnson's London career was ''left in abeyance.''[8]

An unscientific poll was conducted on the night of August 25 by Johnson himself. Dressed to watch but not to perform, he went to the Euston Theatre for the first performance. When he entered his private box, he was loudly cheered by those in the cheaper seats in the gallery and pit. These same supporters interrupted the performance of two female singers who had been vocally opposed to Johnson. Those sitting in the more expensive seats, however, took no part in the outbursts. The same scenario was repeated later that night at the South London Palace. Among the noisier element, cheers outnumbered hisses, and the wealthier patrons sat in cold silence.[9]

By their silence the ''better people,'' those who formed public opinion, had spoken. Only one member of the British aristocracy defended the champion, and he was the quarrelsome and eccentric Marquis of Queensberry. According to Queensberry, as long as laws allowed blacks to perform with, box, and marry whites, Johnson should be treated fairly and allowed to perform, fight, and marry as he wished. Of course, Queensberry favored legislation that would prohibit any such interracial dealings. Until such laws were passed, one should not blame Johnson: "We pride ourselves in this country on fair play. Give the man fair play and take on yourselves . . . the lawmakers, the blame for the present state of affairs." As Queensberry said, and a *New York Times* editorialist affirmed, Johnson was not the primary sinner; rather it was a public that glorified brute acts and allowed the races to mix legally.[10]

Like the grouse season that year in England, public acceptance of Johnson was spotty. Though denied the stage, he was not prohibited from the ring. At the Rosherville Gardens in Gravesend, he boxed exhibitions before cordial crowds. As a boxer—a beast—he was accepted; as a performer—dancer, singer, bass viol player—he was rejected. The irony went unobserved. One writer commented that Johnson's superiority likened him "with brutes rather than with human beings." Yet it was insisted that he act only like a brute, that he not show his humanity. The stereotype was reinforced by the exclusion of any evidence to the contrary.[11]

A few days after sparring at Gravesend, all Johnson's professional activities in England were abruptly halted. While driving with his wife near Victoria Station in London, the champion was broadsided by a drunken taxicab driver. Johnson was injured—he wrenched his back and suffered from "nervous shock"—but not very seriously. The wreck punctuated a sadly disappointing English tour. He had come to Britain expecting to fatten his pocketbook with money earned from stage appearances. He left leaner by one automobile.[12]

Even his title, his last hope for money, was threatened. It was sought not so much by other fighters as by boxing bureaucrats. The French Federation of Boxing Clubs, which governed the sport in that country, stripped Johnson of his title. It was impossible, said Victor Breyer, one of the federation's spokesmen, to allow a convicted criminal to hold such an exalted title. Soon there was a proposal before the even more influential International Boxing Union to follow the federation's example. Although the union rejected the proposal, the period of confusion hurt Johnson's chances for a profitable title defense.[13]

It was winter, and Johnson was broke. Rumors floated back to America that the once proud champion had been humbled and that he had started drinking heavily. In a letter to *Le Matin*, a Parisian daily, he said he would fight any man for a personal stake of between 100,000 and 200,000 francs ($20,000 to $40,000). But there were no takers. The only men willing to battle him were wrestlers. He accepted. He had no choice. He needed the money. The bouts were usually staged at the Nouveau Cirque in Paris. Sometimes Johnson was cast as the hero, as when he fought a German named Urbach. When the German, evil incarnate to the French crowd, used dirty tactics, Johnson laughed in his face. Other times Johnson was the villain. Switching from wrestling to boxing tactics, he knocked out a Liberian named Andre Sproul. Whether fixed or not, the fights were exhibitions in humiliation. But back in the United States few white sportswriters felt sorry for the champion. Reporting on the Sproul bout, Sandy Griswold remarked that Johnson was "tryin' to pick a quarrel with a wrestler. Now waddyeknowaboutthat? We could almost pity the poor old crooked coon." Almost—but not quite.[14]

Wrestling and boxing exhibitions in France and England provided a routine for his exile and furnished spending money. But they did not yield francs and pounds enough for Johnson to live in championship style. To earn that kind of money he had to defend his title, preferably against a white challenger. The British sporting press publicized the talents of their native son, Bombardier Billy Wells. But there were preachers and reformers in England who stood bolt upright and tight-jawed against that interracial match. The best white Frenchman was Georges Carpentier, a dashing, popular boxer. But he was far too light to challenge Johnson. In America there were a number of White Hopes but none who was clearly better than the rest. As for Johnson, he had neither the time nor the money to wait for protest to subside or boxers to grow physically and pugilistically. He needed a fight—immediately.[15]

To meet the expenses of Christmas, Johnson agreed to fight "Battling" Jim Johnson, an undistinguished ring veteran "three shades blacker" than the champion. A reporter for the *London Times* excused his ignorance of Jim Johnson's career by writing that the boxer was "better known in the United States than in Europe." In truth, he was a relative unknown in both places. Except for a few fights against Joe Jeannette, he had battled in quiet obscurity. Now, probably because he was readily available, he was matched for the world's title.[16]

The fight was held in Montmartre. Like all other entertainment in that section of Paris, it was late in getting started. By the time introductions were made, it was almost midnight. The vocal crowd, which had been excited by the previous match, demanded action. Johnson and Johnson did not give it to them. Jack Johnson looked in fine shape but fought with excessive caution, almost as if he were a sympathetic bystander who was raising his hands, palms spread, to break up a fight. Jim Johnson fought out of a crouch said to be even lower than Jim Jeffries's. If that were true, his head must have been barely inches from the canvas. All together, the combination made for, in the words of a proper English critic, "10 inconclusive and most unsatisfactory rounds."

After a few rounds most spectators had lost their patience. Cries of "fake" and other such "outspoken criticism" were sounded. Soon the outraged yells of the crowd drowned out all other sounds. Amid chants of "our money back" the clang of several bells went unheard. When the decision of a draw was announced, another "terrific hubbub" concluded the evening. Parisians had come to praise the champion. They left in a mood to bury him.[17]

Jack tried to account for his poor showing. He said he had broken his left arm, and the next day a physician announced that indeed his radius bone was shattered. The champion said the injury had occurred in an early round, but "the general impression" was that the arm was broken—if, in fact, it was broken—when the two fighters rolled to the canvas in the closing minute of the fight. Yet even if Johnson had fractured his arm, the spectators were still displeased. Jeers and hisses accompanied the announcement of his injury. Parisian crowds, like New York crowds, brooked no excuses.

In the United States black newspapers ran stories of the champion in exile. They read like visions of heaven, reflecting more the wish of the dreamer than any physical reality. Johnson, *Chicago Defender* editorialists reported, was a free man—a *free* black man. He was courted by royalty and idolized by the masses. It was said that he wanted to spend the rest of his life in Europe, that he would become a French citizen. Commenting on the champion's visit to Austria-Hungary, an editorialist observed, "When one sees how like a man [the black] is treated there, he wonders why he remains in America to be treated as a serf." According to many members of the black community, Johnson had found an earthly heaven.[18]

Truth was discrimination, indifference, and increasingly cheap hotels. Wherever he went outside of France, his exhibitions were greeted by protests and jeers. In Gothenburg, Sweden, for example, he was scheduled to wrestle Jess Pedersen. But before the match could take place Johnson insulted a white woman, and Swedes reacted with hostile demonstrations. The contest was canceled, and Johnson left the country. Joe Jeannette, who was traveling in Europe at the time, heard stories of Johnson's drinking. It was said that the champion was going to pieces.[19]

Englishmen, particularly, objected to any appearance of Johnson on a stage or in a boxing ring. Time and again protests forced timid promoters to cancel exhibitions involving the champion. Yet there were Englishmen who hoped to profit from Johnson's misfortune. A. F. Bettinson, promoter for the prestigious National Sporting Club, offered the champion £3,000 to defend his title against Sam Langford, the outstanding Boston heavyweight. Langford and Johnson were the two best fighters of their day, and they violently disliked each other. The match, if arranged, promised to be a classic.[20]

But Johnson would not touch it. Publicly he expressed outrage over the parsimonious offer. Calling the proposal "absolutely ridiculous," Johnson said that he was a "very proud" man and would not consider the National Sporting Club's sanctimonious stand. He had guaranteed Tommy Burns £6,000 and would not defend his title for a nickel less. Behind Johnson's public indignation, however, one senses a certain fear. Although he had defeated Langford eight years earlier, Johnson made every excuse not to fight Sam again. When London reporters asked when he would fight Langford, the champion would laughingly reply that he was "going to draw the color line." In Langford's case it was no joke. Johnson knew he would lose the title someday, and after the Jim Johnson fight he realized that that day might be close at hand, but he would not lose it to Sam Langford. And certainly not for a measly £3,000.[21]

The match Johnson wanted was against Frank Moran, a rugged Pittsburgh Irishman. Since turning professional in 1910, Moran had compiled an impressive record that included a victory over Al Palzer and tough fights with Gunboat Smith and Luther McCarty. There had also been defeats by several lesser heavyweights. In Moran, Johnson saw a white fighter, a respectable fighter, but not a dangerous one. Even though his own ability was fading, Johnson believed that he could still handle Moran. He hoped for a good payday. He knew there would not be many more.[22]

There was some feeling, however, that Johnson's hopes were unfounded. When Johnson signed the contract to meet Moran, he was handed a check for 175,000 francs that was not to be cashed until after the fight. The check was signed by Charles McCarthy, a former

Coney Island showman. The check was worthless. Johnson, Moran, and McCarthy all knew this. The sole purpose of the inflated sum was to ignite interest in the match, give it the aura of a big money fight. In truth, the boxers had agreed to fight for the gate receipts and motion picture rights. Since this was the arrangement, it was commonly believed that the bout was fixed to go at least ten rounds. There would be little interest in a film of a one-round fight.[23]

Johnson trained as if the fight were indeed in the tank. He was supposed to spar daily at Luna Park on the outskirts of Paris. Most days he did not show up. When he did, most of his program consisted of humorous observations concerning his "consumptive condition." There was little boxing and no conditioning. But it was hardly necessary, for Moran was training no harder. As one reporter for the *London Times* observed, "if it is true that American children are praying for Moran's victory, . . . they had better pray very hard."[24]

The fight was staged at the Velodrome d'Hiver, a covered bicycle track in Paris. It was a beastly hot night, and the ring was garishly decorated. Beneath a purple silk canopy, it was bathed in an electric illumination that gave a ghastly greenish tint to everything and everybody around it. Still, recalling the night many years later, Fred Dartnell remembered that it was quite wonderful. Paris was beautiful and gay as perhaps it would never be again. The worlds of beauty, finance, sport, literature, and art were well represented at ringside. There were Goulds and Vanderbilts, counts and earls, Rothschilds and princesses. There was an Eastern prince, coffee-colored, elegant, with wonderful pearls. There were hundreds of women in beautiful silk dresses and expensive jewels. For Dartnell, "It was La Mode."

Keeping order, and cutting the most striking figure, was referee Georges Carpentier, slender and handsome, dressed in a silk shirt and white flannels. For the occasion he had learned a few expressions in English—"break away," "get back," "don't hold." The nationality of his teacher was obvious, for he chewed gum and spoke with an American accent.

The fight started slow and got slower. The lead reporter for the *New York Times* wrote that "it was positively the poorest bout every staged as a championship contest." Other reporters were marginally kinder, but all agreed that the bout was certainly bad. In the early rounds it appeared that Johnson could knock out Moran at any time. In fact, the "cinematograph people" were frightened that the champion might get angry and do just that. But the fear was unnecessary. Johnson smiled throughout the fight and never really tried to hurt his opponent.[25]

Defensively Johnson was still sound, but the crowd of about 7,000 had not come to the fight to admire his defensive skill. There were hoots and howls and cries of "fake," but the commotion did not affect the champion. Although Moran looked jaundiced under the green lights and was cut above both eyes, he was not hit hard. Either Johnson had lost his punch or he had agreed to carry Moran the full twenty rounds. Even his wife's cries of "hit him, Daddy" and "come along, Poppa" failed to excite the champion to action. In twenty rounds there was not one knockdown, and by the time the fight ended, hundreds of spectators had left the arena in disgust. Johnson was the clear winner and was given the decision. But the crowd booed anyway.

The bout began on June 27 but ended after midnight. The fight was but one phase of what a *New York Times* columnist called "the gay Paris season." Still to come was the climax, the Grand Prix. The auto race would be run as Europe sped toward tragedy. Less than twelve hours after Johnson left the ring in Paris, Archduke Francis Ferdinand and his wife Sophie got into a Graefund Stift automobile for a ride along the Miljacka River in the Bosnian capital of Sarajevo. As they passed Schiller's grocery store on the Appel Quay, Gavilo Princip, a Serbian student, stepped out of the crowd and shot the royal couple. At the time newspapers called the event a deep personal tragedy for Emperor Franz Josef. A few years later it would be called the severest tragedy for mankind.[26]

Viewed from this vantage point, the Johnson-Moran fight was the last gathering of the old sporting order before the Great War. To those who were there, in retrospect it seemed better than it really was. But, then, Europe during that summer had taken on a golden glow. England was greener, Paris was gayer, Belgium was drier. Optimism and the belief in progress came easy, at least for some of the people who wrote books. In truth, Johnson was a witness to and an illustration of the hypocrisy, seediness, and meanness of the order. As he left the ring, people crowded around him to shake his hand, to touch him. The next day he was once again an outcast, with creditors and bill collectors knocking at his door.[27]

France, especially Paris, was out of the question. By the end of August Alexander von Kluck's First Army was within 25 miles of Paris. A dark, fierce-looking man whose face was lined with dueling scars and who carried a rifle as well as a pistol, von Kluck led an advance that seemed as inexorable as it was terrifying. The leading French commander, Joseph Jacques Cesaire Joffre, talked of giving up Paris and making a final stand south of the Seine, Aube, and Ormain rivers. In preparation for this decision the French government packed up and left for Bordeaux on the Atlantic coast. Old and able Joseph Simon Gallieni, commander of the ragtag forces in Paris, stood ready for disaster.

It was no place for a boxer, even a champion. Johnson left for London. His attitude toward England was curious; for some unfounded reason he always expected to be treated fairly there, as if the Rugby legends of "fair play" extended throughout English society. When his hopes were shattered by the cold reality of prejudice and racism, he was always disappointed.

As usual, he arrived in London with plans for making money, big money, money that he desperately needed. He was living on credit. He was supposed to have received $14,400 from his fight with Moran, but Johnson claimed that he was not paid a cent. He was corroborated by the promoter Dan McKetrick, who told John Lardner that neither Johnson nor Moran was paid, nor, for that matter, was McKetrick himself. According to this story McKetrick, who was also Moran's manager, developed a dislike for the Pittsburgh fighter—an intense, bitter, Irish dislike. "I'm as bitter a man as there is in the world," he said a few years before his death. Therefore, to pique Moran, McKetrick connived to have the profits of the fight impounded. The Parisian lawyer who arranged the transaction was promptly drafted into the army and killed in the opening engagement of the war. This left the profits of the fight safely in the Bank of France, and McKetrick, Moran, and Johnson broke.[28]

The story may be true, though undoubtedly like most boxing tales it has been refined over the years. At any rate, there is no doubt that Johnson found himself in a pressed financial condition. And in London, where patriotic athletes in droves were answering Kitchener's call for men, Johnson's thespian and pugilistic talents were in little demand. Only on the streets was Johnson able to attract a crowd, and that ability caused problems of its own. Once when a group of people surrounded his automobile, Johnson was arrested for using "obscene language" to scatter the gawkers. Another time he was fined £2 when onlookers gathered around his car and obstructed traffic. Johnson complained that he could not prevent people from looking at him. The magistrate suggested that he had better learn how.[29]

There were some hard times. With no real source of income, his credit rating dropped. Fewer and fewer people were willing to invest in his can't-miss dreams. Even his lies returned to haunt him. In the days after he first arrived in Europe, he told reporters that he had become a French citizen. Now with Frenchmen dying by the thousands in places like Aisne, Artois, Ypres, and the Chemin des Dames, Johnson was questioned about his French citizenship and why he wasn't fighting for France. It had all been a mistake, he said. And to prove the fact, he took an oath at the American Embassy in London that he was a loyal citizen of the United States. No, he had "never even dreamed of expatriating himself." War made such matters extremely serious.[30]

At home Americans carefully followed the war, but in a detached sort of way, as one follows the tragedies reported in the newspapers of people one does not know. The stories of Von Kluck, Joffre, and the Marne were more interesting than real. American dailies still had plenty of space for other subjects. Undoubtedly, millions of men turned to the sports page before the front page and read about the exploits of Ty Cobb before those of General Foch. In America White Hopes could still raise an eyebrow, and though Johnson was out of the country, few had forgotten that he was still champion. This was a remembered and unforgiven fact.

In the years since Johnson defeated Jeffries, a succession of White Hopes had risen, briefly titillated the public's imagination, and then abruptly fallen from grace. Perhaps the best was Luther McCarty. He looked like the real thing. He was big and strong and was managed by Billy McCarney, who was known in boxing circles as the "professor" because of a two-week stint at the University of Pennsylvania law school. McCarty started fighting in 1911, and in less than three years he had defeated all the other major White Hopes, knocking out Carl Morris, Al Kaufman, Jim Flynn, and Al Palzer, from whom he won the white heavyweight championship. McCarney planned to take his fighter to London and Paris, but before they departed it was arranged that McCarty would fight Arthur Pelkey on Queen Victoria's birth date in Calgary, Canada. The fight, which saw no fighting, was held on an overcast day. The bell rang, the two men clinched, and McCarty fell to the ground. The sun came out, McCarney said, as the referee counted, but withdrew behind the clouds on the number 10. Spectators screamed "fake." Eight minutes later McCarty was pronounced dead.[31]

This freak accident made Pelkey the new white heavyweight champion. Never a good fighter, he did not respond well to this unfamiliar exalted position. In his next seventeen fights he was knocked

out twelve times, at which point he prudently retired. The first person
to knock him senseless, Gunboat Smith, became the next of the
White Hope champions. He was far better than Pelkey, though not as
good as McCarty. Besides victories over the best white heavyweights,
he held a decision over Sam Langford in a fight that was probably
fixed. Reporters said he would certainly defeat Johnson. Smith himself was not so sure. As he said years later, "I knew in my heart that I
wasn't the champion of the world. White, yes—but there was Jack
Johnson."[32]

In the spring of 1914 Gunboat crossed the Atlantic, supposedly
wanting to fight Johnson. However, there were serious questions
about the genuineness of Smith's mission. Fred Dartnell went to
Gunboat's training quarters at Harrow. Several times Dartnell asked
the boxer when he would fight Johnson. Smith ignored the question.
Finally, forced to answer, Gunboat said, "Oh, Johnson will wait,"
and he snapped his mouth shut, as if to close the discussion. But as
an afterthought he added, "And the longer he waits, the better."[33]

While Johnson waited, Smith defended his Caucasian title
against France's Georges Carpentier. It was a confusing fight for
Smith. As he recalled, Carpentier "was always on the floor. Every
time you'd go to hit him, he was a fellow that from the legs down
he'd do all his ducking. You didn't know whether he was on the floor
or up. Well, I says, 'I'll fix him. I'll wait till he goes down, then when
he's coming up I'll bat him.' Well, he went down and I thought he
was coming up and I let one go and he goes down again, and he don't
come up at all." Carpentier's manager cried "foul," and after a moment's hesitation referee Eugene Corri agreed. Carpentier was now
the white heavyweight champion.[34]

Carpentier's main problem was physical: he weighed only about
160 pounds. The idea that he might challenge Johnson was ludicrous,
to him as much as to anyone else. Shortly after defeating Smith, Carpentier enlisted in the French army. He let the title of white heavyweight champion, an honor that never seemed to interest him much,
fall into limbo. What had been conceived in the minds of race-con-
scious reporters suffered a fate similar to other dearly held turn-of-
the-century myths. After July 1914 the title was never again mentioned.

If the white title was lost in the confusion of the Great War,
American White Hopes were still anxious to redeem their race and
fatten their bank accounts. The crucial problem was that no clearly
superior White Hope emerged from a singularly undistinguished

group. Al Palzer knocked out Al Kaufman and Bombardier Wells and then was flattened by Luther McCarty and Frank Moran. Carl Morris's star rose and fell swiftly, but not as quickly as Boer Rodel's or Jim Coffey's. As a *London Times* editorial pointed out, part of the problem was the American process of hero selection: "They are always telling us that they have discovered some colossal person of Herculean strength, who has only to learn how to box to become a world's champion. The trouble is that the very heavy heavy-weight cannot learn to box." It was inconceivable to most Americans that bigger was not, *ipso facto*, better.[35]

The biggest of the hopefuls was Jess Willard, who came from Pottawatomie County, Kansas. He was slightly over 6 feet, 6 inches tall and weighed in excess of 250 pounds. As a boxer he was severely handicapped by poor defensive technique and slow hands and feet; but he was as good as, perhaps better than, most of the other White Hopes. After a checkered career that included more than a score of unimpressive victories and a few equally unimpressive defeats, he knocked out two fighters in quick succession. It was at that point that he challenged Johnson, but rather than press his luck and ruin his modest string of victories, he withdrew from active boxing. This enraged other fighters, whose managers proclaimed Willard "no better qualified to fight for the title than the average spermaceti whale." But the cessation had its merits, the most important of which was keeping Willard's stock with the public reasonably high.[36]

Eventually Johnson was notified of Willard's availability as a challenger. Jack Curley, the champion's old friend, arranged the match. Johnson was willing—he needed the money—but finding a location for the bout presented problems. Europe was out of the question. In 1915 European eyes would be focused on other areas, on Gallipoli and Serbia and the miles of trenches in France. There was no demand to watch two Americans fight for a thing as frivolous as a boxing title. Because Johnson was a fugitive, he could not return to the United States to fight. The next best thing, Curley decided, was to hold the fight close to an American border. He decided on Juarez. Johnson agreed, and in early 1915 he left England for Buenos Aires, from which he was to travel to Tampico via Barbados and Havana.[37]

Juarez was a poor choice. In fact, any place in Mexico would have been a foolish choice, for the country was torn by revolution. By February 1915 Alvaro Obregón had captured Mexico City for the Constitutionalists. His chief, Venustiano Carranza, was safe in Veracruz. Together the two controlled the capital and much of the east coast from Matamoros to Veracruz. South of Mexico City was the heart of Emiliano Zapata's country, and north of the capital were the lands of Francisco "Pancho" Villa. Although at any time one leader might join another, no alliance was certain, and confusion and political intrigue were the order of the day. Added to this home-grown anarchy were the Byzantine efforts of German spies, who were preparing to bring the old dictator, Victoriano Huerta, back from exile. North of the border, Americans carefully watched the action in Mexico, but there was no clear consensus about which faction would or should win.[38]

It was probably the high level of disorder that attracted Curley to Mexico. Fight promoters, like hard-core revolutionaries, work best in fluid situations, where your enemy one day might be your closest ally the next. Through serious negotiations, Curley had persuaded Carranza to allow Johnson to land in Veracruz and Villa to permit the fight to take place in Juarez. Both leaders, of course, rightfully demanded and were granted a piece of the action. For a while everything appeared set.[39]

Behind the routine announcements alliances were shifting. In theory, President Wilson and Carranza shared common visions—rule by a constitution. They both expressed their support of law and order. It was A. Bruce Bielaski's hope, therefore, that the United States could persuade Carranza to return Jack Johnson to government officials north of the border. He wrote a Bureau of Investigation agent in San Antonio that it might be possible to get Mexico to deport Johnson as an "undesirable citizen." Toward this end he told his agent to offer a $500 reward for any action that would help return Johnson to the United States. Through the Mexican Secret Service Carranza learned of Bielaski's offer.[40]

Vague rumors of Carranza's change of heart reached Johnson in Havana. He told reporters that he was unconcerned about the stories, but he was in no hurry to depart for Veracruz. When the rumors were confirmed—Carranza announced his intention to arrest Johnson when the boxer set foot in Mexico—Curley started a search for a new route to Juarez, where he still had a solid agreement with Villa. Maps were of no help. Johnson could not reach Juarez from the north, and he could not sail to any of the eastern ports. Short of sailing around Cape Horn to the west coast, there was no way for Johnson to reach Juarez. Once this reality was accepted, the site of the bout was switched from Juarez to Havana.[41]

Although farther from the United States, Cuba enjoyed important advantages over Mexico. It had, for example, a relatively stable government. General Mario Menocal was the sole power in Cuba, and he was enthusiastic about the fight. So was the Cuban Congress. It agreed that on the day of the fight all official business would be postponed to allow the politicians to attend. Even the Cuban people discovered that boxing was exciting, and although unfamiliar with the finer points of the sport, they jammed into railway stations and training quarters to watch the Americans work out.[42]

There were minor difficulties. Most of the first-class hotels drew the color line, which created housing problems for Johnson. And in their haste to arrange the contest promoters unwittingly scheduled the fight for Easter Sunday. The pious objected. One person wrote the *New York Times* asking how a newspaper that "always stands up for what is right and decent" had not protested against the desecration of the Christian celebration. An editor for the *Times* replied that given the deaths in Belgium, France, East Prussia, and the Carpathians, "how can we get excited over the battle of two utterly unimportant human outlaws who have contracted to break each other's noses for hire?" But the Cubans, sensitive to American opinion, took action. When United States Minister to Cuba William Gonzales complained of the Sunday date, the promoters were persuaded to set the fight back from April 4 to April 5. This "concession to American prejudice," if it did not satisfy strait-laced *Times* editors, was applauded by most Americans.[43]

Of a more serious nature were moves to get the champion deported. Bielaski learned through his men in Havana that the Cuban government would be receptive to an official United States request to deport Johnson. With this end in mind, the Assistant Attorney General wrote to Secretary of State Bryan to issue the formal request. Robert Lansing, who was then a counselor for the Secretary of State, did not share the Attorney General's desire to see Johnson deported. Lansing, a cautious, farsighted professional, refused to ask the Cuban government to ship the champion back to America as an "undesirable alien." Even if the Cuban authorities agreed, a circumstance Lansing believed was unlikely, it would set a bad precedent. America could never return the favor. Therefore, once again an impersonal decision by one branch of the United States government protected Johnson's fugitive status.[44]

While the government decided on a policy toward Johnson, the champion trained to defend his crown. But he did not train with real intensity. For a boxer he was old; he turned thirty-seven on March 31, less than a week before he fought Willard. What he needed was about three months of hard work. What he settled for was a month of light workouts. Reporters watched him as he failed to complete his training sessions. He would set out for a 9-mile run and quit after 5 miles. Scheduled sparring sessions were postponed with alarming frequency. Mostly Johnson posed—for stills, for moving pictures, for Cubans who had never before seen a boxing champion. It was if he were a boxer in a side show—all he had to do to defeat the local yokels was look strong and mean. Nat Fleischer, who later started the *Ring* magazine, stayed at the Palace Hotel with Johnson. The champion, Fleischer recalled, was arrogant and confident, but "his carousing in France and Argentina had softened him." Physically, he was a far cry from the man who had defeated Jeffries in 1910.[45]

Willard trained with grim determination. His sparring partners suffered. Walter Menahan, a willing if untalented fighter, repeatedly had his nose broken. Others were so badly cut that Willard occasionally had to cancel sparring sessions to allow his partners time to recuperate. Even in bad weather Willard worked. In outdoor rings made greasy by sweat, blood, and rain, the challenger relentlessly punched his bruised sparring partners. Unlike Johnson, who preferred swimming to sparring and driving race cars to running, Willard took the match seriously. He believed the White Hope hyperbole.[46]

When asked about his erratic training, Johnson smiled. "I am the best judge of my condition, and I am satisfied," he said. Satisfied that he could defeat a man ten years his junior. Satisfied that if necessary he could fight the scheduled forty-five rounds. Some boxing experts, in fact, believed that Johnson was too satisfied, too confident. Rumors that the fight was fixed were rife in Havana bars. According to these stories Johnson's confidence was all a pose, for he had agreed to lose the fight. As early as mid-February the *Chicago Herald* sportswriter Billy Birch, who knew both Johnson and Curley, said the match would probably be a "frame-up." Johnson needed money and wanted to return to the United States, Birch reported. By agreeing to lose, Johnson hoped to pocket more money and receive a reduced sentence when he returned to America.[47]

How much truth there was in the rumors is difficult, if not impossible, to say. Years after the fight Johnson said yes, he had agreed to lose. He had received a promise of $30,000 and a guarantee that his problems in America would be "fixed." He said this, however, in 1919, when he was angling for a rematch with Willard. Even before the fight Johnson had indirectly approached the United States government. Working through Robert Cantwell, a former agent for the Bureau of Investigation, Johnson expressed his willingness to lose if he could get his Mann Act penalty reduced to a heavy fine. He was broke and in a mood to negotiate. Bielaski refused to bargain. He was "very much opposed" to any deal that would allow Johnson to escape a prison term. Johnson, he said, would be treated "as any other fugitive," and the Bureau of Investigation would not place itself in a "compromising position" by dealing in any way with the champion. Whether or not Bielaski's decision was then relayed to Johnson is unknown. If it was, it did not affect his training.[48]

Probably Johnson was willing to take a beating from Willard if it would get him a reduced sentence. But unable to arrange such a deal, he decided to fight honestly. Certainly Jack Welch, who refereed the bout, believed that the fight was not fixed. He said Johnson was so confident that the night before the match he bet $2,500 on himself to win. Undoubtedly the champion underestimated the big, clumsy challenger. Perhaps he also misjudged the effect that age and easy living had had on his own ability. If the fight were fixed, then it was certainly a most curious set-up.[49]

It was hot and still. In the green hills that surrounded the Oriental Race Track in Marianao, 10 miles outside of Havana, no breeze stirred the palm trees. The only activity in the hills was the milling around of roughly 5,000 people who hoped to see the match free. Below, 15,000 to 20,000 others waited for the fighters to enter the ring. Most waved white flags, symbols of their racial preference. It was an orderly crowd, but Cuban officials were taking no chances. Around the ring stood a large contingent of rural guards, pistols and machetes strapped to their sides. It was 12:30 in the afternoon, time for the fighters to make their entrances.[50]

Shortly after one o'clock they began to fight. Willard was slow; his boxing technique was pathetically crude. He stood ramrod straight and stuck out his long left arm in an attempt to keep his opponent at a distance. A few years before Bearcat MacMahon had ignored Willard's left and beaten him soundly. A few years later Jack Dempsey would step inside the extended left and break Willard's jaw. Johnson, however, respected the bigger man. For the first ten rounds there was little action. Willard moved about stiff-legged, looking for an opening in Johnson's defense. The champion smiled, talked to Willard's handlers, and permitted the fight to go a respectable distance for the sake of the cameramen.

After the tenth round Johnson increased the pace of the fight. He started to hit Willard with hard, stinging punches. He landed right-hand leads and digging counters to Willard's ribs and face. He maneuvered Willard into the corners and then beat him unmercifully. It was a boxing lesson. Willard, no longer the challenger, became a punching bag. For about ten rounds Johnson did as he pleased. He failed in only one thing—he could not knock out the hefty challenger. After more than an hour of fighting Willard was still strong and ready.

Johnson was visibly tired. After the twentieth round it seemed as if he knew he could not knock out Willard and he could not last the full forty-five rounds. In short, he knew the fight was lost. For a few rounds he tried to stall in hopes of gaining his second wind. But age and insufficient training had robbed him of his natural stamina. The crowd sensed Johnson's predicament and cheered louder for Willard, who also sensed the champion's plight but was not sure what to do about it.

At the end of round twenty-five Johnson told Curley to take Lucille out of the arena. He was tired, he said, and could not last much longer. He came out slowly for the twenty-sixth. For half the round the two fighters exchanged nothing more serious than glances. Then Willard moved. A left to the face, a right to the stomach, a left to the body, and a right to the jaw. The last was a long, looping punch that landed with full force.

Johnson fell. Spectators close to the action lunged toward the ring but were beaten back by the rural guards, who hit the anxious spectators with the flats of their machetes. Referee Welch began his count. Johnson lay on his back, his knees bent and his hand shading his eyes, as if he were trying to see something close to the sun. But as Welch counted, Johnson's knees flattened against the hot canvas and his arms fell to his sides. In this position he was counted out.

Billy Roche helped Johnson back to his corner. The ex-champion was clearly groggy, and it took five minutes for Johnson to regain full consciousness. As he sat on his stool, cheer after cheer echoed around the race track. White flags were waved by white men. Johnson's long reign was over. Willard had, in the words of a *New York Times* sportswriter, "restored pugilistic supremacy to the white race." Back in America whites rejoiced. As one editorialist wrote, Willard "made it possible for many millions of his fellow citizens to sit down to their dinners . . . with renewed confidence in their eight-inch biceps, flexed, and their twenty-eight inch chests."[51]

Immediately after the fight Johnson made no excuses. He said he had lost to a better fighter. Within a year, however, he had revised his story. In 1916 he sold his "confessions" to Nat Fleischer. According to this account, his wife left the fight to collect the last installment of the payoff money, and when she had it she signaled him that it was time to lie down. He thereupon promptly allowed Willard to win the fight. Johnson swore to the truth of this account "by the Holiness of my Maker and my dear beloved mother."[52]

Because of the prefight rumors that the bout was fixed and the photograph of Johnson "shading" his eyes and a general tendency to believe the worst of anyone, many people believed Johnson's story. Fred Dartnell, for example, remembered watching the film of the fight in a London theater shortly after Johnson's return from Cuba. After seeing the knockout, Dartnell looked at Johnson, whose face was "wreathed in smiles." Fix, Dartnell thought. And the expert boxing trainer William Muldoon had refused to attend the fight because he felt it might be fixed. However, no boxing authority who had been at the fight believed Johnson's "confessions." Tom Flanagan, the Canadian who helped to train Johnson for the contest, said Jack tried for a knockout in the fourteenth round, and when he failed he lost heart. The knockout in the twenty-sixth was "on the level." Nat Fleischer, Jack Welch, Jack Curley, and Jess Willard all agreed. The fight was honestly contested. More recently Jim Jacobs, a fight film collector, acquired the full film of the bout. After watching the fight, especially the knockout, it is difficult to believe Johnson's version.[53]

The roar of the European guns drowned out the controversy over the fight. Johnson had lost. Americans—whites and "intelligent colored folk"—a *New York Times* editorialist reported, were satisfied. But Americans' attitude toward the sport had been dramatically affected by the Great War. In 1908, when Johnson won the near worthless title in Australia, boxing was regarded as a remnant of a more brutal age, a relic of barbarism. Optimistic reformers were sure that people had outgrown—or were certainly rapidly outgrowing—such bloody exhibitions. Civilization and progress, they said, demanded an end to boxing. The Great War changed this pacifist attitude toward boxing and mankind. This growing uneasiness about the world was reflected in the pages of the *New York Times:* "Of course we would all like to feel that prizefights belong only to the crude past, when man was nearer the other animals, before he had become so thoroughly civilized. We would like to feel that way, too, about war. But . . . ." It was a "but" that was shattering a faith built strong over several hundred years.[54]

13

Exile's Return

IT SOUNDED ALMOST like fun. Although he was no longer champion, Johnson boasted that he was still the favorite of people everywhere. In London he lightened the war-heavy mood with his revue, "Seconds Out!" in which he boxed, sang, and played various instruments. He was a huge success, so big in fact that he decided to take his show on the road, where he played to warm, enthusiastic crowds. Summing up his tour, Johnson wrote, "Newspaper accounts of my efforts as an actor were highly favorable, and the capacity houses which greeted us were ample evidence that the reviews met with public approval."[1]

In truth, the years after Johnson lost his title were hardly enjoyable. To begin with, he was tired of Europe and longed to return to America. The day after he was defeated by Willard, Johnson applied for a passport. Under oath he said that no charges were pending against him in America and that he had never been convicted of a felony. Why he bothered to apply for the document—let alone lie—was a mystery. Government officials in the United States had no desire to see Johnson again, not even to punish him. At the direction of Secretary of State Bryan he was denied a passport. His steamer ride back to Europe from Cuba was a sign of failure, not a quest for adventure.[2]

As for his reception in England, it was certainly not warm and friendly. For a few weeks Englishmen were curious to see how the loss had changed Johnson, and they paid to watch his show. They soon discovered that the loss had not humbled him; he even hinted grandly that he had lost by design. His behavior was lighthearted, his smile broad, his movements a study in affectation. Soon Johnson was playing to near-empty houses, at which time he "ceased to be the agreeable gentleman with the settled smile and the shining white teeth." After his show flopped in the industrial town of Preston, Johnson fired Jack du Maurier, his theatrical manager, who had an acting part in "Seconds Out!" When du Maurier went to Jack's dressing room to collect his back pay, Johnson swore at him and violently punched him in the face, "injuring the structure of the eye."[3]

Before long Johnson was drawing more attention in law courts than on stage. Du Maurier sued Johnson and won a £107,5s. judgment. Johnson was also sued for breach of contract when he refused to pay for theatrical posters he had ordered. Again he lost the case. As with his previous visits to England, he ended up owing much more than he earned.[4]

Still, England seemed safer than the Continent. By February 1916 the slaughter at Verdun had started, and Johnson was not eager to leave the relative comfort of Great Britain. The British government, however, viewed the matter differently. Johnson was unpopular in America, a potential ally England did not want to offend, even in trivial ways like harboring famous fugitives. Therefore, Johnson would have to go. On February 29, 1916, the Home Secretary invoked the Aliens Restriction Act and gave Johnson three days to leave the country. Under the act the Secretary was not required to give any reason for his decision, and he didn't.[5]

Thrown out of England and barred from France because of the war, Johnson was now suffering from geographical as well as financial problems. There was no place he could go where he could be safe and still make enough money to maintain his customary life-style. This being the case, he opted for safety. He and his small following traveled to Spain, where internal factionalism made neutrality a necessity. The Army, the Church, and conservatives in general favored Germany, which tempted Spain with the vision of a free hand in Portugal and a Spanish Gibraltar. Liberals, regional minorities, and the bulk of the population were sympathetic to the Allies. The division made neutrality the only logical policy, which suited Johnson well.[6]

For the remainder of the war Johnson stayed in Spain. Times were hard. It was difficult to make much money. Mostly, Johnson just talked about success. It was reported that he had opened a boxing academy in Madrid and that King Alfonso XIII was an enthusiastic patron. The story, used for filler in American newspapers, was unfounded. Johnson opened an advertising agency, which he admitted was "not as successful as I could have wished."[7] Since this admission was the closest he ever came to saying he failed, his agency must have been a total bust. A strange country and an unfamiliar language were not the best circumstances for starting a new business.

Eventually he resorted to what he knew best—fighting. It was a logical move and may very well have succeeded had there been any bullfighters in Spain who knew how to fight without muleta and sword. Unfortunately there were none. In March 1916, before curious spectators, Johnson boxed Arthur Gruhan and Frank Crozier, two unknown fighters, in Madrid. Although the matches were little more than exhibitions, they were more lucrative than Johnson's other business efforts.[8]

Johnson's most interesting opponent in Spain was Arthur Craven, an eccentric avant-garde poet who billed himself as "the nephew of Oscar Wilde." Craven was a pip, a precursor of the later Dadaists. In his magazine, *Maintenant*, he denounced everything, and he was known to deliver lectures wearing only a jockstrap. As a disciple of Mallarmé, Rimbaud, and Baudelaire, he preferred the bohemian world of homosexuals, prostitutes, and thieves to the bourgeois one into which he was born. By 1916 he was as much an outcast as Johnson. Fleeing from a stint in the British military, he was in Spain and intended to go to America. But to do this he needed money.[9]

Craven and Johnson had met in Paris. Johnson liked to think of himself as a boxer and poet, Craven as poet and boxer. Both were flabby and out of shape, though Craven's softness was the more serious. And both were short of funds. The fight, if not a natural, offered interesting possibilities. The match was scheduled for early July, and posters were pasted to walls throughout Barcelona. Craven asked only that Johnson, "his pal Jack," allow the fight to go a few rounds and that he not hit him too hard.[10]

Even Spanish observers unused to boxing realized that the Johnson-Craven fight lacked authenticity. Before the match Craven obtained a large portion of his assured purse, enough to finance his trip to New York, and this left him in a satisfied, uncombative mood. The result was most unsatisfactory for the spectators who paid to see a fight. At the bell Craven covered his face with his fists, lowered his head, pulled his elbows close to his sides, and tried as much as possible to leave no part of his body exposed to a possible blow. He made no attempt to fight or even to look as if he were fighting. Instead, wrote his friend Blaise Cendrars, he "contented himself with turning round and round, *trembling visibly*. The Negro prowled around him like a big black rat around a Holland cheese, tried three times in a row to call him in order by three kicks to the rump, and then in an effort to loosen up the nephew of Oscar Wilde, the Negro thumped him in the ribs, cuffed him a bit while laughing, encouraged him, swore at him, and at last, all of a sudden furious, Jack Johnson stretched him out cold with a formidable punch to the left ear, a blow worthy of a slaughterhouse." In less than one minute the "fight" was over.[11]

The Catalan public roared with protest, invaded the ring, and demanded its money back. The arena was sacked and benches set ablaze, as the descendants of the Visigoths demonstrated their outrage. Johnson, who spent the night in jail for his own protection, was furious, swearing that Craven would pay for his cowardice. Craven, pleased by his showing, left for New York the next day.[12] He would mysteriously disappear a few years later.

The Craven fight satisfied the Spanish curiosity about boxing. In need of money, Johnson had to discover new ways to make a dollar. According to him, he chose a when-in-Rome approach. More specifically, he decided to participate in the *fiesta brava*. At the time Spanish bullfighting was locked in a golden age. There were two great fighters. José Gómez Ortega, "Joselito," worked his classic magic in Madrid. From a family of bullfighters, Joselito summed up the grace and style of the world before the Great War. His rival was the bandy-legged Juan Belmonte. A peddler's son with a nervous stammer, he had none of the classic grace of Joselito; indeed, he was a rebel in a tradition-bound sport, going as far as to cut off his *coleta*, the pigtail that marked a matador. What Belmonte possessed was raw, terrifying courage.[13]

Both Joselito and Belmonte advised Johnson to take up the sport, or at least so he claimed. Johnson wrote friends in America that he was going to fight a bull, and in his autobiography he said that he had one bullfight. He might have. No one ever doubted his courage or the extent to which he would go to become the center of attention. If he did engage in a *corrida*, it was a one-time proposition. It was not a career change.[14]

After a few months his life in Spain, like his life elsewhere, found its own routine. He drank and he talked and he tried to con anyone who would listen to him. United States agents kept a loose watch on him, and their reports detail Johnson's predicament. Major

John Land, military attaché in Madrid, spent a week with Johnson in 1918. Johnson, he said, was surrounded by "a bunch of down-and-outs, cheap gamblers, pimps and prostitutes." They drank in cheap saloons and complained bitterly about America. Most wanted to leave Spain but could not obtain passports and had nowhere to go in any case. So they passed their days complaining and drinking toasts to the German army.[15]

Lang's account contradicts Johnson's. With typical drama, Johnson's autobiography casts him as an important government agent in Spain. Major Lang, wrote Jack, gave him the task of uncovering German submarine bases off the coast of Spain. He was—as he normally was in his own stories—completely successful: "For my work and the information which I obtained I received due recognition from the officials under whose instructions I operated, and I had the great satisfaction of being of service to my native country, even thought I was in exile."[16]

Although his reported deeds were imaginary, he did make tentative efforts to join the American cause. To join, that is, for a price. Once America declared war on Germany, Johnson said he was ready to fight for President Wilson's noble ideals. To this end Frank Armand, a friend of Johnson, wrote Emmett Scott, Special Assistant to the Secretary of War, that Jack was anxious to "win back the good opinion of the American people" and was willing to serve the American forces in France in any capacity. If, however, he "should survive the war" he would expect the government "to wipe out his past record" and give him a full pardon. Since all three men involved in the exchange were Texans, Armand believed that Scott's help would serve the people of the great state of Texas.[17]

State pride, at least in this instance, was not enough. When Scott relayed Armand's request to the Justice Department he was promptly told to forget about the case. Raymond Morris in Justice reported that Johnson's crime was so serious—indeed, "the details of which are in every respect offensive to the ears of decency" and were such that "time cannot efface"—that his department could not consider a deal. This became the official position. The war would have to be won without the services of an aging and overweight ex-champion.[18]

To the American government Johnson, far from a hero, was a suspected enemy. Some believed that he was working for Germany. For example, when he began his advertising agency he hired Moritz Moisevics, a revolutionary anarchist who had spent some time in a French internment camp at the beginning of the war. It was said that

Johnson's agency itself was a "cloak for German activities." It is true that most of Johnson's friends in Barcelona were vocally pro-German, a position Jack adopted when he was snubbed by the American government. It was with distrust and suspicion, then, that American agents and officers in Madrid regarded Johnson.[19]

If Johnson was employed by Germany, the Kaiser did not pay him well. By the end of the war Johnson was broke. Although he still dressed well, his clothes showed signs of wear. His fur coat, which he said had cost $5,000, was now shabby, and he was forced to pawn his wife's diamonds. Even his charm as a big attraction had worn as thin as his shirt cuffs. For a ten-round fight he was lucky to get 1,000 pesetas.[20]

The years had robbed him of his youth. He was fat, short of wind, and well on his way to becoming a sideshow freak. The men he fought in Spain in 1918 and 1919 were often comical and sometimes pathetic. One in particular stands out: Blink McCloskey. Johnson and McCloskey fought a series of matches throughout Spain. Before each fight, Blink removed his glass eye and placed it in his corner. Then Johnson would "cut up" the one-eyed fighter with sharp punches. The Spaniards thought that the whole show was "fine sport."[21]

There must have been pain in this for Johnson. The respect he once commanded was rapidly fading in the strange land where he was living. Back in America, where only prison awaited him, his mother had recently died and her body lay unclaimed in an interment vault. Bitterness became Johnson's closest companion. And when he was drinking he vented his rage. England, France, America—there was no freedom in those countries. He had been in all of them, he said, and he had been treated like a slave. In those countries freedom and fair play were hollow words. The war, he emphasized, proved that. He said he had proof that France and England started the conflict and that the British were the first to use asphyxiating gas. Only the Germans were honorable. "The Germans treat me as a man and my wife as a lady," he told an American military man in Barcelona.[22]

His attitude toward America was illogical but not uncommon among blacks at the time. He despised the way he had been treated in the United States but longed to return. In Spain he was treated fairly well but felt he had no chance for success. Even before the war ended he had decided to leave. In May 1918 he wrote Arthur Craven in Mexico, asking for 5,000 pesetas and three first-class tickets to Veracruz. Once there he believed that he and Craven could make a fortune boxing exhibitions. Craven was all for it and said he would send the money. He never did.[23]

When the war ended Johnson felt he had to leave Spain, even if he could not afford to travel first class. Mexico, so close to America and so far from God, seemed the perfect place. Toward this end, in March 1919 Jack, Lucille, and his nephew Gus Rhodes sailed for Cuba aboard the *Maria Christiana*. Except for a few months in 1915, he had been in Europe since 1913. Now he was headed toward America. United States government officials noted the direction Johnson traveled. Agents in Havana were informed. If Johnson stepped on American soil, lawmen would be waiting for him. There would be no more surprises.[24]

His stay in Cuba was short, hardly long enough for a good meal and a night's sleep. Then he was off for Carranza's Mexico. It was the year that Carranza consolidated his control over the country, the year that saw Villa's army in the north scattered and Zapata gunned down in the south. For a brief time Carranza was alone at the top of the greasy pole of Mexican politics. Of course, a year later he went too far in his quest for absolute power and, like Zapata, was killed. But at the time Johnson disembarked at Vera Cruz, Carranza's word was law.[25]

The American military attaché in Mexico City was told to watch Johnson, but that was the most he could do. Unlike in 1915, American agents could expect no help from Carranza, who by 1919 had turned against the United States. The main source of the conflict was the question of foreign property rights in revolutionary Mexico. In Article 27 of the Constitution of 1917, Mexican legislators proclaimed the rights of villagers to land and the ownership of subsurface deposits. Carranza, an ardent nationalist, supported this fundamental position, a stand that shocked and outraged American capitalists, who believed that the right of private property and the sanctity of contracts should have been the Eleventh and Twelfth Commandments. In short, at a time when oil was tightening its grip on the Western world, Mexico announced that it owned everything below its soil, regardless of previous contracts or practices.[26]

American oil barons reacted as if insulted by a lowly rig worker. Mexico, they said, could not do such a perfidious thing. Senator Albert Fall, a Republican spokesman for oil interests, and even Secretary of State Robert Lansing believed that eventually the military would have to settle the issue. Tempers flared. Mexico's coziness with Germany was bad enough, but this— this involved big money. If the two countries were still far from open conflict, it was difficult to convince Mexican leaders of the fact. America had in the past been all too eager to invade Mexico, and border crossings had followed disputes much less serious than this one. For Zapata, Carranza, and other leaders the Revolution seemed threatened by the money lords of the north.[27]

As an exile from the United States and a known opponent of American policy in general, Johnson was warmly received in Mexico. It was easy for Mexican officials to believe that Johnson was a victim of perverted American justice, and they treated him like an oppressed brother. Even Carranza, whose personality was the direct opposite of Johnson's, found time in his busy schedule to talk with the boxer. This attention was enough to convert Johnson to the Mexican cause. It was even rumored in the American intelligence community that Johnson had accepted a commission under the Carranza government.[28]

Johnson's connections in high places served him well. He was able to demand treatment as a "free man." One afternoon he and a group of friends went to eat at Sanborn's original drugstore and restaurant in Mexico City. Walter Sanborn, the American owner of the beautiful House of Tiles, drew the color line and refused to serve Johnson. Jack left but returned a few hours later with three or four of Carranza's generals. They drew their pistols and demanded that Sanborn apologize. Mexico, they informed him, was not a "white man's country." Sanborn was forced to shake hands, embrace, and finally serve Johnson. By that time a large crowd had gathered, and everyone in the restaurant ate and drank free of charge.[29]

The boxing rings of Mexico were also open to Johnson. There was talk that he would box leading white heavyweights in Mexico. Carl Morris's name was mentioned. So was Porky Flynn's. But these fights never panned out. The men Johnson fought were strictly third-raters: men like Tom Cowler, Paul Sampson, Marty Cutler, and Captain Bob Roper were at best merely sparring partner material. But that sort of fight best suited Johnson's needs. With rolls of fat encasing his midsection and "otherwise entirely out of condition," Johnson was not in the market for a lean and hungry opponent. Although he publicly said he wanted to fight Jack Dempsey for the title (which Dempsey had taken from Jess Willard in 1919), he must have known as he puffed through sloppy exhibitions that he was no longer a first-rate boxer.[30]

The only thing he retained was his unsurpassed ability in self-promotion. As America experienced interracial violence in the summer of 1919, Johnson announced that he had the answer to the race

question. Leave America, he counseled fellow blacks. Leave America
for the free nation of Mexico. In *Gale's Magazine*, an IWW periodi-
cal printed in Mexico City, an advertisement for the Jack Johnson
Land Company read: "Colored People: You are lynched, tortured,
mobbed, persecuted and discriminated against in the 'boasted' land
of liberty; own a home in Mexico, where one [man] is as good as another, and it is not your color that counts, but simply you."[31]

Such statements attracted the attention and hostility of American officials. Johnson had always been a problem, they reasoned, but
only by example. He had never made truly revolutionary speeches.
Now in Mexico all that had changed. He had to be watched closely.
An American spy who had infiltrated the Socialist Party in Mexico
told his United States contacts that Johnson wished to spread race
propaganda and was interested in socialist ideology. E. O., the spy,
arranged to take boxing lessons from Johnson in order to keep close
tabs on him.[32]

Along the border between Mexico and the United States American officials were especially nervous about Johnson's racial-egalitar-
ian pronouncements. One American military officer reported that
Johnson entertained Mexican troops by sparring and then telling
them how much better they were than the "damn American gringos." In a speech given before a cheering crowd in front of the Vega
Hotel in Nuevo Laredo, Johnson said that when and if the gringos invaded Mexico, American blacks would stand alongside their Mexican
brothers. At a time when illegal border crossings were occurring with
irritating frequency—indeed, Villa had fired on El Paso only a month
before Johnson's speech—this kind of talk was seen in itself as a hostile act.[33]

It is difficult to say how many of Johnson's statements were sincere. Certainly he believed—he knew—that he had been mistreated in
the United States and that millions of other American blacks were
similarly, if in less sensational ways, abused. This much he meant, beyond question. But Johnson, though a bitter man, was not a doctri-
naire revolutionary. He had no creed, no ideology, perhaps no absolute beliefs. His ethics were akin to those of a circus barker. For a
price he would, and eventually did, espouse any position. In Mexico
he supported a line that was well grounded in fact and consistent with
his own experiences. It was a position that he could defend comfortably. But he did not defend it for free. As always, he expected something in return. When he arrived in Mexico he was broke. Supporting
Carranza was one way out of that condition. When he spoke about

equality in Mexico, about lynching and suffering in the United States, and about the evil gringo menace, he was paid by the Carranza government and protected by Carranza's generals. As in boxing, he was a professional. He did not take chances for free.[34]

Unfortunately for Johnson, he had tied himself to a powder keg. He would be safe and fêted in Mexico only as long as his patron, Carranza, remained in power. And the lesson of the previous decade was that no Mexican leader lasted for long. In 1920 Carranza, who was supposed to step down as president, refused to relinquish his power. Instead he named Ignacio Bonillas, a puppet, as his personal choice for the presidency. This was going too far. Alvaro Obregón, a former general of Carranza's, rose in revolt. Backed by the Mexican labor organization and a clique of northern chiefs, Obregón forced Carranza to flee Mexico City. Before he could leave the country, he was murdered.

Before Carranza was killed, Johnson had only talked about returning to the United States. He had said that he would return if conditions were right, by which he meant if he could obtain a reduced sentence. But in Chicago District Attorney Charles Cline demanded "unconditional surrender." This had more or less closed the matter, and Johnson had returned to the Mexican boxing rings, where, though out of shape, he was still able to get fights.[35]

In fact, Johnson was settled quite comfortably in Tijuana. There, with the support of Estaban Cantu, governor of Lower California, and Fred Dato, Cantu's brother-in-law and a local boxing promoter, Johnson thrived both as a boxer and a businessman. He boxed only setups and was allowed to open a saloon, the Main Event Café, where he lived with Estelle and Gus Rhodes. The Main Event was not the Café de Champion, and there were no boxers around Tijuana to rival Jim Jeffries, but Johnson was as well off as he had been in years.[36]

Then in May 1920 Carranza was shot, and overnight the political winds shifted. Friends of Carranza were now enemies of the state, or at least suspect. Johnson's comfortable life ended abruptly. His saloon was closed, and he was denied permission to box in Mexico. Governor Cantu, trying to keep his own balance in the shifting gusts, turned his back to Johnson's appeals. *El Monitor*, published in Mexicali, Lower California, reported that Johnson had been ordered to leave Mexico. Governor Cantu said that it was a necessary decision.[37]

Cantu was looking for support both in Mexico and in the United States. Less than two weeks after Carranza was shot, Cantu told

American agents that Johnson's standing in Mexico was no longer good. Indeed, the boxer had become involved in some "crooked transactions," and Cantu was anxious to deport him. If the United States would make a request, Cantu said, as a personal favor he would deliver Johnson to American authorities. Bureau of Investigation agents were justifiably suspicious. Eventually, they realized, Cantu would collect on his personal favor. Rather than put themselves in Cantu's debt they decided to decline the governor's generous offer.[38]

Johnson's status as *persona non grata* remained the same. One way or another, he had to leave Mexico by the end of July 1920. Again, but this time with added urgency, he tried to negotiate with Bureau of Investigation officials. He knew he could not obtain a reduced sentence, but he wished to be arrested and transported to Chicago with dignity. When Special Agent Dave Gershon interviewed Johnson in Tijuana, the former champion told him he would surrender if he were not handcuffed like an "ordinary criminal" and if he could be taken to Chicago by a black officer. He did not wish to be humiliated. Gershon refused to bargain. Beyond treatment in a "civil manner," he would not promise Johnson anything.[39]

Johnson had no choice. He had to leave. An embarrassment to Cantu, he could no longer make any money in Mexico, and he had reached a stage where the likelihood of prison was more attractive than the brutal clarity of Mexican politics. Special Agent W. A. Weymouth, who had visited Johnson several months before, realized the inevitability of the boxer's decision. Only by promoting his own fights could Johnson remain in Tijuana, and along those lines there was no hope for success. "He will soon be ready to return to this country," Weymouth told his superiors.[40]

He was treated with dignity. On the morning of July 20, 1920, he crossed the border into the United States. Waiting for him was U.S. Marshal George Cooley, Special Agent Dave Gershon, and a host of reporters and photographers. Johnson shook hands with Cooley and Gershon. They all smiled for the cameras. Johnson's clothes looked a bit shabby, but not nearly as bad as Cooley's. There were no black officers present, but neither were there any handcuffs. It was altogether a very peaceful surrender.[41]

Johnson chatted with the reporters. He seemed calm, even happy. One journalist wrote that he was in a "joyous mood," which was probably a slight misreading of the scene. Even so, Johnson seemed remarkably relaxed and candid. It was good to be home, he said. "No man, unless he has been through the experience, can realize the relief it brings when he returns to his country after being in exile for five years." One reporter asked him about his anti-American speeches. "You know I have changed my allegiance a number of times, but I am still an American." What would he do now? He would take his punishment and then start over again.

Later, locked in jail in Los Angeles, he talked some more. He wanted to set the record straight on several points. First of all he had made some mistakes, certainly. And he was sorry for them. But, he emphasized, he was still a great boxer and a loyal American. He reaffirmed that he had "laid down to Jess Willard in Havana" and he could still "lick any man in the world today." In addition, during the war he had done valuable secret service work in Spain.[42]

The statement was a plea for recognition. In his own mind he was still the world's champion, as absolutely as the day in July 1910 when he had battered the great Jeffries to the canvas. He still saw himself as "Papa Jack"—the best boxer, automobile racer, talker, and lover in the world. That it was now 1920 and Jack Dempsey was champion did not seem to matter. Mentally, Johnson was still undefeated. He would serve his time and then conquer the world again.

Chicago had changed. Between 1913 and 1920 Southern blacks by the thousands had left their walking plows and sharecropper poverty in search of a better—or, perhaps, less miserable—life. Many had followed the dream to Chicago, the focal point of the Great Migration. There was some substance to dreams. The Great War cut off the flow of poor, uneducated European immigrants into the stockyards, steel mills, foundries, and meat-packing plants of Chicago. Cheap, unskilled labor was in demand, especially after America started to send men as well as arms and food to Europe. Rural Southern blacks satisfied Chicago's industrial need. Daily, cars of the Illinois Central Railroad disgorged hundreds of fresh workers. The black population grew, as did the friction between the races. By 1917 there was serious stress, a result of job and housing competition and the summer heat. In 1919, as white soldiers returned to Chicago and racial competition heightened, a riot burned through the streets and slums of Chicago. For one of the first times in American history, whites and blacks fought each other as, if not equals, competitors. From the riot emerged a renewed sense of black solidarity and isolation. What little hope there was of a peaceful, integrated city was destroyed in the orgy of hate.[43]

For many blacks and whites Johnson was a visible symbol of the state of race relations. Although he had not been in America since 1913, in many black and white minds he still represented the ultimate of black competition and violence. He had, after all, bruised great white fighters and married beautiful white women. The potential for racial violence followed Johnson like an angry energy. Rumors of some sort of racial confrontation spread as the train carrying Johnson rolled across the Western desert toward Chicago. When the California Limited reached the Windy City, several thousand vocal blacks were waiting to greet their hero.[44]

They were disappointed. There was no Jack Johnson aboard the train. Fear of a riot had prompted federal authorities to remove him from the train before it reached Chicago. He was placed in the county jail at Joliet until officials believed he could be taken safely into Chicago. The change of plans seemed not to disturb Johnson. Unruffled, he talked to reporters about his future plans. As he chewed on a large cigar, he announced, "I'm damn glad to be back." And after he settled his legal problems, he intended to "clean up this Dempsey fellow."[45]

Clearly, he was not as repentant as federal lawmen had wished. Nor was he very helpful in solving still unanswered questions about his case. The new head of the Bureau of Investigation, Frank Burke, wanted to know if Johnson had paid any government agents to allow him to escape. Had he bribed DeWoody, Meyer, or Parkin? Under oath, Johnson was supposed to clear up the matter. But he wouldn't. Not, at least, until he had consulted his attorney.[46]

Influential government officials were anxious that Johnson serve his full sentence. As a public service the Department of State confidentially informed Burke that Johnson had offered his services to the "German Espionage organization" in Spain and had been a thoroughly reprehensible American during the Great War. In addition, Johnson's flippant attitude toward the seriousness of his crime upset officials. Johnson took an "I'll-soon-be-free" attitude. This reinforced the government's resolve that he serve his entire sentence.[47]

Show "no leniency in this scandalous case of white slavery," Wilbur Croft, head of the pious International Reform Bureau, counseled the Attorney General. Federal agents agreed. However, county officers in Joliet were charmed by Johnson's smiling presence. Although he could not get out on bail, jailors tried to make his stay pleasant. Soon rumors of Johnson's ice cream soda sprees and joy rides reached Washington. Chicago District Attorney Cline was incensed. Johnson, Cline said, should be treated "like a prisoner, not a hotel guest." To ensure this, Johnson was transferred to Geneva, Illinois. There, despite reports to the contrary, he was jailed in a more orthodox manner.[48]

Summer gave way to fall. Johnson remained in jail, waiting for resentencing. He was visited by friends and business associates, and together they planned his future. He still expected a reduced sentence, and so he boxed daily, looking forward to an early return to the ring. Then the blow landed. No leniency. Johnson had to serve the full year and a day. He sat silent and downcast as Judge Carpenter read his decision. A few days later he was transferred to the federal prison in Leavenworth.[49]

He started his prison term in style. About 500 people greeted the train bearing Johnson when it arrived in Leavenworth. A black chauffeur offered the use of his car to the former champion, and Johnson took over the wheel and drove to the prison himself. Once inside the gates he was assigned number 15,461 and made orderly of the prison baseball park. If he was good, the warden said, he would be appointed athletic director for the entire penitentiary.[50]

He did behave, and he was treated exceptionally well, almost as if he were a talented athlete in a boys' camp. For the most part this was due to the kindness of prison superintendent Denver S. Dickerson. As governor of Nevada, Dickerson had allowed the Johnson-Jeffries fight to be staged in Reno, and during the days before the bout he had enjoyed several talks with Johnson. A rugged, relaxed man, he regarded Johnson's crime rather leniently. Johnson, he reasoned, was a decent enough fellow. As long as the boxer remained decent, his stay was to be made as comfortable as possible.[51]

For the next ten months Johnson boxed and thought inside the prison walls. Prison officials exploited his name; he was used as an example of the way prisoners were treated in a modern system. Before large crowds inside the prison, he fought a series of exhibitions. He battled white fighters and black. The events were filmed, to be included in documentaries about prison life. Always, Johnson said he was well-treated, that he was glad to pay his debt to society.[52]

Johnson understood what was expected of him; by his actions and speech he had to show that he was not longer a threat to white society. Repentance preceded acceptance. A few years later he recalled his thoughts: "My stay in the prison, cutting me off as it did from the perplexities and the strife of life, gave me time to take stock of my friends and my enemies. I came to the conclusion that one of my greatest errors was my flight to Europe."[53] The statement might have been true, indeed probably was, but it was written more to convince and charm the American white public than to record his deepest feelings. He was tired of his life as an exile. He now wanted acceptance.

In some circles the "New Johnson" was welcomed. Sportswriters said he was fit and friendly and ready for Jack Dempsey. Prison officers said he was an ideal inmate. Even Attorney General Harry Daugherty, a close friend of President Harding, was impressed by Johnson's behavior. In late June 1921 Daugherty told reporters that he was considering freeing Johnson a few weeks early so that the boxer could attend the July championship bout between Dempsey and Georges Carpentier. The action, Daugherty emphasized, would be a "liberty bonus" for a "model prisoner."[54]

But it was not to be. In the minds of Bureau of Investigation officials memories of the old Johnson were still fresh. Recalling the boxer's past, one agent reminded Dickerson of Johnson's "recklessness as to his expenditures and . . . life of profligacy," his "mania for young white girls," and his anti-American propaganda work for the Mexican government. Bureau officials also made their appeal to Daugherty, who thereupon had a change of heart. "Considering the crime," Daugherty now told reporters, he could not extend parole privileges to Johnson.[55]

After July 9, however, not even Bureau officials could keep Johnson behind bars. He had served his time. Shortly before ten in the morning he was given five dollars and released. His mood was light. He would frame the money, he said, and then order a dozen suits from a Kansas City tailor. There was no need to worry about the future. He was still in good condition. Although almost forty-two, he felt sure he could whip Jack Dempsey. The public, he lectured, wanted that "draft dodger" Dempsey defeated, and he was the only man who could do it.[56] Johnson was referring to the accusation that Dempsey avoided the draft during World War I. Dempsey was tried for draft dodging and was cleared.

There were lively times and celebrations. In Chicago a large crowd of blacks greeted Johnson and welcomed him home. But this was only the beginning. When the Twentieth Century Limited carrying Johnson arrived in New York, it was met by a small contingent of admirers. Then at 125th Street the real festivities began. Thousands of residents of Harlem celebrated his release and treated him like a "conquering hero." There was even a parade, with Johnson leading the way in a flashy black suit with broad white stripes. He wore a straw hat at a "rakish angle" and carried a silver-mounted cane. Clamped between his gold teeth was a cigar. He looked good, reporters agreed. More like a man of twenty-five than forty-two. He was on his way back to the top. He would win the heavyweight championship again. Or so he and they thought.[57]

14

Ghost in the House

IT WAS 1933 and times were hard everywhere. Hitler had been Chancellor of Germany for less than a half-year, and Roosevelt president of the United States for barely a month. In California you could buy three dozen oranges for a dime and lamb chops for twelve and a half cents a pound. But with perhaps 25 percent unemployment, few people were eating fruit and meat. It was a potato and soup world, and life had changed considerably since Johnson's return to America in 1920. There was more talk of the next meal than of the next million.

Johnson would now become a figure of humiliation in tinsel surroundings. In May 1933 the Chicago World's Fair opened, ironically called "The Century of Progress Exposition." It began with a cacophony of bells, bands, choruses, and symphonies. Cannons thundered and lights swayed over the gathered multitudes. The Chicago Black Horse troops, the 106th Cavalry, led a parade of dignitaries that included Postmaster General Farley, special representative from the White House. Farley talked as a businessman and a politician. Free trade, he believed, would solve the world's economic problems. Capitalism and competition would lead the way to a better, more profitable, more secure future.[1]

Johnson was at the World's Fair not to hear Farley's optimistic intonations but to make a few dollars. He needed money. He was willing to turn sideshow performer—and he did. He boxed exhibitions with children. For a dollar your son could flail away at the once great and proud champion. Philip Rieff, who would go on to become a leading critic of Western culture, fought Johnson at the World's Fair. It was enormous fun for the youth, swinging powerful but errant haymakers at the smiling, encouraging black man. Almost a half-century later, upon reflection, Rieff realized what such exhibitions must have meant to Johnson. For a dollar Johnson had agreed to become a freak. For a dollar he was willing to push aside his challenging, threatening past and become the black man whites wanted to see. The only refuge for the man who recants is the freak show. [2]

This was not the future Johnson saw for himself when he left Leavenworth. More acquiescent, certainly, but still proud, Johnson looked forward to prosperity achieved on his own terms. He was after a future like his past, only devoid of the open, bitter confrontations. He wanted to fight the best boxers in America. He wanted Dempsey. In fact, even before he left prison the ballyhoo for the Dempsey-Johnson match had started. Captain J. W. McCaw, a millionaire California clubman, promised Dempsey at least $200,000 to fight Johnson. It was a lot of money, but not enough to make Dempsey put aside the guiding principle of his championship years. Like the Great John L. a half-century before, Dempsey said he would fight any man—as long as the man was white. [3]

Most states and cities where big fights were held felt the same way about any match involving Johnson. He may have served his time for society, but he had not satisfied boxing officials. They remembered the agony of his victories over Burns, Ketchel, and Jeffries. Now with the development of boxing boards and licensing agencies, they saw a way to bar Johnson officially from major bouts. "Johnson will not be granted a license," said Chairman William Muldoon of the New York Boxing Board. "We believe that the appearance of Johnson in a contest . . . would be derogatory to the sport," echoed Chairman Robert Doherty of the New Jersey State Boxing Commission. It was the same across the country. Over the next two years Johnson was prohibited from boxing in Ohio, Pennsylvania, and several other leading boxing states. [4]

When boxing authorities were quiet, outraged citizens objected to Johnson's presence in the ring. After not fighting in the United States since his release from prison, in 1923 a match was arranged for Johnson in Mingo, West Virginia. However, before the fight could be staged Ku Klux Klan members held a protest in Brilliant, West Vir-

ginia. They said they would "run Jack Johnson into the [Ohio] river"
if he tried to fight in their state. The match was canceled.[5]

Eventually he found some fights. Small fights. Unimportant
fights. He was old. He was starting to look it. His waist was thick, his
arms flabby. His skill—defensive skill—depended upon quickness,
and that advantage of youth deserted him. He was left with only his
knowledge of the craft. For a while it was enough. In May 1923 he
fought two matches in Havana. Both were against weak opponents,
fighters who earned more money as sparring partners than in main
events. In the first, Johnson hit Walter "Farmer" Lodge with a low
blow in the fourth round. Farmer sank to the canvas and refused to
continue. He said he was in too much pain. After some consultation
he was given a week to recover. A few days later he returned to the
United States and Johnson was awarded the victory.[6]

Johnson's second match in Cuba was even less satisfying. In a
fight against Jack Thompson, a Boston heavyweight, Johnson resisted all efforts to make him fight seriously. Thompson was similarly
immune from hostile criticism. For ten rounds the two moved about
the ring, watching each other but seldom throwing a punch. After the
tenth round, referee Villamil quit in disgust and the promoter had to
officiate the last two rounds. The fight ended in a "no decision," and
both boxers were fined $500 for stalling.[7]

Eventually not even craftsmanship was enough. In May 1926
Johnson defeated Pat Lester in a match held in Nogales, Mexico. He
won, but he was far from impressive. Three weeks later he fought
Bob Lawson, a black light heavyweight, in Juarez. Toward the end of
the seventh round Lawson knocked down the former champion.
Tired and hurt, Johnson was unable to continue. His competitive
boxing career was over, although like many great fighters it took him
a few years to realize it. In 1928 he fought twice and was knocked out
twice. That was enough. After that he fought nothing more serious
than peaceful exhibitions.[8]

He still had to eat. Johnson was never a saver. The money he earned
in the ring and on stage he quickly spent. As his ring career died with
a whimper, he turned more than ever toward the stage. It was not
easy. In 1921 he was denied the right to box during his vaudeville
show, and this detracted greatly from his stage appeal. Also, vaudeville and burlesque were dying. Like Johnson, they were remnants
from another age, one before motion pictures and film stars and talk-
ies. Every once in a while Johnson got a role in a play or an opera,

but he rarely obtained any part more important than a general spear-carrier. For example, in 1936 he was given a silent role in the opera *Aïda*. He was dressed like an African king and pranced about, overweight but proud. In his own mind he should have had a bigger part. After all, he told reporters, he could sing and he was a great lover of operas, at least those by Verdi. He admitted he found Wagner "very heavy."[9]

More generally Johnson stayed in pocket money by hustling small jobs in the boxing business. He managed a few boxers, refereed a number of fights, and trained anyone who would pay him a living wage. It was not a place for a man with high ethics or principles, and Johnson was right at home. He was certainly not above becoming involved in fixed fights. In 1927 he was arrested on a charge of participating in a "canned" fight in which Young Stribling faked an injury in a bout with Leo Diebel, whom Johnson seconded. Nothing could be proved, and Jack was released, but in the fight game any match suspicious enough to be investigated is suspicious indeed.[10]

When Johnson could not directly participate in the sport, he readily assumed the role of the worldly wide prognosticator. If a reporter wanted a good quote on a current heavyweight, all he had to do was take Jack to dinner. "About the only thing I can say in favor of Primo Carnera is that he has mighty big feet," Johnson remarked about the lumbering, mob-controlled heavyweight. He was right. George Godfrey, a good black heavyweight in the 1930s, Johnson said looked "like a champ against a colored fighter—but more like a chump against a white opponent." And again he was right. He knew talent, had a fine eye for weaknesses, and a master of the snappy quote.[11]

Johnson's most noted failure as a prognosticator was Joe Louis. The great black champion of the 1930s and 1940s, he said, was just not that good. In fact, Johnson was one of the few people who saw that Louis had serious technical flaws in his defense. "Louis holds his left too low, is off balance, and does not land properly," Jack told unbelieving reporters. Any fighter who circled constantly to Louis's left would defeat the Brown Bomber. This was exactly what Max Schmeling did in 1936, when he defeated Louis.[12]

But that loss was the only one Louis suffered during Johnson's lifetime. In truth, Johnson's aversion to Louis had nothing to do with defensive flaws. Johnson resented and envied Louis's superb abilities. Although he was not jealous of white fighters, Johnson was extremely touchy about black ones, particularly when they were gifted.

He hated Sam Langford, deprecated the talent of Harry Wills, and ridiculed the ability of Louis. Whenever a reporter asked him about Louis, Johnson quickly turned the conversation to himself. He would not share the spotlight with another black.[13]

Louis also resented Johnson. Because of Johnson's life-style, Louis, the second black heavyweight champion, constantly had to reassure the public that he was not another Jack Johnson. He did this in several ways. First, and most important, his sexual energy was directed toward black women. He did not challenge racial taboos as Johnson had done. Second, Louis was a man of few words, dignified and decent in public but verbally unsure of himself. No, he was not Jack Johnson, and you will find few pictures of them together. Louis kept his distance—physically and emotionally. Once when Johnson showed up at Louis's Pompton Lakes training camp, Joe told his manager, "Get that black cat out of here. I don't want him in my camp."[14]

Johnson's relationship with Louis was important. It illustrates his attitude toward himself and his own race. He was black. One senses that he resented this. In the years after he left prison he drifted farther and farther into a white world. Most of his friends were white. When Lucille divorced him in 1924, he rapidly remarried, this time to Irene Marie Pineau, an attractive white woman. His mannerisms became not only more white but absolutely European. In later years he always wore a beret, carried a cane, and spoke in a rich British accent. The dialect of his youth and his race had been trimmed away, like his black friends.[15]

He even took to the stump for white politicians. In 1928, asked when he would fight again, he said "My next fight will be in politics. I am going to enter the ring in behalf of Al Smith." The news was more welcome in Republican campaign headquarters than in Democratic. Senator Carter Glass of Virginia called the release "cheap Republican propaganda." But by the 1930s Democrats, unlike Louis, were glad to have Johnson in their camp. He was an FDR supporter, and on the stump he told blacks, "Franklin D. Roosevelt is champion now and wearing the belt. Abraham Lincoln was a good fighter in his prime, but he can't help us now. Always string along with the champion." Johnson even defended the CIO, calling it the "greatest thing since the Civil War" and "champion of peace, prosperity and happiness for millions of people."[16]

Perhaps Johnson's most useful work as a talker came during World War II. It was a popular war, and everyone wanted to take part. Too old to fight, Johnson encouraged others to enlist. He even fought a peaceful exhibition with his old rival Joe Jeannette to raise money for the war effort. Afterward in a rich English accent he encouraged his fellow Americans to buy war bonds. It was honest work, and he took pride in it.

Glib, articulate, occasionally insightful, Johnson continued to talk and preach. His message, when he was in a serious mood, was that color meant nothing. He did not counsel racial harmony as much as total color blindness. Usually he used his own life as his single text. The Bible, he said, reads " 'Thou shalt take unto thyself a wife.' It doesn't say what kind of wife. Chinese or white or green or black or any other kind. I took unto myself a wife, just as the Bible told me to.'"[17] Book closed. Sermon finished. Man, he believed, was not bound by race, class, or culture. And though his life showed the fallacy of this doctrine, he believed it.

When his mood was light he would discuss anything. Irregularly for the last twelve or so years of his life he talked professionally at Herbert's Museum on 42d Street east of Eighth Avenue in New York. It was a curious low-life place, rich with a seedy sideshow atmosphere. There for a dime you could see Professor Renato, the sword swallower; Madam Catalina, the snake charmer; a live Flea Circus; and an assortment of fat ladies, tattooed men, and such. There also, if you were fortunate, you could meet and listen to Jack Johnson. Standing on a 3-foot platform in the dingy basement that was Herbert's Museum, dressed like a dandy with a bright red tie and a blue French beret, Johnson would use his cane to emphasize certain points in his impromptu lectures. He told his life story—changing parts, creating a living legend. Visitors listened transfixed.[18]

His specialty was answering questions. His voice was soft and cultivated. His smile was warm, his eyes alive. But for many whites there was something vaguely disquieting about Johnson's talks, as if the great boxer would never share his genuine emotions. Bill Corum, a sportswriter for the *New York Journal American*, interviewed Johnson at Herbert's. Johnson was outwardly friendly and very articulate, but Corum instinctively disliked the boxer. "There was a leering and egotistical quality about the way [he] answered my questions that made me wonder when I left if I really believed anything he had said. Whether his testimony . . . meant a thing, and whether for a drink, a few dollars, or just a whim, he might not contradict himself the next day."[19]

The years passed, and he grew old. But he continued to sing his greatness and live recklessly. His recklessness was no longer considered challenging—he was no longer important enough to generate much controversy—only dangerous, mostly to himself. It manifested itself most singularly in his driving. Dan Burley, a columnist for the *New York Daily News*, remembered that as a youth in Chicago he admired Johnson's rakish, "floridly red" automobile, which the then champion "drove expertly but with reckless abandon, either in the street or up on the sidewalk as the notion struck him." He expected people to get out of his way. After all, he was the heavyweight champion of the world.[20]

He never stopped driving or thinking that way. After he was released from Leavenworth his only problems with the law arose over his reckless driving. He was fined for speeding, failure to stop at red lights, passing illegally, driving on sidewalks, and assorted other moving violations. He always had an excuse—either he didn't know the traffic laws of a particular state, or his car was too difficult to control, or he really had to get somewhere in a hurry. Once when riding with Johnson, Ed Sullivan urged him to slow down. "Jiminelly," Johnson protested, "Ed, I drive fast but I'm more careful than slowpoke drivers." In his own mind he probably thought he was.[21]

It happened the afternoon of June 10, 1946. Johnson was driving up Highway 1 en route to New York, where he was going to see the Louis-Conn rematch. He had just finished a tour of personal appearances in Texas. With Johnson was Fred Scott, whom he had employed to go along as company and to share the driving. Just south of the Franklinton line, about 20 miles north of Raleigh, North Carolina, Johnson lost control of his Lincoln Zephyr. It went off the shoulder on the right and smashed into a light pole. The car was demolished. Both Johnson and Scott were thrown out of the vehicle. Scott was fine. Johnson wasn't.

He was taken to St. Agnes Hospital in Raleigh. Doctors looked at him but didn't do much. He died a few hours later, at 6:10 P. M. Dr. W. D. Allison reported the causes as internal injuries and shock.[22]

Some mourned. Some didn't. The preacher who delivered the eulogy when Johnson was buried in Graceland Cemetery in Chicago said "Jack was a hard, clean fighter. He never hit below the belt." In New York Dan Burley said goodby to the man whites hated and blacks feared. Nat Fleischer, the editor of *Ring* and a close friend of Johnson, wrote the most personal and heartfelt obituary. He recalled Johnson's efforts on behalf of wounded soldiers during World War II. After Johnson "paid for his folly," Fleischer wrote, "there was no finer gentleman in the field of sports." A liberal who did much for black boxers, Fleischer noted that Johnson "had a heart as white as that of any man and I took great pleasure in calling him my friend." There was no racist intent in his words.[23]

Other writers remarked on Johnson's boxing ability. But there were few kind words for the man. Joe Louis, interviewed in his Pompton Lakes camp, said Johnson "must have been a great fighter as my trainer, Jack Blackburn, knew him well and said he was great." Yet no boxers attended his funeral or even sent a floral wreath. The sportswriter Bill Corum probably best expressed the feeling of the boxing community: "If there had been anything remotely resembling racial prejudice in this, I'd be ashamed to say it. But Jack Johnson always struck me as a show-off. As pompous and pushing where his background called for modesty and a willingness to stay in the background."[24] Perhaps Corum believed his statement was not racist; indeed, he admired Joe Louis's quiet dignity. Corum, however, missed the point of Johnson's life. Jack believed that a man was free of his background.

The film flickered on the bedsheet hung on the wall. The champion was in a restless mood. "Quarry. He don't have a machine and movies like this. He has nothing to look at today but the walls." The telephone rang constantly, and he answered it himself. "Sidney Poitier, you're my man!" "Whitney Young, my goodness." Often he told the caller that the buses were scheduled to leave the Regency Hotel an hour before the fight and he would personally see to it that all those aboard got into the arena. Between conversations he half watched the film. "Jack Johnson," he said reverently, as if he were whispering the name of a religious hero. The simulated voice of Jack Johnson spoke from the image on the sheet: "If I felt any better, I'd be *scared* of myself." Ali stored the line away. Johnson was fighting Burns. The round ended. As he turned toward his corner, Johnson waved goodby to Burns. "Look at that," Ali said. "He's signifying, 'See you later, partner,' I believe I'll do that with Quarry tonight." Angelo Dundee whispered to George Plimpton: "Just like him to pick up some crazy notion from that film." The first reel ended. Ali got up. He was hungry. He wanted a meal and a walk before the buses left. Jack Johnson was left in the room by himself.[25]

It was 1970, a good year for Muhammad Ali and, perhaps, even a better one for Johnson. Ali had won his battle. He had returned to boxing without serving time in the army. White and black liberals said this was right and just. But they had almost nothing to do with his return. As George Plimpton wrote, "Our efforts had very little to do with Ali's being allowed to fight; it was more that the mood of the times was changing, and the public was beginning to relate to what he had said about having 'no argument with them Vietcong.' " Largely because of Ali, images of Jack Johnson were in bookstores, on the Broadway stage and the silver screen, even on bedsheets and white walls. The parallels between the two black boxers were striking—both confronted legal authority, both suffered through periods of exile, and both were great showmen in and out of the ring.[26]

The buses left the Regency Hotel on time. That night Ali defeated Jerry Quarry. He cut open the white fighter's eye in the third round. It was an awful mess. Throughout the short fight, Drew "Bundini" Brown, Ali's cornerman and alterego, kept repeating, "Jack Johnson's heah!" And, "Ghost in the house! Ghost in the house!" Ali was being vindicated. So was Jack Johnson. Or so it seemed to many.[27]

In 1969 Howard Sackler's *The Great White Hope*, his first Broadway play, was the hit of the season. It won every major award, including the Tony, the Pulitzer Prize, and the New York Drama Critics Circle prize. And its star, James Earl Jones, who played a thinly fictionalized version of Jack Johnson, won rave reviews. The climate was right, and the other plays of the year—*1776, Does a Tiger Wear a Necktie?, George M!*—were obscured by this tribute to white guilt.[28]

Sackler's play was based on Johnson's autobiography, which was itself reprinted in 1969. It was Jack Johnson as Jack Johnson wished to be remembered. And James Earl Jones played Jack as Johnson saw himself—heroic, honest, passionate, intelligent, and a moral force for his generation. It was a Jack Johnson that black radicals and white liberals wanted to see. At a time when black intellectuals were searching American history for their own past and their own heroes, Jack Johnson seemed tailor made, a forceful, independent hero for a generation looking for forceful, independent leaders.

The fact that Jones's idealization of Johnson struck such a deep chord in the white liberal consciousness was seen clearly when Jones left Broadway to star in the movie version of the play. He was replaced on stage by Yaphet Kotto, a bigger, more physical actor. Kotto's Johnson was not nearly so intellectual or gentle or vulnerable as Jones's. He was big and black and projected all the anger of a ghetto-ridden existence. Clive Barnes, the *New York Times* reviewer, praised Kotto for giving the audience "a more physical, a more angry performance than did Mr. Jones." He applauded the threat implicit in

Kotto's rendition. "With Kotto the prizefighter is more of a man and less of a hero." Peter Bailey, an associate editor of *Ebony*, agreed. Kotto, he wrote, was menacing; he "*looks* mean on stage, and when he calls his ex-wife a bitch or tells someone to make tracks, you feel he really means it." Less art, more of Malcolm X, Kotto was closer to the real Jack Johnson. And before 1970 was a month old the play closed. Audiences did not want to be frightened by a specter of hate that was only too real.[29]

But even with Kotto, Sackler's Johnson was still only a shadow of the real thing. Partially, this was because of the play. For all its awards, it was too pat, its characters too stereotyped. "*The Great White Hope*," wrote film reviewer Vincent Canby, "is one of those liberal, well-meaning, fervently uncontroversial works that pretend to tackle contemporary problems by finding analogies at a safe remove in history." In the end, Sackler merely tells his audience that Jack Johnson faced prejudice and if everyone would please look around they could see prejudice still. Solve it and whites and blacks could live in harmony. It was the NAACP and *Guess Who's Coming to Dinner* brought to Broadway.[30]

The real Jack Johnson was not a stereotype. Nor was he the black hero that young black radicals of the 1960s were looking for. He was not the ghost in the house, as the poetic Bundini Brown told Ali. Where Ali was proudly black and political, Johnson's racial attitude was much more confused. His hatred of the white world was almost as deep as his longing to be part of it. Although he was admired by thousands of blacks during his own day, he refused the responsibility of leadership, and he could not lead by example for to follow his example was to court disaster. On only one point was Johnson consistent throughout his life: he accepted no limitations. He was not bound by custom, background, or race. He saw no inconsistency in ridiculing a white boxer in the ring and then celebrating with white friends. And if his conquest of white women was in part a desire to humiliate the white race, it was also because he preferred white women to black women. He was not a simple man.

Johnson's greatest strength was also his most glaring weakness. His life was the result of a supreme ego. It was everything. He always believed he was the best at anything—boxing, lovemaking, cooking, talking, driving, thinking. That any man was capable of defeating him in anything never really crossed his mind. His legendary composure before and during a fight was nothing more than an expression of his ego. In this regard, ego was the one thing that Johnson shared with other great athletes from John L. Sullivan and Babe Ruth to Muhammad Ali and Jimmy Connors. At the highest level of sport, mental toughness normally separates athletes of equal talent. And ego is the basis of that mental advantage.

Ego also affected Johnson's personal relations. He came first. His relations with prostitutes best illustrates his priorities. They serviced him—they were there when he wanted them and gone when he did not. If love was involved at all, it was strictly on his terms. The same attitude characterized his approach toward his own race. When it suited his fancy, he wore the clothes of a black Moses. But he was never really concerned in any deep sense with the advancement of his race. Indeed, he tended to distrust successful blacks.

Taken as a whole, his life inspires respect. He faced a sea of white hate without fear. He refused to consider himself a second class citizen and wrote the rules for his own life. But the self-centeredness that allowed him to do these things left most observers cold. It is only from a safe distance, intellectual as well as physical, that Jack Johnson could honestly be admired as a man.

Notes

1. Flourishing in the Dark

1. John Edward Weems, *A Weekend in September* (College Station, Tex., 1980); Nathan C. Green, *Story of the Galveston Flood* (Baltimore, 1900).

2. *Assessors Abstract of City Lots in Galveston County, 1900–1904,* p. 166.

3. *1900 Census Population Schedules, Texas, Galveston,* roll 1637; Danzil Batchelor, *Jack Johnson and His Times* (London, 1956), p. 9; *Heller's Galveston Directory, 1878–1879* (Galveston, 1878). Before 1878 it is impossible to determine which Henry Johnson was the one who fathered Jack Johnson. See *Heller's Galveston Directory* for 1875–1876 and 1876–1877.

4. *Assessors Abstract of City Lots in Galveston County, 1880–1884,* p. 166. Also see the volumes for 1885–1889, 1890–1894, and 1895–1899. *Sandborn Insurance Maps of Galveston, Texas* (New York, 1899), p. 51; *Morrison and Fourmy's General Directory of the City of Galveston, 1888–1889* (Galveston, 1889). Also see volumes for 1886–1887, 1890–1891, 1891–1892, 1893–1894, 1895–1896, 1896–1897, 1898, and 1899–1900.

5. *1880 Census Population Schedules, Texas, Galveston,* roll 1305. This census report agrees with the 1900 date in everything but the ages of Henry and Tiny Johnson.

231

6. *1880 Census Population Schedules, Texas, Galveston*, roll 1305; *1900 Census Population Schedules, Texas, Galveston*, roll 1637.

7. In every secondary source Jack Johnson's real name is given as John Arthur Johnson. However, in both the 1880 and 1900 census reports he is listed as Arthur Johnson. In addition, the city directories for Galveston between 1896 and 1900 list him as either Arthur Johnson or Arthur J. Johnson. This small point is illustrative of just how little is known of his early life.

8. *Morrison and Fourmy's Directory of the City of Galveston, 1888–1889*; *Galveston Weekly News*, April 1, 1878.

9. *San Francisco Call*, December 27, 1908, Gary Phillips Collection (hereafter referred to as GPC).

10. Jack Johnson, *Jack Johnson Is a Dandy: An Autobiography* (New York, 1969), p. 25.

11. *Ibid.*, pp. 21–24; David McCullough, *The Great Bridge* (New York, 1972), pp. 546–47.

12. George M. Fredrickson, *The Black Image in the White Mind: The Debate on Afro-American Character and Destiny, 1817–1914* (New York, 1971), pp. 228–55.

13. *Ibid.*, pp. 228–29.

14. *San Francisco Call*, December 27, 1908, GPC; Finis Farr, *Black Champion: The Life and Times of Jack Johnson* (London, 1965), pp. 4–13; Johnson, *Jack Johnson Is a Dandy*, pp. 20–35.

15. *Atlanta Constitution*, July 6, 1918, p. 9 and July 7, 1918, sec. II, p. 3; *Galveston Daily News*, February 26, 1901, p. 10.

16. Ralph Ellison, *The Invisible Man* (New York, 1947), pp. 22–27.

17. *San Francisco Call*, January 18, 1909, GPC.

18. *Morrison and Fourmy's General Directory of the City of Galveston, 1896–1897* and *1890*; Johnson, *Jack Johnson Is a Dandy*, pp. 25–27.

19. *1900 Census Population Schedules, Texas, Galveston; Morrison and Fourmy's General Directory of the City of Galveston, 1891–1892, 1893–1894, 1895–1896, 1896–1897, 1898*.

20. Johnson, *Jack Johnson Is a Dandy*, p. 51; *1900 Census Population Schedules, Texas, Galveston*.

21. Johnson, *Jack Johnson Is a Dandy*, pp. 27–34.

22. *Morrison and Fourmy's General Directory of the City of Galveston, 1896–1897, 1898*; *1900 Census Population Schedule, Texas, Galveston*; Bert Sugar, ed., *The 1981 Ring Boxing Encyclopedia and Record Book* (New York, 1981), p. 474 (hereafter cited as *1981 Ring Record Book*).

23. "A Point of Journalism," *The Nation*, March 23, 1893, p. 210; Dale A. Somers, *The Rise of Sports in New Orleans, 1850–1900* (Baton Rouge, 1972), p. 185.

24. Elmer M. Million, "History of the Texas Prize Fight Statute," *Texas Law Review*, vol. 17, pp. 152–59.

25. *Ibid.*, p. 153; *Galveston Daily News*, March 9, 1901, p. 1.

26. Farr, *Black Champion*, pp. 38–40; Batchelor, *Jack Johnson and His Times*, pp. 31–34.

27. *Chicago Tribune*, May 7, 1899, p. 61, and July 3, 1910, sec. III, p. 3.

28. *1981 Ring Record Book*, p. 474; Johnson, *Jack Johnson Is a Dandy*, pp. 31–33.

29. William M. Kramer and Norton B. Stern, "San Francisco's Fighting Jew," *California Historical Quarterly*, vol. 53 (Winter 1974), pp. 333–46.

30. A. J. Liebling, *The Sweet Science* (New York, 1956), p. 252.

31. *Galveston Daily News*, February 26, 1901, p. 10.

32. *Ibid.*, February 27, 1901, p. 1, and March 9, 1901, p. 1.

33. *Ibid.*, February 27, 1901, p. 1; Rupert Richardson, Ernest Wallace, and Adrian Anderson, *Texas: The Lone Star State* (Englewood Cliffs, N.J., 1981), pp. 346–50.

34. *Galveston Daily News*, March 1, 1901, p. 1, and March 3, 1901, p. 1.

35. *Ibid.*, March 5, 1901, p. 1.

36. *Ibid.*, February 28, 1901, p. 1; Rex Lardner, *The Legendary Champions* (New York, 1972), p. 191.

37. *Galveston Daily News*, March 8, 1901, p. 4, and March 9, 1901, p. 1.

38. *Ibid.*, March 9, 1901, p. 1.

39. *Ibid.*, March 21, 1901, p. 1, and March 23, 1901, p. 1.

40. *1981 Ring Record Book*, p. 474.

2. Black Boss Man

1. Dale Somers, *The Rise of Sports in New Orleans, 1850–1900*, p. 183.

2. *Ibid.*, p. 160.

3. *Ibid.*, p. 181.

4. John C. Betts, "Organized Sports in Industrial America," Ph.D. dissertation, Columbia University, 1951, p. 602.

5. Benjamin Quarles, "Peter Jackson Speaks of Boxers," *Negro History Bulletin*, vol. XVIII (October 1976), pp. 39–40; W. C. Heinz, ed., *The Fireside Book of Boxing* (New York, 1961), p. 205.

6. *Chicago Tribune*, June 16, 1910, p. 11.

7. Interview with Gary Phillips, November 16, 1981; *Los Angeles Times*, May 16, 1902, GPC; *1981 Ring Record Book*, p. 475.

8. *Chicago Tribune*, January 18, 1902, p. 18, and January 19, 1902, p. 19.

9. *Oakland Tribune*, March 8, 1902, GPC.

10. *Los Angeles Times*, May 16, 1902, and May 17, 1902, GPC.

11. *Ibid.*

12. *Ibid.*

13. *Ibid.*

14. *Ibid.*, October 6, 1903, and October 2, 1903, GPC.

15. John Lardner, *White Hopes and Other Tigers*, 33–35; *Los Angeles Times*, October 2, 1903, GPC; Alan Lomax, *Mister Jelly Roll: The Fortunes of Jelly Roll Morton, New Orleans Creole and "Inventor of Jazz"* (New York, 1950), p. xi.

16. Peter Gammond, *Scott Joplin and the Ragtime Era* (New York, 1975), p. 162; Larry Neal, "Uncle Rufus Raps on the Squared Circle," *Partisan Review*, Spring 1972, pp. 48–49.

17. For a picture of Kerr see Lardner, *The Legendary Champions*, p. 197; see also Johnson, *Jack Johnson Is a Dandy*, pp. 51–54.

18. Carbarino Report, March 27, 1913, General Records of the Department of Justice, File Number 164211, Record Group 60, National Archives; Carbarino Report, April 28, 1913, RG 60, NA.

19. *Los Angeles Times*, June 21, 1902, GPC.

20. *Ibid.*, October 21, 1902, GPC.

21. Lawrence W. Levine, *Black Culture and Black Consciousness: Afro-American Folk Thought from Slavery to Freedom* (Oxford, Miss., 1977), pp. 356–58.

22. Rhett S. Jones, "Proving Blacks Inferior, 1870–1930," *Black World*, February 1971, pp. 9–11.

23. *1973 Ring Record Book*, pp. 426–31, 436, 450–51; *1981 Ring Record Book*, pp. 471–75.

24. *San Francisco Post*, January 10, 1903, GPC.

25. *Chicago Tribune*, January 18, 1902, p. 18; Batchelor, *Jack Johnson and His Times*, pp. 31–34; *Los Angeles Times*, October 21 and 22, 1902, GPC.

26. *San Francisco Chronicle*, November 1, 1902, GPC; *Bakersfield Daily Californian*, November 2, 1902, GPC.

27. *Los Angeles Times*, December 3, 1902, GPC.

28. *Bakersfield Daily Californian*, December 10 and 11, 1902, GPC.

29. *San Francisco Post*, January 10, 1903, GPC.

30. *Chicago Tribune*, January 18, 1902, p. 18; *Los Angeles Times*, February 6, 1903, GPC.

31. *San Francisco Examiner*, February 6, 1903, GPC; *Los Angeles Times*, February 6, 1903, GPC.

32. *San Francisco Examiner*, February 6, 1903, GPC; *Los Angeles Times*, February 6, 1903, GPC.

33. See picture in Harry Carpenter, *Boxing: A Pictorial History* (Chicago, 1975), 34; see also *1973 Ring Record Book*, 436; *Los Angeles Times*, February 27, 1903, GPC.

34. Winthrop D. Jordan, *White over Black: American Attitudes Toward the Negro, 1550–1812* (Baltimore 1968), pp. 482–511; Bohum Lynch, *Knuckles and Gloves* (New York, 1923), p. 45; *Los Angeles Times*, February 27, 1903, GPC.

35. *Los Angeles Times*, February 27, 1903, GPC.

36. *San Francisco Examiner*, February 6, 1903, GPC; *Los Angeles Times*, April 7, 1903, GPC; *Los Angeles Times*, July 16, 1903, GPC.

37. *Philadelphia Inquirer*, May 11, 1903, p. 10, and May 12, 1903, p. 10.

38. *Ibid.*, August 1, 1903, p. 6.

39. *Los Angeles Times*, September 30, 1903, GPC; *Bakersfield Daily Californian*, August 19, 1903, GPC.

40. *Los Angeles Times*, October 1, 3, and 4, 1903, GPC.

41. *Ibid.*, October 28 and 29, 1903, GPC.

42. *Ibid.*, October 29, 1903, GPC.

43. *Ibid.*, October 30, 1903, GPC.

44. *San Francisco Tribune*, December 12, 1903 GPC; *Oakland Tribune*, December 12, 1903, GPC; *Bakersfield Daily Californian*, December 11, 1903, GPC.

45. *Oakland Tribune*, December 12, 1903, GPC.

46. *Los Angeles Times*, April 23, 1904, GPC.

47. *Chicago Tribune*, June 2, 1904, p. 8, and June 3, 1904, p. 8.

48. *Los Angeles Times*, October 19 and 25, 1904, GPC.

3. Changes in Attitudes, Changes in Latitudes

1. *San Francisco Chronicle*, March 24, 1905, GPC; *San Francisco Post*, March 27, 1905, GPC.

2. *San Francisco Post*, March 14, 1905. GPC.

3. *San Francisco Chronicle*, March 25, 1905, GPC; *San Francisco Post*, March 17 and 25, 1905, GPC.

4. *San Francisco Examiner*, March 29, 1905, GPC.

5. *Ibid.* All descriptions of the fight are taken from Naughton's round-by-round report. See photograph of fight in Allen Ressler, "The One-Eyed Heavyweight Champion," *Boxing Illustrated and Wrestling News*, March 1959, p. 31.

6. *San Francisco Examiner*, March 29, 1905, GPC; *San Francisco Post*, March 29, 1905, GPC.

7. Batchelor, *Jack Johnson and His Times*, p. 53.

8. *Philadelphia Inquirer*, May 12, 1903, p. 10, and April 26, 1905, p. 15.

9. *Ibid.*, May 3, 1905, p. 10.

10. *Ibid.*, May 10, 1905, p. 15; *1981 Ring Record Book*, p. 475.

11. Elmer M. Million, "The Enforceability of Prize Fight Statutes," *Kentucky Law Journal*, vol. 27 (1939), pp. 152–68; O. F. Snelling, *Bedside Book of Boxing* (London, 1972), pp. 59–66.

12. *New York Times*, August 26, 1900, p. 18.

13. *Ibid.*, July 29, 1902, p. 8; Rex Beach, "Fight at Tonopah," *Everybody's*, April 1907, pp. 464–74.

14. E. B. Osborn, "Revival of Boxing," *Nineteenth Century*, October 1911, pp. 771–72; W. R. C. Latson, "Moral Effects of Athletics," *Outing*, December 1906, pp. 389–92; "How Roosevelt Kept Fit," *Literary Digest*, April 19, 1913, p. 917.

15. John R. Tunis, *Sports: Heroics and Hysterics* (New York, 1928), p. 107; Theodore Roosevelt, "The Recent Prize Fight," *Outlook*, July 16, 1910, pp. 550–51.

16. *New York Times*, March 28, 1905, p. 9; May 3, 1905, p. 1; and May 4, 1905, p. 8.

17. *Ibid.*, July 4, 1905, p. 5.

18. Nat Fleischer, *"Fighting Furies": Story of the Golden Era of Jack Johnson, Sam Langford and Their Contemporaries* (New York, n.d.), p. 44.

19. *Philadelphia Inquirer*, June 27, 1905, p. 10.

20. Fleischer, *"Fighting Furies,"* 46–48.

21. *1973 Ring Record Book*, pp. 422–23; George Plimpton, *Shadow Box* (New York, 1977), p. 185; Fleischer, *"Fighting Furies,"* pp. 48–50.

22. *Philadelphia Inquirer*, December 4, 1905, p. 10; *Baltimore Sun*, December 2, 1905, p. 8, and December 4, 1905, p. 8.

23. *1973 Ring Record Book*, 67–68.

24. Fleischer, *"Fighting Furies,"* pp. 55–58; Nat Fleischer, *50 Years at Ringside* (New York, 1958), pp. 78–80.

25. *1973 Ring Record Book*, p. 475; Fleischer, *"Fighting Furies,"* pp. 54, 60.

26. Fred Dartnell, *"Seconds Out!" Chats About Boxers, Their Trainers and Patrons* (New York, n.d.), pp. 161, 171.

27. Carbarino Report, March 24, 1913, RG 60, NA.

28. Johnson, *Jack Johnson Is a Dandy*, p. 54; Carbarino Report, March 24, 1913, RG 60, NA; Charles Herbert Stember, *Sexual Racism: The*

Emotional Barrier to an Integrated Society (New York, 1976), pp. 90–120.

29. Richard Broome, "The Australian Reaction to Jack Johnson, Black Pugilist, 1907–9," in Richard Cashman and Michael McKerman, eds., *Sports in History: The Making of Modern Sporting History* (St. Lucia, Australia, 1979), pp. 344–45.

30. *Ibid.*, p. 349; Fleischer, *"Fighting Furies,"* pp. 60–61.

31. Broome, "The Australian Reaction to Jack Johnson," p. 349.

32. *Ibid.*, pp. 349–50.

33. Fleischer, *"Fighting Furies,"* pp. 61–62.

34. "The Fights of Fitz," *Literary Digest*, November 3, 1917, pp. 81–87.

35. *Philadelphia Inquirer*, July 17, 1907, p. 10; July 18, 1907, p. 10; and July 22, 1907, p. 6.

36. *The United States of America v. John Arthur Johnson*, No. 2017, United States Circuit Court of Appeals for the Seventh Circuit, October Term, 1912, pp. 87–88, (hereafter referred to as *U.S.* v. *Johnson*); Sterling Report, May 11, 1913, RG 60, NA.

37. Farr, *Black Champion*, pp. 47–48.

38. Fleischer, *"Fighting Furies,"* pp. 64–66.

39. Quoted in *ibid.*, 66–67.

40. Alexander Johnson, *Ten—And Out! The Complete Story of the Prize Ring in America*, 3d ed. (New York, 1947), pp. 177–78; Batchelor, *Jack Johnson and His Times*, p. 60; Steven R. Nicholaison, "Tom Burns: The Champ Nobody Remembers," *Ring*, July 1981, pp. 72–79.

41. Johnson, *Jack Johnson Is a Dandy*, p. 54; Fleischer, *"Fighting Furies,"* p. 67.

42. E. B. Osborn, "The Revival of Boxing," *The Nineteenth Century*, October 1911, pp. 775–80.

43. *Ibid.*, pp. 771–81.

44. Dartnell, *"Seconds Out!"*, pp. 259–61, 170–71; Lynch, *Knuckles and Gloves*, p. 149.

45. Farr, *Black Champion*, pp. 55–56.

46. *Ibid.*, pp. 51–52.

47. Broome, "The Australian Reaction to Jack Johnson," p. 351; *New York Times*, December 21, 1908, p. 7.

4. The Days of Tamerlane

1. Quoted in Al-Tony Gilmore, *Bad Nigger! The National Impact of Jack Johnson* (Port Washington, N.Y., 1975), p. 27; *Omaha Daily News*, December 27, 1908, p. 1; quoted in Charles Samuels, *The Magnificent*

Rube: The Life and Gaudy Times of Tex Rickard (New York, 1957), p. 135.

2. *Omaha Daily News*, December 27, 1908, p. 1; quoted in Gilmore, *Bad Nigger!*, pp. 29–32; *Omaha Daily News*, December 28, 1908, p. 6.

3. Broome, "The Australian Reaction to Jack Johnson," p. 345.

4. *Ibid.*, p. 346.

5. *Ibid.*, pp. 345–47; Lardner, *The Legendary Champions*, p. 174; Batchelor, *Jack Johnson and His Times*, pp. 61–62.

6. Broome, "The Australian Reaction to Jack Johnson," pp. 347–48.

7. *Ibid.*, p. 348.

8. Quoted in *ibid.*

9. *New York Times*, December 21, 1908, p. 7; Broome, "The Australian Reaction to Jack Johnson," pp. 350–51; Lynch, *Knuckles and Gloves*, pp. 147–48, 150–53.

10. Quoted in Broome, "The Australian Reaction to Jack Johnson," pp. 351–52; John Hetherington, *Norman Lindsay: Embattled Olympian* (Melbourne, 1973), pp. 74–75.

11. Quoted in Broome, "The Australian Reaction to Jack Johnson," pp. 352–53.

12. Quoted in Jan Morris, *Heaven's Command: An Imperial Progress* (London, 1973), p. 465.

13. Broome, "The Australian Reaction to Jack Johnson," p. 354.

14. *New York Times*, December 25, 1908, p. 8; and December 26, 1908, p. 8. (Unless otherwise noted, the details of the fight come from the December 26 *New York Times* and Broome, "The Australian Reaction to Jack Johnson," pp. 354–56.

15. *San Francisco Call*, December 27, 1908, GPC.

16. Jervis Anderson, "Black Heavies," *American Scholar*, vol. 47, (Summer 1978), p. 387.

17. *San Francisco Call*, December 27, 1908, GPC.

18. Dartnell, *"Seconds Out!"*, pp. 173–74.

19. Fredrickson, *The Black Image in White Minds*, p. 232; Charles F. Woodruff, "The Failure of Americans as Athletes," *North American Review*, October 1907, pp. 200–204.

20. Dartnell, *"Seconds Out!"* p. 174; John D. McCallum, *The Heavyweight Boxing Championship: A History* (Radnor, Pa., 1974), p. 62.

21. Lynch, *Knuckles and Gloves*, p. 149.

22. *Ibid.*, pp. 150–53; Lardner, *Legendary Champions*, pp. 173–76; *San Francisco Call*, December 27, 1908, GPC.

23. *San Francisco Call*, December 27, 1908, GPC.

24. Lynch, *Knuckles and Gloves*, pp. 152–53.

25. Quoted in Broome, "The Australian Reaction to Jack Johnson," p. 356.

26. *Ibid.*, p. 357.

27. *Omaha Sunday Bee*, December 27, 1908, p. 1; *Omaha Evening World-Herald*, December 26, 1908, p. 5.

28. *Omaha Daily News*, December 27, 1908, p. 1.

29. *Ibid.*, p. 2; Scully Report, March 11, 1913, RG 60, NA.

30. Quoted in Broome, "The Australian Reaction to Jack Johnson," p. 358.

31. John Durant, *The Heavyweight Champions* (New York, 1971), p. 57; Scully Report, March 10, 1913, RG 60, NA; Farr, *Black Champion*, pp. 53–55.

5. White Hopes and White Women

1. Quoted in Fleischer, *"Fighting Furies,"* p. 73; *New York Times*, December 28, 1908, p. 5.

2. Lardner, *White Hopes and Other Tigers*, pp. 20–39.

3. H. C. Bearley, "Ba-ad Nigger," *South Atlantic Quarterly*, vol. XXXVIII (1939), pp. 75–81; Samuel M. Strong, "Negro–White Relationships as Reflected in Social Types," *American Journal of Sociology*, vol. LXII (1946), pp. 23–30; William H. Wiggins, "Jack Johnson as Bad Nigger: The Folklore of His Life," *Black Scholar*, January 1971, pp. 4–19.

4. Levine, *Black Culture and Black Consciousness*, pp. 407–20.

5. *Chicago Tribune*, March 3, 1909, p. 8; March 10, 1909, p. 8, and March 11, 1909, p. 6; *Oakland Tribune*, March 10, 1909, GPC.

6. *Chicago Tribune*, March 10, 1909, p. 8.

7. *Vancouver Daily Province*, March 11, 1909, GPC; Farr, *Black Champion*, p. 66.

8. *Los Angeles Times*, March 16, 1909, and March 15, 1909, GPC; *Chicago Tribune*, March 13, 1909, p. 10, and March 16, 1909, p. 8.

9. Mark Connelly, *The Response to Prostitution in the Progressive Era* (Chapel Hill, N.C., 1980), 91–113.

10. Charles Washburn, *Come into My Parlor: A Biography of the Aristocratic Everleigh Sisters of Chicago* (New York, 1936), p. 69.

11. Chicagoan to United States District Attorney, October 28, 1912, RG 60, NA; *U.S.* v. *Johnson*, 81.

12. Belle Schreiber affidavit, October 30, 1911, RG 60, NA; *U.S.* v. *Johnson*, 59; P. P. Schmid Report, March 13, 1913, RG 60, NA; P. O. Schmid Report, March 15, 1913, RG 60, NA.

13. Meyer Report, December 11, 1912, RG 60, NA.

14. Jordan, *White Over Black*.

15. Quoted in Fredrickson, *The Black Image in the White Mind*, pp. 249–52; quoted in James H. Jones, *Bad Blood: The Tuskegee Syphilis Experiment* (New York, 1981), pp. 24–25.

16. Broome, "The Australian Reaction to Jack Johnson," p. 357; story told to Gary Phillips by man who knew Johnson; Gilmore, *Bad Nigger!*, p. 14.

17. James Weldon Johnson, *Along This Way* (New York, 1933), p. 121.

18. Quoted in Samuels, *The Magnificent Rube*, p. 137; quoted in Lardner, *White Hopes and Other Tigers*, pp. 34–35.

19. *Chicago Tribune*, March 20, 1909, p. 10; *U.S.* v. *Johnson*, p. 134.

20. *Chicago Tribune*, March 29, 1909, p. 12, and March 30, 1909, p. 8.

21. Quoted in A. J. Liebling, "Philadelphia Jack O'Brien," *Ring*, November 1980, pp. 76–81.

22. *Chicago Tribune*, April 24, 1909, p. 9; Frank Sutton Affidavit, February 19, 1913, RG 60, NA.

23. *Chicago Tribune*, May 5, 1909, p. 9, and May 19, 1909, p. 13; *Philadelphia Inquirer*, May 16, 1909, p. 10; May 17, 1909, p. 9; and May 19, 1909, p. 10.

24. *Chicago Tribune*, May 20, 1909, p. 9, and June 13, 1909, sec. III, p. 1; *Philadelphia Inquirer*, May 20, 1909, p. 10.

25. *Chicago Tribune*, May 22, 1909, p. 9.

26. Thomas Croak, "The Professionalization of Prizefighting: Pittsburgh at the Turn of the Century," *The Western Pennsylvania Historical Magazine*, vol. 62 (October 1979), pp. 338–40; *Chicago Tribune*, June 30, 1909, p. 13; and July 1, 1909, p. 11.

27. *Chicago Tribune*, July 3, 1909, p. 13, and July 18, 1909, III, p. 1; *U.S.* v. *Johnson*, pp. 16–17.

28. DeWoody to Bagley, May 6, 1913, RG 60, NA; Meyer Report, May 12, 1913, RG 60, NA; *U.S.* v. *Johnson*, pp. 37–40, 16–17; Lins Report, May 7, 1913, RG 60, NA.

29. DeWoody to Bielaski, April 28, 1913, RG 60, NA; Matthews Report, December 23, 1912, RG60, NA.

30. *San Francisco Call*, March 10, 1909, GPC; *Los Angeles Times*, March 10, 1909, GPC.

31. Fleischer, "*Fighting Furies*," p. 78; *San Francisco Bulletin*, September 8, 1909, GPC; Steven A. Riess, *Touching Base: Professional Baseball and American Culture in the Progressive Era* (Westport, Conn., 1980), p. 33.

32. *San Francisco Bulletin*, September 10, 1909, GPC; *San Francisco Examiner*, September 10, 1909, GPC.

33. *U.S.* v. *Johnson*, 134; *San Francisco Examiner*, October 9, 1909, GPC; "Data Relative to Immoral Associations of John Arthur Johnson and Belle Schreiber," RG 60, NA.

34. *San Francisco Examiner*, October 9, 1909, GPC.

35. Johnson, *Along This Way*, p. 208; *San Francisco Examiner*, October 9, 1909, GPC.

36. *San Francisco Examiner*, October 9, 1909, GPC.

37. *Ibid.*, September 8, 1909, GPC; Peter Heller, ed., *"In This Corner. . . .!": Forty World Champions Tell Their Stories* (New York, 1973), pp. 39–44.

38. Lardner, *White Hopes and Other Tigers*, 31; Stanley Weston, "The Killer Who Became a Champion," *Boxing Illustrated and Wrestling News*, September 1960, pp. 26–29, 64; quoted in John D. McCallum, *The World Heavyweight Boxing Championship: A History* (Radnor, Penn., 1974), p. 68.

39. *U.S.* v. *Johnson*, pp. 185–186; Farr, *Black Champion*, p. 65.

40. *San Francisco Examiner*, October 17, 1909, GPC; McCallum, *The World Heavyweight Boxing Championship*, p. 68.

41. *San Francisco Examiner*, October 17, 1909, GPC.

42. *Ibid.*

43. *Ibid.*

44. Heller, ed., *"In This Corner!"* p. 40; Joseph Friscia, "The Forgotten Fight Between Sam Langford and Stanley Ketchel," *Boxing Illustrated and Wrestling News*, August 1964, p. 22.

45. Lardner, *White Hopes and Other Tigers*, p. 30; *San Francisco Bulletin*, October 17, 1909, GPC; *Omaha Daily News*, October 17, 1909, p. 1.

6. The Year of the Comet

1. *Los Angeles Times*, March 10, 1906, GPC; Lardner, *White Hopes and Other Tigers*, p. 30.

2. *Chicago Tribune*, April 4, 1909, sec. III, p. 4.

3. "Data Relative to the Immoral Associations of John Arthur Johnson and Belle Schreiber," RG 60, NA.

4. Farr, *Black Champion*, p. 73.

5. Bielaski to Garbarino, February 21, 1913, RG 60, NA: *U.S.* v. *Johnson*, pp. 45–49.

6. *U.S.* v. *Johnson*, pp. 82, 45–49.

7. Scully Report, March 8, 1913, RG 60, NA; Eurborshaw Report, March 10, 1913, RG 60, NA; Gerard to Horn, March 11, 1913, RG 60, NA; *Chicago Tribune*, January 1, 1910, p. 14.

8. William Stowe, Jr., "Damned Funny: The Tragedy of Bert Williams," *Journal of Popular Culture*, vol. X (Summer 1976), pp. 5–12.

9. Scully Report, March 20, 1913, RG 60, NA; *Chicago Tribune*, January 3, 1910, p. 12.

10. Gerard to Horn, March 11, 1913, RG 60, NA; Eurborshaw Report, March 10, 1913, RG 60, NA.

11. *Chicago Tribune*, January 21, 1910, p. 12; January 22, 1910, p. 10; February 2, 1910, p. 12; and February 3, 1910, p. 9.

12. Farr, *Black Champion*, p. 69; Samuels, *The Magnificent Rube*, pp. 151–54.

13. Samuels, *The Magnificent Rube*, pp. 137–44; "The Making of the Match," *Harper's Weekly*, November 20, 1909, p. 30.

14. Samuels, *The Magnificent Rube*, pp. 143–44; Fleischer, *"Fighting Furies,"* pp. 86–91; Edward B. Moss, "In the Ring for a Million," *Harper's Weekly*, May 14, 1910, p. 13; *Current Literature*, June 1910, p. 607.

15. Samuels, *The Magnificent Rube*, pp. 1–216; Mel Heimer, *The Long Count* (New York, 1969), pp. 103–12; Barton W. Currie, "Prize-Fights as Mine Boomers," *Harper's Weekly*, August 22, 1908, p. 25.

16. Moss, "In the Ring for a Million," p. 13; *Current Literature*, June 1910, p. 605.

17. Harry Carr, "Fighting Father Time," *Collier's*, June 11, 1910, pp. 19, 32; Homer Davenport, "The Modern Caveman," *ibid.*, p. 19.

18. Samuels, *The Magnificent Rube*, pp. 147–48.

19. *Chicago Tribune*, May 1, 1910, sec. III, p. 3; May 2, 1910, p. 13; May 4, 1910, p. 13; May 6, 1910, p. 13; May 8, 1910, sec. III, p. 3; May 11, 1910, p. 15; May 12, 1910, p. 9; June 16, 1910, p. 11; June 19, 1910, sec. III, p. 1; and June 23, 1910, p. 11.

20. Stuart Mews, "Puritanicalism, Sport and Race: A Symbolic Crusade of 1911," in *Studies in Church History*, ed. O. J. Cuming and Derek Baker, vol. VIII (Cambridge, England, 1972), pp. 305–8.

21. *New York Times*, June 6, 1910, p. 9, and June 16, 1910, p. 2; Mews, "Puritanicalism, Sport, and Race," p. 307; Farr, *Black Champion*, pp. 85–89.

22. *Chicago Tribune*, June 16, 1910, p. 11.

23. *Ibid.*,; *New York Times*, June 16, 1910, p. 2; Mews, "Puritanicalism, Sport, and Race," p. 308.

24. *Chicago Tribune*, June 18, 1910, p. 13; quoted in McCallum, *The World Heavyweight Boxing Championship*, pp. 57–59.

25. Samuels, *The Magnificent Rube*, pp. 160–66; *Chicago Tribune*, June 20, 1910, p. 11.

26. *Chicago Tribune*, June 25, 1910, p. 13, and June 27, 1910, p. 9.

27. *Ibid.*, June 27, 1910, p. 9, and June 28, 1910, p. 11; "California's Conversion," *Independent*, June 23, 1910, pp. 1404–5; quoted in Farr, *Black Champion*, p. 106.

28. Quoted in Gilmore, *Bad Nigger*, p. 36; *Omaha Daily News*, July 3, 1910, p. 1.

29. Quoted in Gilmore, *Bad Nigger*, p. 34.

30. Quoted in *Current Literature*, June 1910, pp. 606–7; *Omaha Daily News*, July 2, 1910, p. 6.

31. Scott to Wheaton, *Booker T. Washington Papers*, vol. X, p. 75; *Current Literature*, June 1910, pp. 606–7.

32. Arthur Ruhl, "The Fight in the Desert," *Collier's*, July 23, 1910, p. 22; H. Hamilton Fyle, "What the Prize-Fight Taught Me," *Outlook*, August 13, 1910, p. 827; Harris Merton Lyon, "In Reno Riotous," *Hampton's Magazine*, September 1910, p. 387.

33. Lyon, "In Reno Riotous," pp. 386–96; Fyle, "What the Prize-Fight Taught Me," p. 827.

34. Lyon, "In Reno Riotous," pp. 386–96.

35. Ruhl, "The Fight in the Desert," p. 12; *Chicago Tribune*, July 3, 1910, p. 1.

36. Lyon, "In Reno Riotous," p. 387; Farr, *Black Champion*, p. 97.

37. Lyon, "In Reno Riotous," pp. 387–89.

38. *Chicago Tribune*, June 29, 1910, p. 13; quoted in Gilmore, *Bad Nigger*, p. 37.

39. McCallum, *The World Heavyweight Boxing Championship*, p. 7; *Chicago Tribune*, June 24, 1910, p. 13.

40. Edward Van Every, *Muldoon: The Solid Man of Sport* (New York, 1929), p. 306.

41. Farr, *Black Champion*, pp. 98–99.

42. Ruhl, "The Fight in the Desert," p. 22; *Chicago Tribune*, May 16, 1910, p. 12.

43. *Omaha Evening World-Herald*, July 2, 1910, p. 3; *Omaha Daily News*, June 25, 1910, p. 10; "The Psychology of the Prize Fight," *Current Literature*, July 1910, p. 57; *Chicago Tribune*, July 4, 1910, p. 1; Farr, *Black Champion*, p. 93.

44. *Omaha Evening World-Herald*, July 2, 1910, p.1; *Omaha Daily News*, July 2, 1910, p. 6.

45. Gilmore, *Bad Nigger*, p. 41; *Booker T. Washington Papers*, vol. X, p. 76.

46. Ruhl, "The Fight in the Desert," p. 22; *Chicago Tribune*, July 5, 1910, pp. 1, 6.

47. "Johnson Wins the Great Fight," *Harper's Weekly*, July 9, 1910, p. 8; *Chicago Tribune*, July 5, 1910, p. 6; Ruhl, "The Fight in the Desert," p. 22.
48. Farr, *Black Champion*, p. 107; *Current Literature*, August 1910, p. 129.
49. Van Every, *Muldoon*, pp. 313–15; *Chicago Tribune*, July 5, 1910, p. 6.
50. Farr, *Black Champion*, p. 111; "Johnson Wins the Great Fight," p. 8.
51. Heinz, ed., *The Fireside Book of Boxing*, p. 256; *Chicago Tribune*, July 5, 1910, pp. 1, 6. (Except when otherwise noted, the description of the fight is from the various accounts in this paper.)
52. Van Every, *Muldoon*, pp. 308–9.
53. Ruhl, "The Fight in the Desert," p. 13.

7. *The Demons of the* Hexenlehrling

1. Gilmore, *Bad Nigger*, p. 65.
2. *Chicago Tribune*, July 5, 1910, p.1.
3. *Omaha Daily News*, July 5, 1910, pp.1–2; *Omaha Evening World-Herald*, July 5, 1910, p. 1; *Omaha Daily Bee*, July 5, 1910, p. 1; *Chicago Tribune*, July 5, 1910, p. 1; *New York Times*, July 5, 1910, p. 1; *Independent*, July 7, 1910, p. 3.
4. *Omaha Evening World-Herald*, July 5, 1910, p. 1; Gilmore, *Bad Nigger*, pp. 59–72.
5. Gilmore, *Bad Nigger*, pp. 71–2; *New York Times*, July 5, 1910, p. 1; *Chicago Tribune*, July 5, 1910, p. 1; *Independent*, July 7, 1910, p. 49.
6. *Omaha Daily News*, July 9, 1910, p. 4; *Literary Digest*, July 16, 1910, p. 85; quoted in Gilmore, *Bad Nigger*, p. 48.
7. *Life*, July 28, 1910, p. 137.
8. H. Hamilton Fyle, "What the Prize-Fight Taught Me," *Outlook*, August 13, 1910, pp. 327–30.
9. *The Nation*, July 7, 1910, p. 2; *Literary Digest*, July 16, 1910, pp. 84–5; Theodore Roosevelt, "The Recent Prize Fight," *Outlook*, July 16, 1910, p. 551.
10. *Independent*, July 14, 1910, p. 99; *Literary Digest*, July 16, 1910, pp. 85–86; *Independent*, July 14, 1910, p. 58; Gilmore, *Bad Nigger*, pp. 75–90; *Omaha Evening World-Herald*, July 6, 1910, p. 1.
11. Quoted in Gilmore, *Bad Nigger*, p. 81.
12. *Omaha Evening World-Herald*, July 7, 1910, p. 8; Gilmore, *Bad Nigger*, pp. 75–90.
13. Gilmore, *Bad Nigger*, pp. 84–88; Fred Silva, ed., *Focus on the Birth of a Nation* (Englewood Cliffs, N.J., 1971), pp. 1–15.

14. *Chicago Tribune*, July 5, 1910, p. 10.

15. *Chicago Defender*, January 1, 1910, p. 1; August 6, 1910, p. 1; April 23, 1910, p. 1; February 19, 1910, p. 6 and July 30, 1910, pp. 1, 3.

16. *Chicago Tribune*, July 6, 1910, p. 11; July 8, 1910, p. 13; and July 9, 1910, p. 11.

17. Farr, *Black Champion*, p. 80.

18. *Chicago Tribune*, July 12, 1910, p. 11; Fleischer, *50 Years at Ringside*, pp. 75-77.

19. *Chicago Tribune*, July 21, 1910, p. 11; July 26, 1910, p. 9; and July 27, 1910, p. 11.

20. *Ibid.*, July 28, 1910, p. 9; Fleischer, *50 Years at Ringside*, p. 77; Heller, ed., *In This Corner*, p. 42.

21. Pigniuola Report, November 20, 1912, RG 60, NA; Meyer Reports, December 12, 1912, and January 4, 1913, RG 60, NA, Carbarino Report, February 28, 1913, RG 60, NA.

22. Carbarino Reports, March 27 and February 28, 1913, RG 60, NA; Carbarino to Bielaski, February 24, 1913, RG 60, NA.

23. Carbarino Report, February 28, 1913, RG 60, NA; Carbarino to Bielaski, February 24, 1913, RG 60, NA; "Data Relative to Immoral Associations of John Arthur Johnson and Belle Schreiber," RG 60, NA.

24. *Chicago Tribune*, July 24, 1910, sec. III, p. 4.

25. Eberstein Report, February 27, 1913, RG 60, NA; Scully Report, March 19, 1913, RG 60, NA; Prince Hunley affidavit, February 21, 1913, RG 60, NA.

26. Meyer Reports, December 12, 1912, and January 4, 1913, RG 60, NA; Julia Allen affidavit, December 16, 1912, RG 60, NA; "Chicagoan" to United States District Attorney in Chicago, October 12, 1912, RG 60, NA.

27. Eberstein Report, February 28, 1913, RG 60, NA.

28. *New York Times*, October 12, 1910, p. 10.

29. *Ibid.*, October 21, 1910 p. 9; October 24, 1910, p. 7; and October 26, 1910, p. 6.

30. *U.S. v. Johnson*, pp. 101-2; Meyer Report, January 2, 1913, RG 60, NA; *New York Times*, November 19, 1910, p. 13.

31. *New York Times*, November 26, 1910, p. 2.

32. *Ibid.*, December 22, 1910, p. 2.

33. *U.S. v. Johnson* pp. 115-17; *Ibid.* pp. 26-27; Meyer Report, January 4, 1913, RG 60, NA; Frank Sutton Affidavit, February 19, 1913, RG 60, NA.

34. *U.S. v. Johnson* pp. 50-53, 117-18; Meyer Report, January 8, 1913, RG

60, NA; Sterling Report, March 6, 1916, RG 60, NA; Meyer Report, December 10, 1912, RG 60, NA; Lins to Offley, December 10, 1912, RG 60, NA.

35. Sterling Report, March 6, 1913, RG 60, NA.

36. *U.S.* v. *Johnson*, pp. 94–111.

37. Sterling Reports, May 8, 1913, RG 60, NA; and May 9, 1913, RG 60, NA; *U.S.* v. *Johnson*, pp. 119–23.

38. *U.S.* v. *Johnson*, pp. 94–99.

39. *Ibid.*, pp. 141–43; 119–23; Belle Schreiber Affidavit, October 31, 1912, RG 60, NA.

40. Sterling Report, May 9, 1913, RG 60, NA; application and marriage certificates of John A. Johnson and Etta Duryea, January 18, 1911, Orphan's Court, Pittsburgh.

8. *A Brunette in a Blond Town*

1. *San Francisco Call*, February 6, 1911, GPC; *San Francisco Bulletin*, February 10, 1911, GPC.

2. "Data Relative to Immoral Associations of John Arthur Johnson and Belle Schreiber," RG 60, NA; Murdock Report, November 2, 1912, RG 60, NA.

3. *Los Angeles Times*, March 22, 23, and 16, 1911, GPC; *San Francisco Post*, March 22, 1911, GPC.

4. *San Francisco Post*, March 26, 1911, GPC; *San Francisco Call*, March 26, 1911, GPC; *New York Times*, March 26, 1911, p. 6 and April 3, 1911, p. 7; *San Francisco Bulletin*, March 29, 1911, GPC; *San Francisco Examiner*, March 28, 1911, GPC; March 30, 1911, GPC; April 4, 1911, GPC; April 23, 1911, GPC; and April 24, 1911, GPC.

5. *New York Times*, May 16, 1911, p. 11.

6. *Ibid.*, May 17, 1911, p. 3; Carbarino Report, May 7, 1913, RG 60, NA.

7. Lardner, *White Hopes and Other Tigers*, p. 32; *New York Times*, May 27, 1911, p. 8.

8. Lardner, *White Hopes and Other Tigers*, p. 33; *New York Times*, June 6, 1911, p. 18, and June 7, 1911, p. 20.

9. *London Times*, July 4, 1911, p. 14; *New York Times*, July 18, 1911, sec. 5, p. 16; July 30, 1911, sec. 3, p. 2 and August 25, 1911, p. 4; *Chicago Defender*, June 17, 1911, p. 1.

10. *London Times*, July 4, 1911, p. 14; Mews, "Puritanicalism, Sport, and Race: A Symbolic Crusade of 1911," *Studies in Church History*, pp. 311–12.

11. Mews, "Puritanicalism, Sport, and Race: A Symbolic Crusade of 1911," *Studies in Church History*, pp. 312–16.

12. *New York Times*, September 16, 1911, p. 2; *London Times*, September 16, 1911, p. 8; Mews, "Puritanicalism, Sport, and Race: A Symbolic Crusade of 1911," *Studies in Church History*, p. 322.

13. *New York Times*, September 14, 1911, p. 10; *London Times*, September 19, 1911, p. 2, and September 22, 1911, p. 6.

14. *New York Times*, September 20, 1911, p. 8; Mews, "Puritanicalism, Sport, and Race: A Symbolic Crusade of 1911," *Studies in Church History*, p. 328.

15. *New York Times*, September 24, 1911, sec. 3, p. 4, and September 26, 1911, p. 11; *London Times*, September 17, 1911, p. 5.

16. *New York Times*, September 29, 1911, p. 8.

17. *Ibid.*, p. 11; September 24, 1911, sec. III, p. 4, and October 2, 1911, p. 9; *London Times*, September 30, 1911, p. 10, and October 2, 1911, p. 13.

18. *London Times*, October 24, 1911, p. 3; *New York Times*, December 22, 1911, p. 15.

19. Lardner, *White Hopes and Other Tigers*, pp. 24–39; *Omaha Daily News*, October 25, 1912, p. 21; Fleischer, *50 Years at Ringside*, pp. 55–62.

20. Lardner, *White Hopes and Other Tigers*, pp. 24–26; *1973 Ring Record Book*, p. 443.

21. *1973 Ring Record Book*, 417.

22. Raymond Wilson, "Another White Hope Bites the Dust: The Jack Johnson–Jim Flynn Heavyweight Fight in 1912," *Montana: The Magazine of History*, vol. 29 (Winter 1979), p. 32; *New York Times*, January 5, 1912, p. 10; January 17, 1912, p. 9; April 9, 1912, p. 8; and April 18, 1912, p. 14.

23. *New York Times*, February 9, 1912, p. 10; Wilson, "Another White Hope Bites the Dust," p. 32.

24. Wilson, "Another White Hope Bites the Dust," p. 33.

25. Gordon Report, May 5, 1913, RG 60, NA; *New York Times*, April 25, 1912, p. 11; *Chicago Defender*, April 27, 1912, p. 1.

26. Lins Report, July 14, 1912, FBI Microfilm, reel 33749, NA; *New York Times*, April 4, 1912, p. 1; May 2, 1912, p. 8; and June 22, 1912, p. 10; *Chicago Defender*, April 6, 1912, p. 5.

27. Quoted in Wilson, "Another White Hope Bites the Dust," pp. 34–35.

28. *New York Times*, June 22, 1912, sec. 4, p. 9; *San Francisco Examiner*, June 18, 1912, GPC; *San Francisco Call*, June 18, 1912, GPC; *Los Angeles Times*, July 10, 1912, GPC.

29. Quoted in Wilson, "Another White Hope Bites the Dust," pp. 33–34; *New York Times*, June 23, 1912, sec. 4, p. 9.

30. *Chicago Defender*, June 15, 1912, p. 1, and June 29, 1912, p. 1; Wyn Craig Wade, *The Titanic: End of a Dream* (Middlesex, England, 1979), pp. 434–37; Gilmore, *Bad Nigger*, p. 20.

31. *Chicago Defender*, June 15, 1912, p. 1; Wilson, "Another White Hope Bites the Dust," p. 35.

32. Wilson, "Another White Hope Bites the Dust," p. 36.

33. *Ibid.*

34. *New York Times*, July 5, 1912, p. 9; *Omaha Evening World-Herald*, July 5, 1912, p. 11; *Chicago Defender*, July 6, 1912, p. 7; Wilson, "Another White Hope Bites the Dust," p. 36. (Unless otherwise noted the description of the fight comes from the above sources.)

35. *New York Times*, July 5, 1912, p. 12; Wilson, "Another White Hope Bites the Dust," pp. 36–38.

36. *Los Angeles Times*, July 10, 1912, GPC; Gilmore, *Bad Nigger*, pp. 88–90; U.S. Congress, House, H.R. 24962, 62d Cong., 2d sess., 1912; S. Res. 7027, 62d Cong., 2d. sess., 1912; U.S. Congress, Senate, *Congressional Record*, 62d Cong., 2d. sess., June 15, 1912, p. 8235, and July 1, 1912, p. 8551.

37. U.S. Congress, House, *Congressional Record*, 62d Cong., 2d sess., July 19, 1912, p. 9305; *New York Times*, July 16, 1912, p. 9, and July 20, 1912, p. 1.

9. Trouble with the Mann

1. Farr, *Black Champion*, pp. 121–24.

2. Johnson, *Jack Johnson Is a Dandy*, pp. 47–49; *New York Times*, July 12, 1912, p. 10; *Chicago Defender*, April 20, 1912, p. 1, and July 13, 1912, p. 1.

3. *Chicago Defender*, July 13, 1912, p. 1.

4. Allan Spear, *Chicago: The Making of a Negro Ghetto* (Chicago, 1967), pp. 81–82; *Chicago Defender*, December 16, 1911, p. 1; December 23, 1911, p. 2; February 3, 1912, p. 3, and December 28, 1912, p. 3.

5. Lins Report, July 15, 1912, FBI Microfilm, Reel 33749, NA; DeWoody Report, July 15, 1912, FBI Microfilm, Reel 33749, NA; *New York Times*, July 13, 1912, p. 6.

6. *New York Times*, July 26, 1912, p. 10.

7. *Ibid.*, September 12, 1912, p. 6; *Omaha Evening World-Herald*, September 12, 1912, p. 1.

8. *Chicago Defender*, September 14, 1912, p. 107; *New York Times*, September 12, 1912, p. 6.

9. *Chicago Defender*, September 14, 1912, pp. 1–7; *New York Times*, September 13, 1912, p. 6.

10. *Chicago Defender*, September 14, 1912, p. 1; *Omaha Evening World-Herald*, September 13, 1912, p. 12.

11. *Chicago Defender*, September 28, 1912, p. 1; *New York Times*, September 13, 1912, p. 6.

12. *New York Times*, September 14, 1912, p. 12, and September 13, 1912, p. 6; *Omaha Daily Bee*, September 13, 1912, p. 1; *Los Angeles Times*, September 13, 1912, GPC.

13. *Chicago Defender*, September 21, 1912, p. 1; *New York Times*, September 15, 1912, p. 12.

14. The most striking picture of Lucille is in the Chicago Historical Society, Graphic Collection.

15. Lins Reports, October 21 and 24, 1912, RG 60, NA; Bowen Report, November 15, 1912, RG 60, NA.

16. Johnson, *Jack Johnson Is a Dandy*, p. 57; Lins Reports, October 21 and 24, 1912, RG 60, NA.

17. *New York Times*, October 19, 1912, p. 4, *Chicago Defender*, October 19, 1912, p. 3.

18. *Chicago Tribune*, October 19, 1912, p. 3; Lins Report, October 21, 1912, RG 60, NA.

19. William Seagle, "The Twilight of the Mann Act," *American Bar Association Journal*, vol. 55 (1966), pp. 641–47.

20. *Ibid.*, p. 643; Connelly, *The Response to Prostitution in the Progressive Era*, pp. 46–66, 114–35; Daniel J. Leab, "Women and the Mann Act," *Amerikastuden/American Studies*, vol. 21 (1976), pp. 55–65; Roy Lubove, "The Progressives and the Prostitute," *Historian*, vol. 24 (1962), pp. 308–20.

21. Quoted in Seagle, "The Twilight of the Mann Act," p. 644.

22. Wickersham to Wilkerson, October 19, 1912, RG 60, NA.

23. *New York Times*, October 20, 1912, p. 12; *Chicago Tribune*, October 20, 1912, p. 3.

24. Quoted in Gilmore, *Bad Nigger*, pp. 96–98.

25. Quoted in *ibid.*, pp. 98–100.

26. *Chicago Tribune*, October 20, 1912, p. 3; Meyer Report, October 21, 1912, RG 60, NA.

27. Meyer Report, October 18, 1912, RG 60, NA; Lins Report, October 19, 1912, RG 60, NA; Garber Reports, October 19, 1912; October 20, 1912; and October 21, 1912, RG 60, NA.

28. Meyer Report, October 22, 1912, RG 60, NA; Lins Report, October 22, 1912, RG 60, NA; Bowen Report, November 13, 1912, RG 60, NA; *Chicago Tribune*, October 27, 1912, p. 3.

29. Lins Report, October 23 and 26, 1912, RG 60, NA; Meyer Report, October 25, 1912, RG 60, NA.

30. Lins Report, October 26, 1912, RG 60, NA; *Chicago Tribune*, October 22, 1912, p. 3.

31. Memorandum for Attorney General from Bielaski, October 19, 1912, RG 60, NA; *New York Times*, October 27, 1912, p. 11; *Omaha Sunday Bee*, October 27, 1912, p. 1.

32. Meyer Report, October 23, 1912, RG 60, NA; *Booker T. Washington Papers*, Washington to United Press International, October 23, 1912, Con. 614, DLC; quoted in Gilmore, *Bad Nigger*, 102.

33. *Chicago Defender*, October 26, 1912, p. 1; *Chicago Tribune*, October 24, 1912, p. 3.

34. *New York Times*, October 21, 1912, p. 1, and November 2, 1912, p. 1.

35. *Chicago Tribune*, October 22, 1912, p. 3; *Chicago Defender*, November 2, 1912, p. 1.

36. *Chicago Defender*, November 23, 1912, p. 8.

37. Meyer Report, October 26, 1912, RG 60, NA.

38. Meyer Reports, October 26 and 28, 1912, RG 60, NA.

39. Marshall Report, October 30, 1912, RG 60, NA; Belle Schreiber Affidavit, October 31, 1912, RG 60, NA; Lins Report, October 29, 1912, RG 60, NA.

40. Bielaski to Lins, October 31, 1912, RG 60, NA.

41. Seagle, "The Twilight of the Mann Act," pp. 644–45.

42. Levine, *Black Culture and Black Consciousness*, pp. 407–20.

43. Lins to Bielaski, November 4, 1912, RG 60, NA.

44. Ambrose Report, November 6, 1912, RG 60, NA; Bielaski to Lins, November 6, 1912, RG 60, NA; Ambrose to Bielaski, November 7, 1912, RG 60, NA.

45. Indictment, *U.S.* v. *Johnson*, November 7, 1912, RG 60, NA.

46. Lins Report, November 7, 1912, RG 60, NA; Meyer Report, November 7, 1912, RG 60, NA; Lins to Bielaski, November 7, 1912, RG 60, NA.

47. *Chicago Tribune*, November 8, 1912, p. 2; *New York Times*, November 8, 1912, p. 3.

10. Love and Hate

1. *Chicago Tribune*, November 9, 1912, pp. 1,4.

2. *Ibid.*; Meyer Report, November 8, 1912, RG 60, NA; *United States* v. *Albert Jones*, RG 60, NA (this Record Group contains all of the material relating to the Jones trial); Lins Report, November 8, 1912, RG 60, NA.

3. *Chicago Tribune*, November 9, 1912, p. 1; unidentified newspaper clipping, November 9, 1912, RG 60, NA; Lins to Bielaski, November 8, 1912, RG 60, NA; *Omaha Daily Bee* November 9, 1912, p. 11; *New York Times*, November 9, 1912, p. 22.

4. *Chicago Tribune*, November 10, 1912, p. 3; *Omaha Sunday Bee*, November 10, 1912, p. 1; *Omaha Evening World-Herald*, November 9, 1912, p. 1.

5. *Los Angeles Times*, November 8, 1912, GPC; *Chicago Tribune*, November 9, 1912, p. 1.

6. *Chicago Tribune*, November 11, 1912, p. 3; November 12, 1912, p. 3 and November 13, 1912, p. 5.

7. *Ibid.*, November 16, 1912, p. 7; Lins Report, November 16, 1912, RG 60, NA; McInerney to Wallace, May 12, 1912, RG 60, NA; Wallace to McInerney, May 12, 1915, RG 60, NA.

8. *Chicago Tribune*, November 17, 1912, p. 5; Meyer Report, November 19, 1912, RG 60, NA.

9. *Chicago Tribune*, November 17, 1912, p. 5; Lins Report, December 6, 1912, RG 60, NA; Meyer Report, November 18, 1912, RG 60, NA.

10. *New York Times*, November 8, 1912, p. 3; *Chicago Tribune*, November 8, 1912, p. 2; *Omaha Daily Bee*, November 19, 1912, p. 1; *Omaha Daily News*, October 28, 1912, p. 1; *Chicago Defender*, November 23, 1912, p. 1; Meyer Reports, December 21, 1912; December 2, 1912, RG 60, NA.

11. *New York Times*, December 3, 1912, p. 1, and December 4, 1912, p. 11; *Chicago Tribune*, December 1, 1912, p. 6, and December 4, 1912, p. 3; *Omaha Evening World-Herald*, December 4, 1912, p. 9; *Chicago Defender*, December 7, 1912, p. 2.

12. Quoted in Gilmore, *Bad Nigger*, pp. 106-8; "Messrs. Blease and Johnson," *Crisis*, January 1913), pp. 123-24.

13. *Chicago Tribune*, December 12, 1912, p. 9; U.S. Congress, House, *Congressional Record*, 62d Cong., 3d sess., December 11, 1912, pp. 502-4.

14. Quoted in Gilmore, *Bad Nigger*, p. 109; "Jack Johnson," *Crisis*, December 1912, pp. 72-74; "Intermarriage," *Crisis*, February 1913, pp. 180-81.

15. U.S. Congress, House, *Congressional Record*, 62d Cong., 3d sess., January 30, 1913, p. 2312.

16. Gilmore, *Bad Nigger*, p. 109; Rayford Logan, *The Betrayal of the Negro*, (New York, 1965), p. 364.

17. "Jack Johnson," *Crisis*, December 1912, pp. 72-74; "Messrs. Blease and Johnson," *Crisis*, January 1913, pp. 123-24; "Intermarriage," *Crisis*, February 1913, pp. 180-81; *Chicago Tribune*, November 23, 1912, p. 4; quoted in Gilmore, *Bad Nigger*, p. 111.

18. *New York Times*, December 22, 1912, p. 1; December 24, 1912, p. 18; and December 25, 1912, p. 6.

19. *Ibid.*, December 24, 1912, p. 18; *Chicago Tribune*, December 27, 1912, p. 2.

20. Meyer Report, January 4, 1913, RG 60, NA.

21. Wilkerson to Wickersham, November 8, 1912, RG 60, NA; Wickersham to Wilkerson, November 9, 1912, RG 60, NA.

22. Joan M. Jensen, *The Price of Vigilance* (Chicago, 1968), p. 16.

23. Lins Report, November 15, 1912, RG 60, NA; Ambrose Report, November 20, 1912, RG 60, NA; Offley Report,, November 19, 1912, RG 60, NA; Offley to Bielaski, November 19, 1912, RG 60, NA.

24. Belle to "My Dear," November 19, 1912, RG 60, NA; Belle to Grace, November 19, 1912, RG 60, NA; Offley to Bielaski, November 20, 1912, RG 60, NA.

25. Adams Report, November 20, 1912, RG 60, NA; Offley Report, November 23, 1912, RG 60, NA; Craft Report, November 26, 1912, RG 60, NA.

26. Bielaski to Belle, November 20, 1912, RG 60, NA.

27. Offley Report, December 5, 1912, RG 60 NA; Rosen Reports, November 29 and December 5, 1912, RG 60, NA; Poulin Report, December 11, 1912, RG 60, NA.

28. Poulin Report, December 11 and 16, 1912, RG 60, NA; Rosen Report, December 19, 1912, RG 60, NA; Craft Report, December 19, 1912, RG 60, NA.

29. Craft Report, December 19, 1912, RG 60, NA; Offley Report, December 16, 1912, RG 60, NA; Offley to Bielaski, December 15, 1912, RG 60, NA; Grgurevich Report, December 19, 1912, RG 60, NA.

30. Belle to Horn, December 24, 1912, RG 60, NA; Belle to Horn, undated, RG 60, NA; Grgurevich Reports, December 21, 1912; December 28, 1912; January 23 and February 10 and 27, 1913, RG 60, NA.

31. Grgurevich Reports, December 19, 28, and 30, 1912, and January 6, 7, 10, and 13, 1913, RG 60, NA.

32. Craft Report, March 24, 1913, RG 60, NA; Bielaski to Offley, April 29, 1913, RG 60, NA; Bielaski to DeWoody, April 29, 1913, RG 60, NA; Pigniuola to Bielaski, May 27, 1913, RG 60, NA.

33. Bielaski to Lins, December 17, 1912, RG 60, NA; Lins to Bielaski, December 17, 1912, RG 60, NA; Lins Reports, December 20, 1912, and February 20, 1913, RG 60, NA.

34. Lins Reports, November 1 and December 5, 6, 11, and 14, 1912, RG 60, NA; Meyer Report, December 10, 1912, RG 60, NA; Lins to Bielaski, December 6, 1912, RG 60, NA; Bielaski to Offley, December 7, 1912, RG 60, NA; Hoy to Wickersham, December 10, 1912, RG 60, NA;

Wickersham to Hoy, December 15, 1912, RG 60, NA; Marsales to Wickersham, December 21, 1912, RG 60, NA, and January 14, 1913, RG 60, NA; Wickersham to Marsales, January 27, 1913, RG 60, NA.

35. DeWoody to Bielaski, November 16, 1912, RG 60, NA; Lins to Offley, December 11, 1912, RG 60, NA; Lins to Bielaski, December 13, 1912, RG 60, NA; Lins Report, December 18, 1912, RG 60, NA; Offley Report, December 16, 1912, RG 60, NA; Meyer Report, December 21, 1912, RG 60, NA.

36. *Chicago Defender*, December 28, 1912, p. 3; Lins Report, January 7, 1913, RG 60, NA.

37. *New York Times*, January 10, 1913, p. 12; January 11, 1913, p. 12; and January 15, 1913, p. 6; DeWoody Report, January 15, 1913, RG 60, NA.

38. Lins Report, November 20, 1912, RG 60, NA; Meyer Report, November 19, 1912, RG 60, NA; DeWoody to Bielaski, January 14, 1913, RG 60, NA; DeWoody Reports, January 15, 1913, and January 15, 1913, RG 60, NA.

39. *New York Times*, January 15, 1913, p. 6; DeWoody Report, January 15, 1913, RG 60, NA; Meyer Report, January 21, 1913, RG 60, NA.

40. DeWoody Reports, January 15, 1913, and January 15, 1913, RG 60, NA.

41. Meyer Reports, January 27 and 29 and February 4 and 20, 1913, RG 60, NA; Lins Report, March 24, 1913, RG 60, NA; DeWoody Report, February 2, 1913, RG 60, NA.

42. Bragdon Report, February 11, 1913, RG 60, NA; DeWoody to Bielaski, February 4, 1913, RG 60, NA.

43. DeWoody Report, January 20, 1913, RG 60, NA; Meyer Reports, February 20 and 24, 1913, RG 60, NA; DeWoody to Bielaski, February 24, 1913, RG 60, NA; Lins Report, February 25, 1913, RG 60, NA.

44. DeWoody Report, February 25, 1913, RG 60, NA; Lins Report, February 25, 1913, RG 60, NA; *Chicago Defender*, February 22, 1913, p. 1; *New York Times*, February 25, 1913, p. 10; unidentified newspaper report, February 26, 1913, RG 60, NA.

45. Meyer Report, March 4, 1913, RG 60, NA; *New York Times*, February 26, 1913, p. 9; DeWoody to Bielaski, March 4, 1913, RG 60, NA; Bielaski to DeWoody, March 5, 1913, RG 60, NA; DeWoody Reports, March 11 and 24, 1913, RG 60, NA.

46. Moses to Taft, November 11, 1912, RG 60, NA; Harris to Taft, November 12, 1912, RG 60, NA; Tennyson to Taft, January 3, 1913, RG 60, NA; DeWoody Report, March 12, 1913, RG 60, NA; Meyer Report, February 14, 1913, RG 60, NA.

47. *Chicago Tribune*, April 25, 1913, p. 3; *New York Times*, April 22, 1913, p. 6, and April 24, 1913, p. 1; *Chicago Defender*, April 26, 1913, p. 8.

11. A Fit of Blues

1. DeWoody to Bielaski, May 1, 1913, RG 60, NA; *New York Times*, May 1, 1913, p. 5.

2. DeWoody to Bielaski, May 1, 1913, RG 60, NA; Lins to Offley, December 10, 1912, RG 60, NA; Offley Report, December 11, 1912, RG 60, NA; Meyer Report, December 10, 1912,RG 60, NA.

3. Bielaski to Offley, April 29, 1913, RG 60, NA; Bielaski to De Woody, April 13, 1913, RG 60, NA; DeWoody to Bielaski, May 1, 1913,RG 60, NA; Pigniuola Report, May 6, 1913, RG 60, NA; Pigniuola to Bielaski, May 2, 1913, RG 60, NA; Bielaski to Pigniuola, May 3, 1913, RG 60, NA; Pigniuola to Bielaski, May 5, 1913, RG 60, NA; Bielaski to Pigniuola, May 9, 1913, RG 60, NA.

4. Bragdon Report, May 7, 1913, RG 60, NA; DeWoody Report, May 6, 1913, RG 60, NA.

5. DeWoody to Bielaski, April 15, 1913, RG 60, NA; Bielaski to De-Woody, April 16, 1913, RG 60, NA; DeWoody Reports, April 28, and May 1, 1913, RG 60, NA; DeWoody to Bielaski, April 28, 1913, RG 60, NA; Meyer Reports, April 30, 1913; November 15, 1912; and May 7, and 12, 1913, RG 60, NA; Lins Report, May 7, 1913, RG 60, NA; De-Woody to Bagley, May 6, 1913, RG 60, NA; Callah Report, May 8, 1913, RG 60, NA; *Chicago Tribune*, May 7, 1913, p. 3; *New York Times*, May 8, 1913, p. 20.

6. *Chicago Tribune*, May 8, 1913, p. 1; Barbara Tuchman, *The Zimmermann Telegram* (New York, 1958), pp. 36–50.

7. *Chicago Tribune*, May 6, 1913, p. 6; *Chicago Defender*, May 10, 1913, p. 1.

8. *U.S.* v. *Johnson*, pp. 9–14.

9. *Ibid.*, pp. 14–16.

10. *Ibid.*, pp. 16–37; *Chicago Tribune*, May 8, 1913, p. 8.

11. *U.S.* v. *Johnson*, pp. 37–85; *Chicago Tribune*, May 9, 1913, p. 16, and May 10, 1913, p. 14.

12. *U.S.* v. *Johnson*, pp. 86–87; Meyer Reports, December 18, 1912, and January 4, 1913; RG 60, NA; Lins Report, December 20, 1912, RG 60, NA; Hillard Report, November 6, 1912, RG 60, NA.

13. *U.S.* v. *Johnson*, pp. 87–88; Pray Report, May 6, 1913, RG 60, NA; Sterling Reports, May 11, 1913, and May 13, 1913, RG 60, NA.

14. *U.S.* v. *Johnson*, pp. 89–94; *Chicago Tribune*, May 13, 1913, p. 5.

15. *U.S.* v. *Johnson*, pp. 115–41; unidentified newspaper clipping, May 14, 1913, RG 60, NA.

16. Brearley, "Ba-ad Nigger," pp. 78–81.

17. *U.S.* v. *Johnson*, pp. 115–41; *Chicago Tribune*, May 7, 1913, p. 3.

18. *U.S.* v. *Johnson*, pp. 153–59.

19. *Ibid.*, p. 160; *Chicago Tribune*, May 14, 1913, p. 1; Meyer Report, May 14, 1913, RG 60, NA.

20. *Chicago Tribune*, May 14, 1913, p. 1; *New York Times*, May 14, 1913, p. 1.

21. *New York Times*, May 14, 1913, p. 1; *Chicago Tribune*, May 14, 1913, p. 1.

22. *Chicago Tribune*, May 14, 1913, p. 1.

23. Quoted in Gilmore, *Bad Nigger*, p. 123.

24. *Chicago Tribune*, May 14, 1013, p. 1; *New York Times*, May 14, 1913, p. 1; *Chicago Defender*, May 17, 1913, p. 1; *Omaha Evening World-Herald*, May 14, 1913, p. 10; Gilmore, *Bad Nigger*, p. 121.

25. DeWoody to Bielaski, May 19, 1913, RG 60, NA.

26. *New York Times*, May 30, 1913, p. 4; *Crisis*, July 1913, p. 121.

27. John Hope Franklin, *From Slavery to Freedom: A History of Negro Americans* (New York, 1967), p. 454; *Chicago Tribune*, June 5, 1913, p. 1.

28. *U.S.* v. *Johnson*, pp. 161–64; *Crisis*, July 1913, p. 121; *Chicago Tribune*, June 5, 1913, p. 1; *New York Times*, June 5, 1913, p. 1; *Chicago Defender*, June 7, 1913, p. 1.

29. Johnson, *Jack Johnson Is a Dandy*, p. 60.

30. *Chicago Tribune*, June 28, 1913, p. 2; *New York Times*, June 27, 1913, p. 3; DeWoody Report, June 23, 1913, RG 60, NA.

31. *New York Times*, June 28, 1913, p. 2; *Chicago Tribune*, June 28, 1913, p. 2.

32. DeWoody Report, June 16, 1913, RG 60, NA.

33. Johnson, *Jack Johnson Is a Dandy*, pp. 60–61; DeWoody Report, June 30, 1913, RG 60, NA.

34. DeWoody Report, June 30, 1913, RG 60, NA; *New York Times*, June 27, 1913, p. 3, and July 4, 1913, p. 3.

35. DeWoody Report, June 30, 1913, RG 60, NA; Lins Report, January 23, 1914, Federal Bureau of Investigation, released under Freedom of Information Act (hereafter cited as FBI); *Chicago Examiner*, January 19, 1914, FBI; Bielaski to Offley, February 3, 1914, RG 60, NA.

36. Offley to Bruff, February 16 and 17, 1914, FBI.

37. Lins Report, January 23, 1914, FBI; Offley Reports, February 7, 1914, and February 8, 1914, FBI; Bielaski to Offley, February 3, 1914, RG 60, NA; Craft Report, February 9, 1914, RG 60, NA; Baker Reports, February 11 and 14, FBI; Bruff Reports, February 4, 5, 6, 7, and 12, 1914, FBI; *New York Times*, January 25, 1914, sec. III, p. 6.

38. Tiny Johnson deposition, RG 60, NA; Jennie Rhodes deposition, RG 60, NA; M. Evalyn Kritzinger deposition, RG 60, NA.

39. Dennenberg to Bielaski, October 17, 1913, FBI; Brown to McReynolds, February 14, 1914, FBI; Bruff Reports, February 7 and 12, 1914, FBI; Bruff to Bielaski, February 14, 1914, FBI; Wilkerson to Wickersham, March 8, 1914, RG 60, NA; *New York Times*, February 12, 1914, p. 18.

40. *Chicago Examiner*, January 22, 1917, RG 60, NA; DeWoody to Brolaski, April 7, 1917, RG 60, NA.

41. *Chicago Tribune*, June 28, 1913, p. 2; *New York Times*, June 28, 1913, p. 2; Brady to Bryan, June 30, 1913, RG 60, NA; Wilkerson to Wickersham, July 2, 1913, RG 60, NA; Hart to Wilkerson, July 8, 1913, RG 60, NA.

42. *New York Times*, June 30, 1913, p. 6; quoted in "McReynolds and Caminetti," *Crisis*, August 1913, p. 177.

12. The Hollow Crown

1. *New York Times*, July 13, 1913, sec. II, p. 5, and July 11, 1913, p. 3.

2. *Chicago Defender*, July 12, 1913, p. 1, and August 9, 1913, p. 1.

3. *New York Times*, July 19, 1913, p. 4, and July 11, 1913, p. 3.

4. *London Times*, August 22, 1913, p. 6.

5. *New York Times*, August 20, 1913, p. 1; August 21, 1913, p. 1; and August 22, 1913, p. 4; *London Times*, August 20, 1913, p. 3, and August 22, 1913, p. 6.

6. *New York Times*, August 22, 1913, p. 4; *London Times*, August 23, 1913, p. 6.

7. *New York Times*, August 25, 1913, p. 3; *London Times*, August 25, 1913, p. 3.

8. *London Times*, August 26, 1913, p. 4.

9. *Ibid.*; *New York Times*, August 26, 1913, p. 3.

10. *New York Times*, August 26, 1913, p. 3, and August 27, 1913, p. 6.

11. Farr, *Black Champion*, pp. 178–84; *London Times*, September 4, 1913, p. 4; *New York Times*, August 27, 1913, p. 6.

12. *London Times*, September 5, 1913, p. 2.

13. *New York Times*, October 29, 1913, p. 9; November 6, 1913, p. 9; and December 13, 1913, p. 11; *London Times*, November 7, 1913, p. 13.

14. *New York Times*, May 13, 1914, p. 13; November 26, 1913, p. 1; and November 30, 1913, sec. IV, p. 3; *London Times*, November 12, 1913, p. 12; *Omaha Evening World-Herald*, December 1, 1913, p. 8.

15. *London Times*, December 2, 1913, p. 5, and December 17, 1913, p. 5.

16. *Ibid.*, December 20, 1913, p. 7.

17. *Ibid.*; *New York Times*, December 20, 1913, p. 1. All descriptions of the fight are from these two sources, which were more detailed than most other papers.

18. *Chicago Defender*, November 15, 1923, p. 1; October 4, 1913, p. 2; April 11, 1914, p. 7; and April 25, 1914, p. 3; *New York Times*, October 13, 1913, p. 3.

19. *New York Times*, March 13, 1914, p. 10, and May 13, 1914, p. 13; *Chicago Defender*, March 21, 1914, p. 4.

20. *London Times*, January 20, 1914, p. 6; January 22, 1914, p. 6; January 23, 1914, p. 6; January 28, 1914, p. 11; February 6, 1914, p. 6; and February 7, 1914, p. 8.

21. *Ibid.*, February 17, 1914, p. 13; *New York Times*, August 25, 1913, p. 5.

22. *1973 Ring Record Book*, p. 442; *London Times*, January 15, 1914, p. 11; *New York Times*, May 7, 1914, p. 9.

23. *New York Times*, June 7, 1914, sec. V, p. 4, and July 15, 1914, p. 7.

24. *Ibid.*, *London Times*, June 26, 1914, p. 14.

25. Dartnell, *"Seconds Out!"*, pp. 123–24; *London Times*, June 29, 1914, p. 15; *New York Times*, June 28, 1914, sec. I, p. 1, and sec. II, p. 3. The description of the fight comes from these two newspapers.

26. *New York Times*, June 28, 1914, sec. II, p. 14, and June 29, 1914, p. 1.

27. *Ibid.*, July 1, 1914, p. 1; *London Times*, July 2, 1914, p. 14.

28. Johnson, *Jack Johnson Is a Dandy*, pp. 127–31; Lardner, *White Hopes and Other Tigers*, pp. 42–48.

29. *New York Times*, September 24, 1914, p. 7, and October 14, 1914, p. 6; *London Times*, September 22, 1914, p. 11.

30. *New York Times*, September 19, 1914, p. 6.

31. *1973 Ring Record Book*, p. 392; Lardner, *White Hopes and Other Tigers*, pp. 35–38; Stanley Weston, "How the Great White Hope Died," *Boxing Illustrated and Wrestling News*, June 1961, pp. 27–29, 62; Barney Negler, "Ten Seconds of Sunlight," in W. C. Heinz, ed., *The Fireside Book of Boxing* (New York, 1961), p. 302.

32. *1973 Ring Record Book*, p. 399; Heller, ed., *In This Corner*, p. 42; Jim Allan, "Gunboat Smith: The Man and the Legend," *Boxing Illustrated and Wrestling News*, April 1963, pp. 22–27, 65–66, and May 1963, pp. 38–43, 67–69.

33. Dartnell, *"Seconds Out!"*, p. 181.

34. Heller, ed., *In This Corner*, p. 43.

35. *London Times*, July 24, 1914, p. 15.

36. Lardner, *White Hopes and Other Tigers*, p. 49.

37. *New York Times*, February 19, 1915, p. 10; *Chicago Daily Tribune*, February 19, 1915, RG 60, NA.

38. Robert Quirk, *The Mexican Revolution, 1910–1915: The Convention of Aguascalientes* (New York, 1963), pp. 150–99; Barbara Tuchman, *The Zimmerman Telegram* (New York, 1958), pp. 63–84.

39. Farr, *Black Champion*, pp. 200–201.

40. Bielaski to Barnes, February 19, 1915, RG 60, NA; Guy Report, January 26, 1915, RG 60, NA.

41. *New York Times*, February 22, 1915, p. 7; February 23, 1915, p. 11; and February 26, 1915, p. 10; Johnson, *Jack Johnson Is a Dandy*, p. 70.

42. *New York Times*, March 26, 1915, p. 11; and April 2, 1915, p. 12.

43. *Ibid.*, February 23, 1915, p. 11; March 26, 1915, p. 12; March 28, 1915, p. 11; and March 29, 1915, p. 8.

44. Assistant Attorney General to Secretary of State, March 1, 1915, RG 60, NA; Lansing to Attorney General, March 9, 1915, RG 60, NA.

45. *New York Times*, February 26, 1915, p. 10; March 28, 1915, p. 11; April 2, 1915, p. 12; and April 3, 1915, p. 10; Fleischer, *50 Years at Ringside*, pp. 82–85.

46. *New York Times*, March 28, 1915, p. 11; April 2, 1915, p. 12; and April 3, 1915, p. 10; Fleischer, *50 Years at Ringside*, pp. 82–86.

47. *New York Times*, April 3, 1915, p. 10; Wheeler Report, February 20, 1915, RG 60, NA.

48. *New York Times*, March 14, 1919, p. 10; Clabaugh to Bielaski, February 19, 1915, RG 60, NA; Bielaski to Clabaugh, February 23, 1915, RG 60, NA; Johnson, *Jack Johnson Is a Dandy*, pp. 133–37.

49. *New York Times*, March 14, 1919, p. 10.

50. *New York Times*, April 6, 1915, pp. 1, 8. (Unless otherwise noted, the description of the fight is taken from this *Times* account and the *Omaha Morning World-Herald*, April 6, 1915, p. 12.)

51. McCallum, *The World Heavyweight Boxing Championship*, p. 83; *New York Times*, April 6, 1915, p. 1; quoted in Gilmore, *Bad Nigger*, p. 138.

52. Al-Tony Gilmore, "Towards an Understanding of the Jack Johnson Confession," *Negro History Bulletin*, vol. XXXV (May 1973), pp. 108–9.

53. Dartnell, "*Seconds Out!*" pp. 138–39; Van Every, *Muldoon: The Solid Man of Sport*, p. 315; Fleischer, *The Heavyweight Championship*, pp. 152–53; Fleischer, *50 Years at Ringside*, pp. 82–89; McCallum, *The*

World Heavyweight Boxing Championship, pp. 77–83; *New York Times*, March 14, 1919, p. 10; Jim Jacobs, "Don't Tell Me Jack Johnson Took a Dive," *Boxing Illustrated and Wrestling News*, November 1961, pp. 40–43, 60.

54. *New York Times*, April 6, 1915, p. 8.

13. Exile's Return

1. Johnson, *Jack Johnson Is a Dandy*, p. 72.

2. *New York Times*, April 8, 1915, p. 11; April 10, 1915, p. 9; and April 21, 1915, p. 10.

3. *London Times*, March 2, 1916, p. 4; Dartnell, *"Seconds Out!"* pp. 138–39.

4. *London Times*, March 1, 1916, p. 3, and March 2, 1916, p. 4.

5. *Ibid.*, February 29, 1916, p. 3.

6. William Atkinson, *A History of Spain and Portugal* (Harmondsworth, England, 1960), p. 322.

7. *New York Times*, June 1, 1916, p. 12; Johnson, *Jack Johnson Is a Dandy*, p. 73.

8. *New York Times*, June 1, 1916, p. 12.

9. Farr, *Black Champion*, p. 215; Plimpton, *Shadow Box*, p. 57.

10. Plimpton, *Shadow Box*, p. 58.

11. Quoted in *ibid.*, pp. 58–59.

12. *Ibid.*, p. 59.

13. Larry Collins and Dominique Lapierre, *Or I'll Dress You in Mourning* (New York, 1968), pp. 26–27.

14. Johnson, *Jack Johnson Is a Dandy*, pp. 73–75; *New York Times*, June 20, 1916, p. 13.

15. Lang to Dunn, December 9, 1918, RG 165, NA.

16. Johnson, *Jack Johnson Is a Dandy*, pp. 75–77.

17. Armand to Scott, June 29, 1918, RG 165, NA.

18. "Memorandum for Mr. Fitts," July 11, 1918, RG 60, NA; Uterhart to Scott, August 5, 1918, RG 165, NA.

19. "Army Staff Joint Records," January 22, 1919, RG 165, NA.

20. *New York Times*, February 17, 1919, p. 3.

21. *Ibid.*

22. Allen Report, April 1, 1919, RG 60, NA; Lang to Dunn, January 18, 1919, RG 165, NA.

23. Johnson to Craven, May 15, 1918, RG 165, NA; Uterhart to Scott, August 20, 1918, RG 165, NA.

24. Allen to Dunn, March 7, 1919, RG 165, NA; Dunn to Davis, March 12, 1919, RG 165, NA; Dunn to Allen, March 14, 1919, RG 165, NA; Reichmann to Dunn, August 13, 1918, RG 165, NA.

25. William Johnson, *Heroic Mexico: The Narrative History of a Twentieth Century Revolution* (Garden City, N.Y. 1968), pp. 262–356; Dunn to Brown, March 21, 1919, RG 165, NA; Dunn to Allen, March 22, 1919, RG 165, NA; Dunn to Allen, March 22, 1919, RG 165, NA; Allen to Dunn, March 26, 1919, RG 165, NA.

26. War Department to Military Attaché, Mexico City, March 21, 1919, RG 165, NA.

27. Karl Schmitt, *Mexico and the United States: Conflict and Coexistence* (New York, 1974), pp. 153–59; John Wamack, *Zapata and the Mexican Revolution* (New York, 1969), pp. 179–80, 299–300, 311–12.

28. Johnson, *Jack Johnson Is a Dandy*, p. 78; Brennan to Burke, October 15, 1919, RG 165, NA.

29. Woodruff to Military Intelligence, October 15, 1919, RG 165, NA; Barnes to Allen, May 7, 1919, RG 165, NA; Brennan to Burke, October 15, 1919, RG 60, NA; *New York Times*, June 18, 1920, p. 5; *New York Tribune*, undated, RG 165, NA.

30. *New York Times*, November 21, 1919, p. 12; July 21, 1919, p. 19; and June 24, 1919, p. 11; *1981 Ring Record Book*, p. 475.

31. Woodruff to Military Intelligence, October 15, 1919, RG 165, NA; Brennan to Burke, October 15, 1919, RG 60, NA; *New York Times*, June 18, 1920, p. 5; *New York Tribune*, undated, RG 165, NA.

32. E.O. Report, November 24, 1919, RG 165, NA; Woodruff to Military Intelligence, October 15, 1919, RG 165, NA.

33. Gallagher to Military Intelligence, August 8, 1919, RG 165, NA; Brennan to Burke, October 15, 1919, RG 165, NA.

34. Gallagher to Military Intelligence, August 8, 1919, RG 165, NA.

35. Weymouth Report, April 27, 1920, FBI; *New York Times*, July 21, 1919, p. 27; January 30, 1920, p. 16; February 5, 1920, p. 2; March 31, 1920, p. 12; April 2, 1920, p. 18; April 18, 1920, p. 12; and April 23, 1920, p. 11.

36. Johnson, *Jack Johnson Is a Dandy*, p. 84; *New York Times*, April 2, 1920, p. 18; April 8, 1920, p. 12; and April 23, 1920, p. 11; Cantu to Dato, March 12, 1912, RG 165, NA.

37. *New York Times*, June 16, 1920, p. 23, and July 4, 1920, p. 16.

38. Gershon Report, June 21, 1920, RG 60, NA; Connell Reports, June 16 and 24, 1920, FBI, and June 30, 1920, RG 60, NA; Connell to Gershon, June 26, 1920, RG 60, NA.

39. Gershon Reports, July 13 and 16, 1920, FBI; Connell Reports, July 9, 1920, FBI, and July 13, 1920, RG 60, NA; *New York Times*, July 10, 1920, p. 15; Hall Report, July 9, 1920, RG 60, NA.

40. Weymouth Report, April 10, 1920, FBI.

41. Unless otherwise noted, the description of Johnson's surrender comes from Gershon Report, July 22, 1920, FBI; unidentified newspaper clipping, July 21, 1920, RG 60, NA; *San Francisco Examiner*, July 21, 1920, GPC; and *New York Times*, July 21, 1920, p. 16.

42. *New York Times*, July 22, 1920, p. 13.

43. Spear, *Chicago*, pp. 129–229.

44. *New York Times*, July 26, 1920, p. 11; Johnson, *Jack Johnson Is a Dandy*, pp 85–86; Brennan to Burke, July 26, 1920, FBI.

45. *New York Times*, July 26, 1920, p. 11.

46. Burke to Brennan, July 24, 1920, FBI; Statement of John Arthur Johnson, July 24, 1920, FBI.

47. Burke to Brennan, July 22, 1920, FBI.

48. Craft to Attorney General, March 2, 1920, RG 60, NA; *New York Times*, July 25, 1920, p. 4; July 27, 1920, p. 5; July 29, 1920, p. 28; September 4, 1920, p. 7; and September 5, 1920, sec. XIII, p. 22.

49. *New York Times*, September 15, 1920, p. 17, and September 19, 1920, sec. II, p. 1.

50. *Ibid.*, September 21, 1920, p. 16.

51. Johnson, *Jack Johnson Is a Dandy*, p. 88.

52. *New York Times*, September 22, 1920, p. 8; November 26, 1920, p. 19; December 16, 1920, p. 23; May 29, 1921, p. 20, and June 18, 1921, p. 11.

53. Johnson, *Jack Johnson Is a Dandy*, p. 87.

54. *New York Times*, June, 1921, p. 4.

55. Balsy to Dickerson, January 20, 1921, RG 60, NA; *New York Times*, June 29, 1921, p. 11.

56. *New York Times*, July 10, 1921, p. 9.

57. *Ibid.*, July 15, 1921, p. 12, and July 23, 1921, p. 8.

14. Ghost in the House

1. *New York Times*, May 28, 1933, pp. 1, 16.

2. Conversation with Philip Rieff, summer 1981.

3. *New York Times*, July 7, 1921, p. 12, and July 9, 1921, p. 10.

4. *Ibid.*, October 17, 1922, p. 17; July 7, 1921, p. 12; July 13, 1922, p. 17; December 7, 1923, p. 27, and March 8, 1922, p. 13.

5. *Ibid.*, August 24, 1923, p. 11.

6. *Ibid.*, May 8, 1923, p. 13; May 12, 1923, p. 12; and May 15, 1923, p. 16.

7. *Ibid.*, May 22, 1923, p. 16, and May 30, 1923, p. 12.

8. Johnson, *Jack Johnson Is a Dandy*, p. 95; *New York Times*, May 3, 1926, p. 19; May 31, 1926, p. 12; and June 11, 1946, p. 46; *Chicago Whip*, June 12, 1926, Jack Johnson Vertical Files Folder, Schomburg Collection, New York City Public Library (hereafter referred to as Schomburg Collection).

9. *New York Times*, August 17, 1921, p. 8, and October 21, 1922, p. 15; *New York Post*, September 30, 1936, Schomburg Collection; *New York Times*, undated, Schomburg Collection.

10. *New York Times*, September 8, 1927, p. 33, and September 9, 1927, p. 22.

11. *Pittsburgh Courier*, May 3, 1930, Schomburg Collection; *Chicago Whip*, April 26, 1930, Schomburg Collection.

12. *Afro-American*, June 27, 1936, Schomburg Collection; *Chicago Defender*, July 4, 1936, Schomburg Collection; Fleischer, *50 Years at Ringside*, pp. 80-81.

13. Anderson, "Black Heavies," *American Scholar*, p. 395.

14. *New York Journal American*, undated, Alexander Gumby Collection, Folder 50, Special Collection Division, Columbia University, New York (hereafter referred to as Gumby Collection).

15. *New York Times*, February 16, 1924, p. 17; Farr, *Black Champion*, pp. 228-29; *New York Journal American*, undated, Gumby Collection.

16. *New York Times*, September 14, 1928, p. 4, and September 18, 1928, p. 6; *New York Sun*, November, 1934, Schomburg Collection; *Daily Worker*, June 26, 1940, Schomburg Collection.

17. *New York Times*, August 1, 1921, p. 6, and September 6, 1921, p. 13.

18. For good discussions of Johnson at Herbert's Museum, see John Realdine, "Boxing's Master Storyteller," *Ring*, July 1982, pp. 62-64, and Stanley Weston, *The Heavyweight Champions* (New York, 1970), pp. 69-70.

19. *New York Journal American*, June 1936, Gumby Collection.

20. *New York Daily News*, June 12, 1946, Gumby Collection.

21. *New York Times*, December 29, 1922, p. 14; January 26, 1922, p. 36; January 29, 1922, p. 21; January 23, 1930, p. 25; and January 24, 1930, p. 21; *New York Daily News*, June 15, 1946, Gumby Collection.

22. *New York Times*, June 11, 1946, p. 1; Farr, *Black Champion*, p. 236.

23. Farr, *Black Champion*, pp. 236-37; *New York Daily News*, June 12, 1946, Gumby Collection; Nat Fleischer, "Johnson, Craftiest Boxer," *Ring*, August 1946, pp. 20-21, 30.

24. *New York Times*, June 11, 1946, p. 46; Farr, *Black Champion*, p. 237; *New York Journal American*, June 1936, Gumby Collection.

25. Plimpton, *Shadow Box*, pp. 152–54.

26. *Ibid.*, pp. 51–52.

27. *Ibid.*, p. 164.

28. *New York Times*, April 21, 1969, p. 56; May 6, 1969, p. 1; and May 16, 1969, p. 37.

29. *Ibid.*, May 18, 1969, sec. II, p. 29; September 27, 1969, p. 26; October 26, 1969, sec. II, p. 3: and January 24, 1970, p. 23.

30. *Ibid.*, October 12, 1970, p. 46.

Bibliographical Note

This note is intended not as a list of materials consulted or used in the writing of *Papa Jack*, but rather as a guide to those works that were particularly helpful. Because of the government's interest in Jack Johnson, I was able to base this book on primary sources, most of which had been previously unavailable to the public. Most important was the file on Johnson declassified and released to the National Archives in the spring of 1981. Listed under the General Records of the Department of Justice, File Number 164211, Record Group 60, it contains several thousand enclosures, including field reports of Bureau of Investigation agents, letters between branches of the government, affidavits, pictures, newspaper articles, and the record of Johnson's trials and appeals. The records of the War Department, especially those on "Negro Agitation in Mexico," Record Group 165, were also helpful, especially for Johnson's activities during World War I. In addition, the Federal Bureau of Investigation acted promptly on my Freedom of Information request and declassified another group of Department of Justice records on Johnson. Finally, the Federal Bureau of Information microfilms, reel 33749, contain information on Johnson's career.

Johnson's public career can be followed in the newspapers and magazines of his day. The *Chicago Tribune, Chicago Defender,* and *New York Times* were helpful, as were *Everybody's, Outing, The Nation, Literary Digest, Outlook, Nineteenth Century, Collier's, Current Literature, Harper's Weekly, Hampton's Magazine, Independent, Life,* and *Crisis.* I used several collections of newspaper articles about Johnson. The most important was the Gary Phillips Collection, a private collection housed in Phillips's home in Yuba City, California. For any topic that touches upon boxing on the West Coast for the first quarter of the twentieth century this collection is essential. Also helpful were the Jack Johnson Vertical Files Folder, Schomburg Collection, New York Public Library; the Alexander Gumby Collection, Folder 50, Special Collection Division, Columbia University, New York; and the photographs of Johnson in the Graphic Collection of the Chicago Historical Society.

There are a handful of biographies about Johnson. All of them, however, depend heavily on Johnson's autobiography, *Jack Johnson Is a Dandy* (New York, 1969), which is an odd mixture of fact and fancy. To use it as a basis of a biography is to be hopelessly misled. Given this caution, the best biography of Johnson is Finis Farr's *Black Champion: The Life and Times of Jack Johnson* (London, 1965). Also of interest are Danzil Batchelor's *Jack Johnson and His Times* (London, 1956) and Robert H. deCoy's *The Big Black Fire* (Los Angeles, 1969). Two other books, although not full biographies, were useful. Al-Tony Gilmore's *Bad Nigger! The National Impact of Jack Johnson* (Port Washington, N.Y., 1975) is a carefully detailed and documented public reaction study. Nat Fleischer's *"Fighting Furies": Story of the Golden Era of Jack Johnson, Sam Langford and Their Contemporaries* (New York, n.d.) details Johnson's early career quite nicely.

Several articles on Johnson aided my study: Stuart Mews, "Puritanicalism, Sport and Race: A Symbolic Crusade of 1911," in O. J. Cuming and Derek Baker, eds., *Studies in Church History*, vol. 8 (Cambridge, England, 1972), pp. 303–31; Richard Broome, "The Australian Reaction to Jack Johnson, Black Pugilist, 1907–09," in Richard Cashman and Michael McKerman, eds., *Sports in History: The Making of Modern Sporting History* (St. Lucia, Australia, 1979) pp. 343–63; William H. Wiggins, "Jack Johnson as Bad Nigger: The Folklore of His Life," *Black Scholar,* January 1971, pp. 4–19; Raymond Wilson, "Another White Hope Bites the Dust: The Jack Johnson–Jim Flynn Heavyweight Fight of 1912," *Montana: The Magazine of History,* vol. 29 (1979), pp. 30–39; and my own "Heavyweight Champion Jack Johnson: His Omaha Image, a Public Reaction Study," *Nebraska History,* vol. 52 (1976), pp. 226–41.

For Johnson's Galveston career, the material available is largely of an impersonal nature. Johnson's father can be found in both the *1880 Census Population Schedules, Texas, Galveston,* microfilm 1305, and the *1900 Census Population Schedules, Texas, Galveston,* microfilm 1637. Henry Johnson's financial and employment status can be traced through the *Assessor's Abstracts of City Lots in Galveston County,* the *Sanborn Insurance Maps of Galveston, Texas* (New York, 1899), *Heller's Galveston Directory,* and *Morrison and Fourmy's General Directory of the City of Galveston.* Texas and national prizefighting laws are well covered in two articles by Elmer M. Million: "History of the Texas Prize Fight Statute," *Texas Law Review,* vol. 17 (1938), pp. 152–59, and "The Enforceability of Prize Fight Statutes," *Kentucky Law Journal,* vol. 27 (1939), pp. 152–68. Johnson's most important fight in Galveston is covered in William M. Kramer and Norton B. Stern, "San Francisco's Fighting Jew," *California Historial Quarterly,* vol. 33 (1974), pp. 333–46.

Boxing in the first decade of the twentieth century is still a largely unexplored but fascinating subject. Probably no period in the sport saw more fixed fights or shady deals. Probably in no other era were the boxers themselves so ruthlessly exploited. This can be seen in Rex Beach, "Fight at Tonopah," *Everybody's,* April 1907, pp. 464–74; Benjamin Quarles, "Peter Jackson Speaks of Boxers," *Negro History Bulletin,* vol. 18 (1976), pp. 39–40; and Peter Heller, ed., *"In This Corner. . . .!" Forty World Champions Tell Their Stories* (New York, 1973). More analytical are E. B. Osborn, "Revival of Boxing," *Nineteenth Century,* October 1911, pp. 771–81; Thomas Croak, "The Professionalization of Prizefighting: Pittsburgh at the Turn of the Century," *The Western Pennsylvania Historical Magazine,* vol. 62 (October 1979), pp. 333–43; and Dale Somers, *The Rise of Sports in New Orleans, 1850–1900* (Baton Rouge, 1972). Helpful biographies include Edward Van Every, *Muldoon: The Solid Man of Sport* (New York, 1929), and Charles Samuels, *The Magnificent Rube: The Life and Gaudy Times of Tex Rickard* (New York, 1957). Johnson's place in these years is detailed mostly in West Coast newspapers, but a more personal view of the boxer is provided in James Weldon Johnson, *Along This Way* (New York, 1933). Finally, one dissertation and two record books were helpful: John C. Betts, "Organized Sports in Industrial America," Ph.D. dissertation, Columbia University, 1951; Nat Loubet et al., *The 1973 Ring Boxing Encyclopedia and Record Book* (New York, 1973); and Bert Sugar, ed., *The 1981 Ring Boxing Encyclopedia and Record Book* (New York, 1981).

Once Johnson won the championship he was seldom far from the public eye. However, few of the contemporary newspaper or magazine articles written about him are very insightful. Several exceptions are Harris Merton Lyon, "In Reno Riotous," *Hampton's Magazine,* September 1910, pp. 386–96; and H. Hamilton Fyle, "What the Prize-Fight Taught Me," *Outlook,* August 13, 1910, pp. 827–30. Firsthand impressions of Johnson can be found in Nat Fleischer, *50 Years at Ringside* (New York, 1958); Fred Dartnell, *"Seconds Out!": Chats About Boxers, Their Trainers and Patrons* (New York, n.d.); Bohun Lynch, *Knuckles and Gloves* (New York, 1923); and Jerome Holtzman, ed., *No Cheering in the Press Box* (New York, 1975). John Lardner, *White Hopes and Other Tigers* (New York, 1951), is more a history, but he knew Johnson and left a telling portrait, as well as one of the finest books on boxing.

Several general histories of boxing were useful: Rex Lardner, *The Legendary Champions* (New York, 1972); Alexander Johnson, *Ten—and Out! The Complete Story of the Prize Ring in America,* 3d ed. (New York, 1947); John D. McCallum, *The Heavyweight Boxing Championship: A History* (Radnor, Pa., 1974); John Durant, *The Heavyweight Champions* (New York, 1971); and Harry Carpenter, *Boxing: A Pictorial History* (Chicago,

1975). W. C. Heinz, ed., *The Fireside Book of Boxing* is the best collection of boxing articles, a few of which deal with Johnson. Three of the most entertaining books on boxing are A. J. Liebling, *The Sweet Science* (New York, 1956); George Plimpton, *Shadow Box* (New York, 1977); and O. F. Snelling, *Bedside Book of Boxing* (London, 1972). Also insightful are two articles: Jervis Anderson, "Black Heavies," *American Scholar,* vol. 47 (1978), pp. 387–95; and Larry Neal, "Uncle Rufus Raps on the Squared Circle," *Partisan Review,* Spring 1972, pp. 44–52.

The literature on prostitution is extensive and includes books and articles that range from outstanding to worthless. I was aided by Mark Connelly, *The Response to Prostitution in the Progressive Era* (Chapel Hill, N.C., 1980), which is a fine starting point on the subject. Charles Washburn, *Come into My Parlor: A Biography of the Aristocratic Everleigh Sisters of Chicago* (New York, 1936), a popular history of the house where Belle worked, deals less with numbers than with atmosphere. William Seagle, "The Twilight of the Mann Act," *American Bar Association Journal,* vol. 55 (1966), pp. 641–47, is the best legal discussion of the White Slave Traffic Act. Daniel J. Leab, "Women and the Mann Act," *Amerikastuden,* vol. 21 (1976), pp. 55–65, and Roy Lubove, "The Progressives and the Prostitute," *Historian,* vol. 24 (1962), pp. 308–20, were also useful.

Finally, Johnson can be put into perspective only by reading widely in volumes written about black life in America. Novels by black writers who lived during Johnson's time provide a sensitive exploration of what it is like to live in a culture dominated by white men and white values, and no novel does this better than Ralph Ellison, *The Invisible Man* (New York, 1947). Lawrence W. Levine, *Black Culture and Black Consciousness: Afro-American Folk Thought from Slavery to Freedom* (Oxford, 1977), was invaluable to my study. Similarly, I was aided by a number of books on black-white relations, the most outstanding of which are Winthrop D. Jordan, *White over Black: American Attitudes Toward the Negro, 1550–1812* (Baltimore, 1968); George M. Fredrickson, *The Black Image in the White Mind: The Debate on Afro-American Character and Destiny, 1817–1914* (New York, 1971); Thomas F. Gossett, *Race: The History of an Idea in America* (New York, 1975); William Stanton, *The Leopard's Spots: Scientific Attitudes Toward Race in America, 1815–1859* (Chicago, 1960); John S. Haller, Jr., *Outcasts from Evolution: Scientific Attitudes of Racial Inferiority, 1859–1900* (Urbana, Ill., 1971); and Charles Stember, *Sexual Racism: The Emotional Barrier to an Integrated Society* (New York, 1976). Dan T. Carter, *Scottsboro: A Tragedy of the American South* (Baton Rouge, La., 1969), and James H. Jones, *Bad Blood: The Tuskegee Syphilis Experiment* (New York, 1981), are two studies whose implications are far broader than their titles suggest. Allan Spear, *Chicago: The Making of a Negro Ghetto* (Chicago, 1967), details the community where Johnson lived, and Rayford Logan, *The Betrayal of the Negro* (New York, 1965), remains a useful study on the history of black Americans during Johnson's time.

Index

1

P-84